TRADERS PRESS, INC.

P.O. BOX 6206
GREENVILLE, SOUTH CAROLINA 29606

BOOKS AND GIFTS FOR
INVESTORS AND TRADERS

800-927-8222

Gold Investment

Gold Investment

Theory and Application

Eugene J. Sherman

New York Institute of Finance
Prentice-Hall

Library of Congress Cataloging-in-Publication Data

Sherman, Eugene J.
  Gold investment.

  Includes index.
  1. Gold. 2. Investments. I. Title.
HG293.S47 1986   332.63   85-32089
ISBN 0–13–357823–2

This publication is designed to provide accurate and authoritative information in regard to the subject matter covered. It is sold with the understanding that the publisher is not engaged in rendering legal, accounting, or
other professional service. If legal advice or other expert assistance is required, the services of a competent professional person should be sought.

*From a Declaration of Principles Jointly Adopted by
a Committee of the American Bar Association and a
Committee of Publishers and Associations*

Printed in the United States of America

10 9 8 7 6 5 4 3 2

New York Institute of Finance
(NYIF Corp.)
70 Pine Street
New York, New York 10270

Contents

Foreword, vii

Preface, ix

I
Supply, Demand, and Above-Ground Stocks, 1

1
Gold: An Economic Analysis
of Supply and Demand: 1972–83, 3

Summary and Implications for
Gold Investment, 4
Method of Analysis, 14
Gold Supply, 21
Fabricated Gold Demand, 28
Nonfabricated or Gold Bullion
Demand, 64
Data Notes, 68

iii

2
**Above-Ground Stocks of Gold:
Amounts and Distribution, 71**

Estimating Procedures, 73
Distribution of Private Gold Stocks
    Between Bullion and Coin, 79
The Geographical Distribution of Private
    Stocks of Bullion and Coin, 82
Summary of Investment Stocks, 87
Jewelry, 88
Secondary Recovery from Scrap, 88
Update on Above-Ground Stocks:
    Year-End 1984 Estimates, 92

II
The Determinants of the Gold Price, 97

3
A Gold Pricing Model: 1985 Update, 99

Model Enhancements, Statistical Problems,
    and Analytical Issues, 101
The New Sample Period, 107
Empirical Results of the Revised Gold
    Pricing Model, 110
Projections, 117

4
**Gold: The Transition from Commodity
to Currency Form: 1968–73, 121**

Premises, 122
Summary and Conclusions, 123
Annual Chronology, 127

III
The Role of Gold in a Large Portfolio, 139

5
The Application of Modern Portfolio Theory to Gold: 1974–83, 141

Investor Philosophy in the 1980s, 141
Conclusions, 142
Statistical Measures, 144
The Results of Statistical Analysis
   of Gold Price Variability, 146
Summary of Portfolio Simulations, 148
Methodology and Terms Used
   in Simulations, 151
The Prudent Man Rule and Its Evolution, 165

IV
Gold in Relation to Major Currencies, 171

6
Performance of Gold Vs. Stocks, Bonds, and Money Markets in Six Countries: 1968–83, 173

Purpose, 174
Summary, 175
Implications for Gold Investment, 178
Summary: Total Return and
   Correlation (R^2) of Each Asset
   Vs. Gold Across Six Countries, 180
United States Summary, 182
Canada Summary, 190
United Kingdom Summary, 198
Germany Summary, 206
Switzerland Summary, 214
Japan Summary, 222
Summaries for All Six Countries, 230
Definitions and Sources of Data, 232

V
Gold in the International Monetary System, 235

7
Gold in the Monetary System—
A Re-Examination, 237

Summary and Conclusions, 238
The Use of Gold as Money in History, 240
The International Gold Standard, 241
The Gold Exchange Standard, 249
The Bretton Woods System, 253
The Search for an Alternative, 256
A Multicurrency Reserve System, 261

8
Gold in the International Monetary System:
Current and Prospective Official Roles, 265

U.S. Gold Commission Findings, 268
Gold's Current Role—Official
    International Institutions, 269
The Future Official Role of Gold, 282
International Monetary System Update, 288

Index, 291

Foreword

Since its inauguration in 1980, the Gold-Economics Service of International Gold Corporation has published several original studies on gold investment and its role in a balanced portfolio along four avenues of inquiry: a macroeconomic gold pricing model, supply/demand analysis, multicurrency analysis, and modern portfolio theory. The favorable response generated from these publications has encouraged us to compile these papers into a book of readings designed to assist economists, professional investors, and anyone else who takes a serious interest in gold. Readers will find here all the results of the major studies undertaken by the Gold-Economics Service with updating and some modification, for the sake of avoiding duplication. The articles in this book were written by the following people:

Mr. Eugene J. Sherman	Vice President, Economist International Investment Manager
Dr. Peter I. Berman	Former Second Vice President Investment Division
Dr. Richard A. Stuckey	Former Assistant Vice President Investment Division

Introductory remarks at the beginning of each chapter and two "update" addendums were written by the editor.

Last but not least, we should acknowledge the special pioneering efforts made by Mr. Eugene J. Sherman, who established the Service of the International Gold Corporation in 1980 and spearheaded high-quality theoretical and statistical works in the field of gold investment. Indeed, two of these studies have appeared in learned journals. Before joining Intergold, he served in various high-ranking posts on Wall Street, including the Bank of New York, Merrill Lynch, and the Federal Reserve Bank of New York. His background as an established economist was instrumental in attracting the attention of institutional investors to the sphere of gold investment.

ITSUO TOSHIMA
Manager/Investment Division
International Gold Corporation
Japan

Preface

In 1980, the International Gold Corporation established the Gold-Economics Service to expand its marketing effort to encompass money management professionals. Virtually none of the enormous amount of money under professional management in the United States at that time was invested in gold, and subsequent research demonstrated that surprisingly little was invested in gold by professionals elsewhere in the world. Clearly there was a huge potential here.

It was obvious that in order to attract investment professionals to the concept of gold investment, sophisticated analysis would be necessary. The first mission, therefore, became one of developing a body of literature that addressed this need. We assumed that portfolio managers and analysts would approach our studies with a healthy dose of skepticism, and rightly so. Accordingly, special pains were taken to assure objectivity and accuracy.

This book is the accumulation of the latest versions of the major investment papers prepared by the Gold-Economics Service. We believe it to be the only book of its kind which applies the tools of economic and investment analysis to gold. Certainly, as time passes, more data accumulate and other analysts with fresh imagination approach the subject, new studies will be forthcoming. Our hope is that this volume will stimulate unconventional thinking on the part of investors and analysts.

EUGENE J. SHERMAN

Gold Investment

I
Supply, Demand, And Above-Ground Stocks

We embark on our research of the gold market with fundamental microeconomic analysis of supply, demand, and above-ground stocks in Chapter 1, followed by the macroeconomic approach in Chapter 2.

Dr. Peter Berman carried out a conventional demand and supply analysis over the 1972–83 period, using the Consolidated Gold Fields PLC annual data. Supply/demand-price elasticities for the various gold components are estimated. This study reveals unique characteristics of the gold market, namely, the inelasticity of aggregate gold supply, unconventional positive elasticities of gold investment demand, and normal negative elasticities of karat jewelry demand. It leads to the conclusion that the gold market is demand-driven and that gold coin and bullion demand play a key role in the price formation.

"Above-Ground Stocks of Gold," written by Eugene J. Sherman in collaboration with Economic Consulting

Services, Inc., buttresses these findings with the analysis of the amount, form, and distribution of the existing stock of above-ground gold. It is pointed out that the pattern of gold supply and demand began to change radically since the 1950s. Particularly noteworthy is a substantial increase of private accumulation of bullion and coin. This suggests a growing and diversified world demand for gold.

To bring the statistics up-to-date, the latest "Update on Above-Ground Stocks: Year-End 1984 Estimates" is also reproduced at the end of the part.

1

Gold: An Economic Analysis of Supply and Demand: 1972–83

The most basic technique in the discipline of economics is demand and supply analysis. This study analyzes the components of gold demand and supply for the last 12 years during which gold was allowed to trade completely unrestricted. Of particular interest are the estimates of demand/supply-price elasticities for the various gold components over this period. In many respects, the gold market is a textbook example of the usefulness of this type of analysis.

We believe this study has important implications for gold investors, fabricators, manufacturers, producers, and portfolio managers. Some conventional wisdom is confirmed. But there are more than a few important surprises, including some unusually well developed relationships between major gold components and the dollar gold price. The analysis clearly identifies the gold market as demand driven with special importance attached to investor demands for gold bullion and gold coins.

The first chapter presents a comprehensive "Summary and Implications for Gold Investment," which stands on its own. After a chapter on methodology, the subsequent chapters describe the analyses in detail. Of special interest are the charts presenting supply and demand schedules for the major gold components.

DR. PETER I. BERMAN

Former Second Vice President/Investments
September, 1984

Summary and Implications for Gold Investment

This study subjects the gold market to a conventional demand and supply analysis over the 1972–83 period, using the Consolidated Gold Fields PLC annual data. This period reflects a free market that evolved after the central bank gold pool was broken in 1968 and the United States ended official convertibility between gold and the dollar in August 1971. The basic tools of demand and supply analysis provide a rich variety of insights about gold. Indeed, in many respects the gold market is a textbook example on the usefulness of conventional demand and supply analysis towards understanding market behavior.

Summary

Our study finds that analytically the gold market is demand-driven and has stable relationships in terms of the nominal dollar gold price. A highly inelastic, downward-sloping aggregate supply schedule cuts a unit elastic aggregate demand schedule from above. Thus shifts, or changes, in the aggregate gold demand schedule primarily impact the market determined nominal dollar gold price rather than the physical quantity of gold cleared by the market. In contrast, shifts in the aggregate gold supply schedule will ordinarily impact the physical quantity of gold rather than the nominal dollar gold price. Only very substantial shifts in the aggregate gold supply schedule will significantly affect the price.

The gold market is distinguished by some unconventional demand and supply-price relationships; it also has some unusually well defined demand schedules. The two components most closely associated with gold investment activities, bullion and gold coins, have unconventional upward sloping relationships with the dollar gold price; demand increases as the price increases, opposite the conventional response. Similarly, aggregate gold supply and its principal component, new mine production, slope downward; lower production is associated with a higher price. In conventional supply schedules, higher prices are required to induce greater quantities to the market.

Instability in the gold market principally arises from the demand for nonfabricated or bullion gold in all forms, and on the supply side from official agency activities and, to a lesser extent, communist sector sales. Ordinarily, these three unstable factors do not account for large portions of gold demand or supply. Fabricated gold products, accounting for 85 percent of aggregate gold demand, are stable and well defined in terms of the dollar gold price. In particular, karat jewelry has an unusually close fitting, linear relationship with the dollar gold price. New mine production, accounting for about 80 percent of aggregate gold supply, is not a well defined function of the dollar gold price. However, it is the least volatile of any of the individual gold demand or supply components.

Gold demand and supply became less elastic in the latter half of the sample period. This means that a given change in demand or supply was associated with a larger proportional change in the dollar gold price than previously, that is, more volatility. This finding analytically confirms the observation in recent years that dollar gold prices have become more volatile. These elasticity changes primarily accompanied the upward shifts in fabricated gold demand in 1977–78, and probably reflect global income and employment gains. However, our study did not investigate the reasons for these structural changes.

Our study finds that the 1973–74 and 1979–80 major dollar gold price increases had different origins. The first increase was completely demand-driven, originating from unusually large increases in bullion and gold coin demands. In 1974 these two investment demands accounted for 65 percent of aggregate gold demand in sharp comparison to a combined small net decumulation in 1972. In contrast, the 1979–80 major dollar gold price increase was both demand and supply driven. Gold bullion demand again increased in 1979, but aggregate gold supply contracted by 50 percent with official agencies primarily responsible. During these periods fabricated gold demand and its components generally maintained stable relationships with respect to the dollar gold price, that is, their demand schedules did not change. Also, there were no significant changes in new mine production. Our study implies that in both periods external influences, that is, disturbed international financial and economic conditions, upon gold coin and gold bullion demands, rather than mysterious inner forces, were primarily responsible for the large dollar gold price increases.

The two gold demands most closely associated with investment—gold bullion and gold coin—are quite different from one another. Bullion was three times as volatile as gold coin. In contrast, gold coin was moderately stable, shifting only in 1979–81. Its price elasticity changed from 2.5 to 1.5 in recent years. Previously a 1 percent increase in the dollar gold price was associated with an increase of 2.5 percent in gold coin demand. More recently the increase was only 1.5 percent. Elasticity estimates for the volatile bullion demand ranged between 2 and 5, that is, physical demand for bullion is very sensitive to changes in the dollar gold price.

Karat jewelry, with a 60-percent market share of fabricated gold products, is unusually well defined with a close-knit linear relationship in terms of the dollar gold price. It is difficult to find another major commodity market, using annual data, with a similarly well defined linear relationship for the major demand component. Large dollar gold price increases induced strong changes in the opposite direction for karat jewelry with a delayed response. Indeed, the study of fabricated gold demand is mostly a study of karat jewelry demand. Changes in fabricated gold volume from year to year largely reflect changes in karat jewelry volume.

The conventional view is that karat jewelry demand is markedly different as between developed and less developed countries, with the lines between adornment and investment or hoarding blurred in the latter group. Our study finds no substantially different demand-price relationships between these groups. Interestingly, during periods of karat jewelry, decumulation in 1974 and 1980 in the less developed countries— that is, melt down—changes in karat jewelry demand took place along previously established demand-price schedules.

Aggregate karat jewelry shifted in 1978, becoming substantially less elastic, from −2.5 to −0.6. Before the shift a 1 percent increase in the dollar gold price accompanied a 2.5 percent decline in the physical quantity of karat jewelry demanded. Afterwards the decline was only 0.6 percent. This 1978 shift was also observed upon disaggregation into developed and less developed countries. However, the change in elasticities originated in the latter group. Developed country elasticities remained largely unchanged at about −1.2. For this group, karat jewelry dollar sales volume (at the fabricator/manufacturer level) tended to remain the same as changes in the dollar gold price were offset by changes in the physical quantity of karat jewelry demanded.

Aggregate industrial gold demand, comprising 20 percent market share of fabricated gold products, had a fairly well defined linear demand schedule with a price-elasticity of about -0.5. A 1 percent increase in the dollar gold price was associated with a 0.5 percent decrease in the physical quantity of aggregate industrial gold demanded. Electronic and decorative gold demands had similarly defined demand schedules and elasticities. Dentistry demand, the third component, was unstable in terms of the dollar gold price. Other factors determine dentistry gold demand. As a group, aggregate industrial gold demand was the least volatile of the major fabricated gold products.

New mine production, accounting for about 80 percent of aggregate gold supply, was well defined in terms of the dollar gold price until about 1978 but subsequently shifted repeatedly. Disaggregation finds that upward shifting, unconventional downward sloping supply schedules apply both to South African mine production and production outside South Africa. Shifts in the new mine production schedule, becoming more inelastic, are another factor behind recent increased volatility in the dollar gold price.

Official agency gold activities do not have any meaningful relationship with the dollar gold price. This is not an unexpected finding since these figures are reported on a net basis involving diverse government units. While the agencies were only modest contributors of aggregate gold supply on average over the sample period, their activities on both sides of the market were associated with considerable dollar gold price instability.

Communist sector sales, primarily by the Soviet Union, supply about 20 percent of aggregate gold supply and are believed determined mostly by foreign exchange considerations. There was no sustained dollar gold price relationship although their supply schedules were also unconventionally downward-sloping.

In summary, our study finds that the gold market is stable. Three components, the most important of which is gold bullion demand, that usually account for only moderate amounts of gold demand or supply, were the major determinants of the large 1973–74 and 1979–80 dollar gold price increases. A supply contradiction had a major role in 1980 also. In contrast, fabricated gold demand, accounting for 85 percent of aggregate gold demand, is a well defined, linear, stable function of the dollar gold price with unit elasticity in recent years. By inference, aggregate gold demand is also unit elastic. New mine production is highly price inelastic, not well defined in terms of the dollar gold price, and has an unconventional downward sloping schedule. By inference, aggregate gold supply is highly inelastic and downward sloping. Recent structural shifts in both demand and supply are responsible for greater dollar gold price volatility. The activities most closely associated with investment—gold bullion and gold coins—are more properly viewed as hoarding demands, increasing with the dollar gold price and vice versa. New external disturbances to the international economic and political order could readily bring about a predictable change in the direction of the dollar gold price. Our analysis suggests that those disturbances will primarily impact the gold market by significantly increasing the demand for gold bullion and gold coins.

Implications for Gold Investment

The gold market is demand-driven with a split personality. Ordinarily it is stable, but there are three usually modest components that can generate large dollar gold price increases. Relatively few market participants will be able to track directly these unstable components—bullion demand (the most important), official agency activities, and communist sector sales. This puts a premium on keeping abreast of ongoing international economic and political developments. These are the primary determinants of major moves in the dollar gold price.

Increased new mine production outside South Africa, averaging about 40 metric tons annually, receives much attention. Current production aggregates about 1,100 tons annually in the non-communist world. However, keeping closely abreast of these mining developments will not provide especially helpful insights on future gold price movements. Nor will focusing on the changing production mix vis-a-vis South Africa be especially helpful. Aggregate gold supply is highly inelastic. Our analysis suggests that even a 10-percent mine production increase by itself would decrease the dollar gold price by only about 2 percent. Substantially larger increases in production than experienced in the early 1980s would be required for even a moderate impact on the dollar gold price.

While there is undoubtedly substantial speculative and short-term trading in gold bullion, our analysis suggests that these activities are, from the vantage of annual data, overshadowed by hoarding and investment. Gold bullion and gold coins, the two activities most closely associated with gold investment, are more properly viewed as unique hoarding demands rather than investment in the traditional sense. These demands increase as the dollar gold price increases and vice versa. Associated with long-term asset accumulation and cautionary considerations to preserve capital values, hoarding demand is likely, on balance, to continue dominating gold investment activities over the intermediate term.

Our analysis implies that privately held above-ground gold stocks pose only small risk to the dollar gold price. These stocks were estimated at approximately 10,000 metric tons in 1980, equally divided between coin and bullion.[1] They represent an inventory

[1]*Above Ground Stocks of Gold—Amounts and Distribution* (New York: International Gold Corporation Ltd., 1982), p. 9.

equal to about 25 years at current rates of coin and bullion accumulation. While changes in the dollar gold price over our sample period have substantially increased the value of these stocks, there is no evidence of substantial net dishoarding to reap windfall gains, particularly in 1973–74 and 1979–80. And the liquidation accompanying the 25-percent 1981 dollar gold price decrease was modest, less than $1 billion, compared to a $50-billion reduction in the market value of all privately held above-ground gold stocks. Bullion and coin demand appear to be true hoarding phenomena, sensitive to changes in the external international environment, rather than the size of existing above-ground stocks.

Our analysis provides analytical support for the conventional view that the dollar gold price has become more volatile in recent years. Major components of demand, as well as of supply, have shifted upward since 1977–78, becoming more price inelastic. These upward demand shifts primarily impact the dollar gold price. If the current global economic recovery substantially surpasses the previous peak, the new gains in income and employment may bring about another upward shift in fabricated gold demand. That would place upward pressure on the dollar gold price.

Analytically there is no reason why unusual external conditions could not again induce another major dollar gold price increase as in 1973–74 and 1979–80. Our analysis suggests these increases were primarily driven by bullion and gold coin demands, with an unusual supply contraction in 1980. The major components of fabricated demand did not shift during those periods. Gold bullion and coin demands continue to remain highly sensitive to external economic and political circumstances.

Our study implies that the increased availability of gold coins and its positively sloped, stable demand schedule with a 1.5 elasticity, has increased aggregate gold demand on balance. It is unlikely that coin demand has simply displaced bullion demand; the former is stable, the latter is unstable. Also, there was moderate bullion decumulation in 1972 and 1981, but none for gold coins over the entire sample period.

Aggregate gold demand over the sample period has tended to decrease as the decline in fabricated products, principally karat jewelry demand, has more than offset the increase in the only two demands with positively sloping demand schedules—gold coin and bullion. If the dollar gold price does tend to secularly increase over time, the distribution of privately held gold stocks will tend to favor bullion and coins rather than karat jewelry. (Currently karat jewelry stocks outnumber coin/bullion stocks by about 3:1.) This will be more noticeable in the developed than in the less developed countries. The karat jewelry elasticity is about -1.0 in the former group, -0.6 in the latter. Furthermore, since gold coin demand is only one-third the size of karat jewelry demand, and the elasticities are $+1.5$ and -0.6, respectively, aggregate fabricated gold demand is likely to decline in the face of a continued secular increase in the dollar gold price.

The stable relationship of the dollar gold price largely reflects the unusual stability of fabricated gold product demand. However, the mix is changing away from the most stable component—karat jewelry. By itself that suggests additional dollar gold price volatility. Moreover, with increased investor attention to gold as a financial asset, the structure of aggregate gold demand is likely to change over time, away from the traditional fabricated gold products towards bullion and coin. In time it is possible that the investment nature for gold may shift from principally a hoarding function to a traditional investment role. That development, too, would increase the volatility of the dollar gold price.

Our analysis suggests that a large reduction in the dollar gold price would not create an excess supply situation where new mine production was not completely absorbed. A major price decline would encourage substantially increased fabricated gold product demand, far overshadowing the presumed associated reduction in investor interest in coin and bullion. The karat jewelry industry, particularly in the developed countries with its unit price elasticity, is especially well positioned to take advantage of large price declines. Additionally, a price decline would induce some additional industrial demand. Since 1972 fabricated product demand has exceeded new mine production on average by 10 percent, or about 100 metric tons annually. (In only four years, 1973–74, 1980 and 1983, did new mine production exceed fabrication demand; unusually large price increases spurred by investor demand occurred in three of those years.) Furthermore, given the hoarding nature of investor demand for bullion and coins, it is quite possible that a sufficiently large price decrease would induce significant "bargain-price" stockpiling. Thus, the demand and supply characteristics of the gold market suggest that an excess supply condition is unlikely to develop. In other words, demand for fabricated gold products, the primary use of gold, is sufficiently price sensitive as to preclude a major deterioration in the gold price.[2]

In contrast, on occasion the gold market is subject to excess demand conditions (1973–74 and 1979–80). Investors bidding for bullion and official coin against an inelastic supply price fabricated gold products out of the market. An unusual feature of the gold market is that, owing to the hoarding nature of investor demand, previously accumulated stocks tend not to be liquidated when excess gold demand generates large price increases. Gold is truly unique in this respect

---

[2]Of course, with large official gold stocks used as reserves, there is always the potential for artificially creating an excess supply market condition. But it is difficult to imagine a set of conditions fostering substantial sell-off from official stocks. A concerted effort by the I.M.F. and U.S. Treasury in 1976–79 against a rising market was markedly unsuccessful. As a practical matter there seems to be an effective floor to the dollar gold price. However, our study has not been directed at quantifying that level.

among all other major financial and commodity markets. Unlike excess supply, excess gold demand is an observable market condition and is effectively resolved through price rationing. At a sufficiently high price, the market clears, and excess demand for gold is completely satisfied.

Method of Analysis

A sample of only 12 years of annual data points is a small sample indeed with which to make any meaningful inferences about the demand, supply, and price characteristics for a major market, especially one freely traded on a global basis, subject to a broad range of external influences.[3] Annual data itself precludes study of intra-year dynamics, a *sine qua non* for analysis of financial and commodity markets with their rapid adjustments to external disturbances. And regression analysis, the economist's panacea for quantitative analysis, is hardly applicable for such a small sample.[4] We need other, less restrictive tools.

Our approach has two steps. First, we make comparisons of the signs of year-to-year changes in the dollar gold price with changes in each of the gold demand or supply components, paying particular attention to signs accompanying the major changes in the dollar gold price during our sample period, such as 1973–74 and 1979–80. Examining sign changes is an important tool when working with small samples where familiar large-sample statistical procedures are not applicable.

[3]Demand and supply data, with country and industry detail, on the global gold market on a yearly basis is prepared by Consolidated Gold Fields PLC, London. No other source is believed to prepare and distribute more frequent and more complete data.

[4]Regression analysis is a large sample based procedure and requires at least 25 observations (with due allowance for degrees of freedom). No valid inferences ordinarily can be obtained from applying the regression statistic to small samples, certainly not to samples as small as 12 observations.

The purpose of the sign analysis is to identify whether conventional demand/supply-price responses for gold demand and supply components exist and which ones predominate. The conventional supply-price response is for changes in supply and price to be coincident in the same direction; the demand-price response is for opposite changes in direction. *Ex ante*, for gold demand and supply components, we do not know whether opposite or coincident signs predominate. However, if the gold market does have price dynamics similar to freely traded markets generally, sign change comparisons should reveal some conventional demand/supply-price responses. Also, it is especially important to learn in advance of undertaking scatter diagram analysis, our second step, whether current changes in gold demand or supply are associated with current changes in the dollar gold price.[5] (If lagged relationships predominate, and this has not been predetermined, then the scatters will provide incorrect inferences.)

Our second step examines dated scatter diagrams of gold demand or supply components and the dollar gold price for evidence of identifiable demand and supply relationships suggested by our analysis of sign changes. Unfortunately, scatter diagrams often cannot

[5]In effect, we postulate a binomial distribution for sign changes where the signs of changes in preselected gold demand (supply) components compared with the changes in the dollar gold price have equal probability, one-half, of being opposite (coincident) with each other for demand (supply) relationships. The 12 year sample corresponds to 12 trials, some of which may not be useful if there is no significant change in price or demand (supply) from one year to the next. An observed frequency of opposite sign changes greater than one-half the number of trials, say seven instances out of ten years, for an expected demand-price relationship would be important evidence supporting the existence of such a relationship for that component. Of course, the 12 year sample is too small for formal statistical testing, but the binomial-model is intuitively applicable and the results are important. The existence of identifiable demand/supply-price responses from sign change analysis aids our interpretation of demand/supply schedules from the scatter diagrams.

be interpreted unambiguously, particularly if only 12 sample points are involved.[6] The scatter diagrams plot 12 pairs of points corresponding to the dollar gold price (vertical axis) and demand or supply in metric tons (horizontal axis).[7] The scatter diagrams are dated to identify each point because it is the sequence of movements from year to year that merits close attention. Indeed, incorrect inferences in a number of the scatter diagrams in our study can be made if the date sequence is ignored.

Generally there are four alternative interpretations of scatter diagram plots. Points may be traced out along a downward-sloping direction formed by the:

1. intersection of a shifting supply schedule along a stable demand schedule; or

2. by the intersection of both shifting demand and supply schedules with the demand influence predominating.

Points may be traced out along an upward sloping direction formed by the:

3. intersection of a shifting demand schedule along a stable supply schedule; or,

---

[6]This is the familiar "identification problem" concerned with identifying demand and supply schedules from observed intersection points where the schedules cross each other. We cannot observe aggregate demand or supply schedules (though we can conceptualize about them), but by studying scatter points of major components we can sometimes draw inferences about them. In the gold market, inferences about new mine production and fabricated gold products enable us to make some inferences about aggregate gold supply and demand. These components comprise 80–85 percent of aggregate gold demand and supply. In particular we are interested in making inferences about the slope and elasticity of aggregate gold demand and supply. These inferences need be obtained from examination of the major components.

[7]The dollar gold price is the average of daily London fixings, averaged over the year.

4. by the intersection of both shifting supply and demand schedules with the supply schedule predominating.

In cases 2 and 4, the demand and supply schedules are not readily identifiable, a not infrequent problem when attempting to estimate demand/supply-price relationships. In cases 1 and 3, respectively, demand and supply schedules potentially can be identified and some approximate estimates can be made of their elasticity parameters and stability characteristics. Well defined series of downward-sloping scatter points can be interpreted as suggestive evidence of a stable demand schedule with the scatter points generated by the intersection of shifting supply curves upon stable demand schedules. A similar statement can be made for upward-sloping scatter points and supply.

In examining the scatter diagrams, it is important to distinguish between movements along a given demand or supply schedule traced out by the scatter points, and shifts from one demand or supply schedule to another. Shifts are properly called changes in demand or supply, reflecting a new set of tastes (for demand) or a new set of production costs (for supply). These need to be distinguished from a change in demand or supply accompanying a change in price along a pre-existing or given demand or supply schedule. In this case, tastes or production costs have not changed; movements are made along the same demand or supply schedule.

In practice judgment, rather than mechanical rules of thumb, is needed to distinguish between movements along existing schedules and shifts in scatter diagrams. We would not expect stable demand or supply relationships over the entire 12-year sample for the major gold demand or supply components, that is, scatter points uniformly along readily identifiable demand or supply schedules. Shifts or changes in gold demand or supply are inevitable, given the unusual disturbances to international financial markets during the sample period and the length of the sample itself.[8] Rather, the question is whether changes in gold demand or supply—that is, shifts in demand or supply schedules—were frequent over the 12 years, or occurred only occasionally.

Especially important is determining whether shifts in demand or supply schedules occurred during the years of the major dollar gold price increases, 1973–74 and 1979–80. In a real sense the question of whether demand/supply-price analysis can contribute to our understanding of the gold market is a question of whether major gold demand/supply-price relationships remained fairly stable over 1973–74 and 1979–80.

To abstract away from the scale used in constructing the scatter diagrams, the elasticity concept is helpful—defined as a proportional change in supply or demand (metric tons) divided by a small proportional change in the dollar gold price. The elasticities can be computed for each scatter point (pairs of prices and quantities). But it is more useful to replot the scatters on log-log paper and then compute elasticities for straight-line segments, if any. After conversion into logs, the slopes of the scatters plotted on log-log paper can then be calculated. Those figures approximate the various point elasticity values surrounding the scatter points on the charts in Figures 1–1 through 1–17.[9]

[8]Few quantitative relationships between important economic variables hold unchanged over periods as long as a decade. Shifts or structural changes in demand and supply should not be unexpected. The task is to identify them.

[9]These log-log scatters and the detailed calculations are not presented here but they can readily be constructed by the interested reader using Table 1–1 and similarly for the demand components, Table 1–6.

A 1 percent change in price associated with less than a 1 percent change in quantity demanded or supplied is called an inelastic price response. A change larger than 1 percent in quantity demanded and/or supplied is called an elastic price response. A quantity percent change equal to the percent price change is called a unit elasticity response. Since demand-price schedules ordinarily slope downward, demand-price elasticities are negative. Since

Note that some evidence of stability for at least one major gold demand or supply component is necessary before any reliable inferences can be made about the relative instability of the other components. Stable relationships over the crucial 1973–74 and 1979–80 years are particularly helpful in identifying unstable demand or supply components. Thus, a combination of analytical tools is used in making inferences in this study— comparisons of sign changes, and scatter diagrams of various demand and supply components. Additionally, a study of the response of market shares to changes in the dollar gold price will be helpful.

A number of *caveats* are in order. Our study is limited by design to analyzing gold demand and supply- nominal dollar gold price relationships and is not intended as a complete study of gold demand and supply. That study requires inclusion of many other variables, both nominal and real, that are believed to impact the gold market, such as changes in the major currencies, inflation, interest rate differentials, relative rates of return of internationally traded financial instruments, changes in disposable income, political tensions, and so on. If some major components of gold demand or supply do appear to have well identified and reasonably stable relationships with the dollar gold price, then our study will have provided useful insights. However, variables not analyzed in this study may be important in identifying shifts in gold demand and supply independent of the dollar gold price.[10] Alternatively, the absence of identifiable demand/supply-price relationships implies that the excluded variables are the potentially important determinants.[11] As a practical matter, the limitation of only an-

supply-price schedules ordinarily slope upward, supply-price elasticities are positive. Elasticities on demand-price schedules usually are different for each point along the curve.

[10]A gold demand or supply component may not be stable in terms of the dollar gold price but it could well be stable in terms of some other variable(s), including other currencies.

[11]See Sections II, III, and IV of this book.

nual available data on gold demand and supply, and the small sample itself effectively preclude inclusion of all major potentially important variables required for a complete analysis of the gold market during the tumultuous 1970s. The list of potentially important variables is almost as large as our 12-year sample of annual gold data!

Another limitation is that the gold price is expressed in dollars. However, for many gold market participants, the relevant price of gold is expressed in local currency. Given recent years' foreign exchange volatility, an analysis of gold demand or supply in terms of the dollar gold price abstracts away from the impact of currency fluctuations. Reliable relationships concerning aggregate gold demand or supply may not apply to individual country gold demand or supply relationships expressed in local currencies.

Note that the global annual data gathering effort undertaken by Consolidated Gold Fields PLC is a very large undertaking indeed, relying upon a broad spectrum of private, confidential sources as well as official government records. In particular, data on net sales by the communist sector and net sales by official government agencies are obtained from mostly nonpublished sources. Inevitably there are omissions and errors from reporting difficulties, the extent of which is not known.

Finally, note that the data are collected on a net basis for both private and public sectors. The public sector enters only on the supply side—official agency and communist sector sales. The private sector enters on the supply side—new mine production (not entirely privately produced) and on the demand side for fabricated products (karat jewelry, industrial, and coins/medals), and for nonfabricated or bullion gold in all forms. The last is obtained as a residual, subtracting fabrication from aggregate supply data. Also, the data for fabricated products are net of recycling. And note that data are on a source of production basis, not location of final demand, as would be desired for a demand and supply analysis. Thus, there are the inevitable data limitations. But this is true for other major global markets as well.

The order of presentation is as follows:

1. Gold supply.

2. Fabricated gold demand.

3. Nonfabricated or gold bullion demand.

Nonfabricated or bullion gold demand data are obtained only as a residual, subtracting fabricated gold from the aggregate supply figures. However, it may include changes in inventory and goods in transit, if any, among gold fabricators/manufacturers, and also errors and omissions and losses.

In each section we begin with a summary, followed by a general discussion of the characteristics of that particular component, including an analysis of market share. An analysis of sign change follows, and then a discussion of the sensitivity of the supply or demand component to dollar gold price changes and an examination of scatter diagrams. Some brief notes on the data collection, categories, and limitations are described in "Data Notes."

Gold Supply

Summary

Aggregate gold supply is an unconventional, downward-sloping, inelastic function of the dollar gold price. Over the sample period, aggregate gold supply has been fairly volatile from year to year. The average absolute yearly change was 227 metric tons or about 17 percent of average aggregate gold supply. Two-thirds of this variation originated in official agency activities with the balance largely from communist sector sales. In only one year was new mine production the primary source of variation in aggregate gold supply.

New mine production, accounting for 80 percent of aggregate gold supply, was a well defined, unconventional, downward-sloping function of the dollar gold price for 1972–78, but has subsequently shifted. In recent years its price elasticity was −0.2, implying that aggregate gold supply is highly inelastic. Disaggregation finds that downward-sloping inelastic supply schedules are characteristic of gold production within South Africa and of production in the rest of the noncommunist world. Recent increases in production outside South Africa, averaging about 40 metric tons annually, are not yet sufficiently large to significantly impact aggregate gold supply over the intermediate term.

Communist sector sales, the second major component of aggregate gold supply, has only a loose-fitting, unconventional, inelastic downward-sloping relationship with the dollar gold price. Sales are generally believed to reflect the Soviet Union's foreign exchange requirements.

Official agency activities, on net balance, were the primary source of year-to-year variation in aggregate gold supply even though they supplied on average only 54 metric tons annually. They were the most unstable of any gold demand or supply component in this study. Agency sales were especially large in 1977–79, reflecting IMF and U.S. Treasury sales, while other central banks and official institutions in general were net purchasers in those years. The swing from large net sales in 1979 to large net purchases in 1980 by official agencies, on balance, contracted aggregate gold supplies by almost 50 percent. By inference, this contraction was a significant causal factor in the doubling of the dollar gold price from 1979 to 1980. As with communist sector sales, agency activities are primarily driven by nonmarket forces. They reflect the balance of a broad variety of diverse political and economic decisions by various government agencies.

Overview

Over the 1972–83 period, on average, 1,309 metric tons of gold were supplied annually with a high of 1,744 tons in 1978 and a low of 812 tons in 1980 (Table 1–1). Aggregate supply in 1983 was about the same as in 1972, but was fairly volatile from year to year over the period. The average absolute change from one year to the next (ignoring sign) was 227 tons or about 17 percent of average aggregate supply for the period (Table 1–2). Supply rose 330 tons in 1976 and declined 890 tons in 1980. Excluding these two large yearly changes, the average absolute year to year change in aggregate supply was 136 tons.

In terms of market share, new mine production accounted for 79 percent on average, communist sector sales 19 percent, and the small remainder by official agency net sales (Table 1–3). Market share was volatile over the period. New mine production accounted for less than 60 percent of aggregate supply between 1977 and 1979, but approximately 100 percent in 1972, 1980, and 1981. Communist sector sales ranged from 29 percent in 1976 and 1981 to a low of 7 percent in 1983. And the official agency market share swung substantially from supplying 32 percent in 1979 to removing about 28 percent in 1980–81 through net purchases.

Reflecting long lead times, new mine production varied by only about 4 percent annually, averaging 38 metric tons (ignoring sign) over the period as the dollar gold price rose more than six times. Tonnage hardly varied at all between 1975 and 1980 as the annual dollar gold price quadrupled. Production during

Table 1–1
Gold Supply.

Supply Category	1972	1973	1974	1975	1976	1977
New mine production	1177	1111	996	946	964	962
–South Africa	910	855	759	713	713	700
–Other	267	256	237	233	251	262
Communist sector net sales	213	275	220	149	412	401
Official agency net sales (+) or purchases (−)	−151	6	20	9	58	269
Aggregate Gold Supply	1239	1392	1236	1104	1434	1632
Gold Price: $U.S.	58	97	159	161	125	148

Source: Consolidated Gold Fields PLC
Note: Data in metric tons.

Table 1–2
Year-to-Year Changes in Gold Supply.

Supply Category	1973	1974	1975	1976	1977	1978
New mine production	−66	−115	−50	+18	−2	+10
–South Africa	−55	−96	−46	0	−13	+6
–Other	−11	−19	−4	+18	+11	+4
Communist sector net sales	+62	−55	−71	+263	−11	+9
Official agency net sales (+) or purchases (−)	+157	+14	−11	+49	+211	+93
Aggregate Gold Supply	+153	−156	−132	+330	+198	+112
Gold Price: $U.S.	97	159	161	125	148	193
Change in $U.S. Gold Price	+39	+62	+2	−36	+23	+45

Note: Data in metric tons.

1978	1979	1980	1981	1982	1983	Average	Range
972	959	952	973	1023	1088	1010	946 to 1177
706	705	675	658	664	680	728	658 to 910
266	254	277	315	360	408	282	233 to 408
410	199	90	280	202	92	245	90 to 412
362	544	−230	−276	−85	119	54	−276 to 544
1744	1702	812	977	1140	1299	1309	812 to 1744
193	305	612	460	375	424	260	58 to 612

1979	1980	1981	1982	1983	Absolute Average	Range
−13	−7	+21	+50	+65	38	−115 to +65
−1	−30	−17	+6	+16	26	−96 to +16
−12	+23	+38	+45	+48	21	−19 to +48
−211	−109	+190	−78	−110	106	−211 to +263
+182	−774	−46	+191	+204	176	−744 to +211
−42	−890	+165	+163	+159	227	−890 to +330
305	612	460	375	424	278	+ 97 to +612
+112	+307	−152	−85	+49	83	−152 to +307

Table 1–3
Gold Supply Market Share (in Percent).

Supply Category	1972	1973	1974	1975	1976	1977
New mine production	95	80	81	86	67	59
—South Africa*	77	77	76	75	74	73
—Other*	23	23	24	25	26	27
Communist sector net sales	17	20	18	14	29	25
Official agency net sales (+) or purchases (−)	− 12	0	2	1	4	16
Aggregate Gold Supply	100	100	100	100	100	100
Gold Price: $U.S.	58	97	159	161	125	148

Note: Data in metric tons.
   *Expressed as a percent of new mine production.

the sample period was the highest in 1972 at 1,177 tons, with a low in 1975 at 945 tons.[12] Ordinarily, changes in new mine production were overshadowed by the two nonmarket driven supply factors. Despite considerable industry attention to new sources, in only one year, 1974, was the change in new mine production the major factor in aggregate gold supply change from the previous year. Since 1980, new mine production has increased about 14 percent or 3.4 percent annually on average; it is now about 8 percent below the 1972 high point for our sample of 1,177 tons.

South African production accounted for 72 percent of new mine production over the period. Market share declined from 77 percent in 1972 to 71 percent in 1980, and then subsequently fell to 63 percent in 1983. Production declined from 910 metric tons in 1972 to 658 tons in 1981, and stood at 680 tons in 1983. Conse-

[12]Note that production averaged 1,252 tons during 1963–71 although the dollar gold price was considerably lower.

1978	1979	1980	1981	1982	1983	Average	Range
56	56	117	100	90	84	81	56 to 117
73	74	71	68	65	63	72	63 to 77
27	26	29	32	35	38	28	23 to 38
24	12	11	29	18	7	19	7 to 29
21	32	−28	−28	−7	9	1	−28 to 32
100	100	100	100	100	100	100	
193	305	612	460	375	424	260	58 to 612

quently, production outside South Africa boosted its market share to 38 percent in 1983 from 23 percent in 1972. That increase is a 1980s phenomenon; prior to 1980 production outside South Africa ranged between 233 and 267 tons. The largest declines in South African production during the sample period studied occurred in 1973–75; modest increases occurred in 1982–83. Production outside South Africa has increased about 40 tons on average over each of the last 3 years. As is well known, South Africa is geared towards extending mine life, working lower-grade ores as the dollar gold price rises. Production outside South Africa in recent years has been spurred by a variety of factors, including the attractiveness of the dollar gold price itself, and the strong U.S. dollar accompanying major real currency devaluations in Latin America.

Communist sector sales, the second largest supply factor to the gold market, averaged 245 metric tons over the period. The low of 90 tons was in 1980 and the high of 412 tons in 1976. The Soviet Union dominates sector sales. Its market activities are broadly thought to reflect foreign exchange requirements. Over the sample period, sector sales have earned about 25 billion dollars. In turn, that is a function of the wheat crop, natural energy prices, sales of armaments, political concerns, and the like. Sector sales were the major determinant of changes in aggregate gold supplies in four years when they accounted for about a 25 percent market share—1976–78, and 1981. Most recently, in 1983, the share was 7 percent. Changes in sector sales from one year to the next were substantial, ranging from a 263 ton increase in 1976 to a 211 ton decline in 1979. Ignoring sign, the average absolute change in sector sales averaged 106 tons, nearly one-half their average level over the entire period.

Official agency activities were by far the most volatile supply component. They accounted for about two-thirds of the average absolute change in aggregate gold supplies from one year to the next, even though their net sales over the sample period averaged only 54 metric tons. A swing from unusually large sales of 544 tons in 1979 to a 276 tons purchase in 1980 was primarily responsible for collapsing aggregate gold supply by 50 percent in 1980. In 1980, net purchases by official agencies removed about 28 percent of aggregate supplies from the market as the dollar gold price doubled.

The reported official agency figures are the combined net balance of activities on both sides of the gold market by noncommunist central bank and multinational official agencies. Over the sample period, net sales occurred in 8 years, purchases in 4. However, sales were substantial only in 3 years, 1977–79, averaging almost 400 metric tons or about 25 percent of the aggregate gold supply. These sales reflected concerted IMF and U.S. Treasury efforts to demonetize gold. The IMF disposed of 1,555 tons between 1977–80 and the U.S. Treasury sold 530 tons between 1978–80.[13]

---

[13]*Gold Investment Handbook—A Guide for Institutional Portfolio Managers* (New York: International Gold Corporation Ltd., 1981), p. 8–9.

On average the IMF and U.S. Treasury were supplying 522 tons yearly during 1977–80, a time when the
annual dollar gold price rose from $148 to $612. Over
this period official agency net sales were 236 tons. By
inference, other official institutions and central banks
were net purchasers of 286 tons annually. Also, by inference, other institutions and central banks in toto
were net purchasers in 7 of the 12 years. Thus, aside
from the concerted IMF and U.S. Treasury activities in
1977–80, official agencies tended not to favor any particular side of the market during the 1972–83 period.
We should not expect a stable relationship between
official agency sales or purchases and the dollar gold
price.

Sensitivity to Dollar Gold Price Change

Over the 12-year period the signs of changes in aggregate gold supply, and for the two major components, were mostly opposite the sign of changes in the
dollar gold price (Tables 1–4 and 1–5). Importantly,
this generally occurred during the years of the large
dollar gold price increases. Large dollar gold price
changes (more than 50 percent) were observed in
1973–74 and 1979–80 with a very large increase in 1980
(more than 100 percent). Thus, the gold supply-price
response was the reverse of the conventionally observed supply relationship in markets for freely traded
goods in which a higher price is necessary to encourage a larger quantity to the market. In the gold market,
higher dollar gold prices encourage smaller supplies of
gold to the market; sign change analysis suggests gold
supply schedules will be downward-sloping.
    Changes in the sign of new mine production, ac-
counting for about 80 percent of aggregate gold supply, were opposite the sign of dollar gold price
changes in seven out of nine years, including all of the
four large dollar gold price increase years—1973–74
and 1979–80. This suggests a downward-sloping new

Table 1-4
Signs of Year-to-Year Changes in Gold Supply.

Supply Category	1973	1974	1975	1976	1977	1978	1979	1980	1981	1982	1983
New mine production											
-South Africa	−	−	−	+	n.a.	+	n.a.	−	+	+	+
-Other	−	−	−	+	+	+	−	+	+	n.a.	+
Communist sector net sales	+	−	−	+++	−	+	−	−−	+++	−	−−
Official agency net sales (+) or purchases (−)	+++	+++	−−	+++	+++	+	++	−−	−	++	+++
Aggregate Gold Supply	+	−	−	+	+	+	++	−−	+	+	+
Gold Price: $U.S.	97	159	161	125	148	193	305	612	460	375	424
Sign of change	++	++	n.a.	−	+	+	++	+++	−	−	+

Notes: (a) + and − denote increase or decrease in gold supply (metric tons) or dollar gold price from one year to the next.
(b) ++ and − − denote a percentage change exceeding 50% but less than 100% from one year to the next.
(c) +++ and − − − denote a percentage change exceeding 100% from one year to the next.
(d) n.a. denotes not applicable—less than one percent change.

Table 1–5
Comparison of Signs of Year-to-Year Changes in Gold Supply with Signs of Changes in Dollar Gold Price.

Supply Category	Classification of sign changes			Co-incident sign changes		Opposite sign changes
	Plus	Minus	No change	Plus	Minus	
Supply Category						
New mine production	5	5	1	2	n.a.	7
–South Africa	1	6	4	1	1	4
–Other	7	4	n.a.	4	n.a.	6
Communist sector net sales	4	7	n.a.	2	1	7
Official agency net sales (+) or purchases (−)	8	3	n.a.	6	1	3
Aggregate Gold Supply	7	4	n.a.	4	n.a.	6
Gold Price: $U.S.	7	3	1	n.a.	n.a.	n.a.

Notes: (a) n.a. denotes not applicable.

mine production supply schedule. Changes in South African production were opposite the sign of changes in three of the large dollar gold price increase years. Changes in production outside South Africa were opposite the sign of changes in the dollar gold price in six out of nine years, including three of the large dollar gold price increase years. Thus, the opposite sign of supply and price changes is characteristic of mine production generally, not a function of the changing mix in production from South Africa to increased production elsewhere in recent years. Changes in the sign of communist sector gold sales were opposite the sign of changes in the dollar gold price in seven out of ten years, including three of the four large gold price increase years. Large communist sector supply changes occurred in two of those years, 1979–80. This suggests a downward-sloping supply schedule. Evidently, on an annual basis, communist sector sales are not determined by high dollar gold prices.

Changes in the sign of official agency net sales were coincident with the sign of changes in the dollar gold price in seven out of ten years including very large supply changes (exceeding 100 percent) in three of the large dollar gold price increase years. Thus, with respect to sign change, official agencies expressed the conventional supply-price response.

Changes in the sign of aggregate gold supply were opposite the sign of changes in the dollar gold price in six out of ten years. Opposite sign changes were observed in the four years of large dollar gold price changes. In one of those years, 1980, a large aggregate gold supply change (50 percent or more) occurred. This suggests that the aggregate gold supply schedule will be downward-sloping. However, the aggregate gold supply schedules will not be visible from a scatter diagram since those points reflect the intersection of both aggregate gold demand and aggregate gold supply. Inferences about these schedules in our study

need be made from scatters of their major components.[14]

Gold Supply-Price Schedules

NEW MINE PRODUCTION. New mine production has a
well defined, linear, unconventional, stable, downward-sloping schedule for 1972–78 and then shifts upward to a less stable schedule for 1980–82 (Figure 1–1).
Ordinarily, supply schedules slope upward. The

[14]The aggregate gold demand/supply scatter does show well
defined downward-sloping linear schedules for 1973–77, and an
upward shift to 1980–82 with approximately unit elasticity. Shifts
occurred in 1973, 1978, 1980, and 1983; thus, shifts in at least one of
the schedules occurred during major dollar gold price increases.

Figure 1–1
New Mine Production vs. Dollar Gold Price.

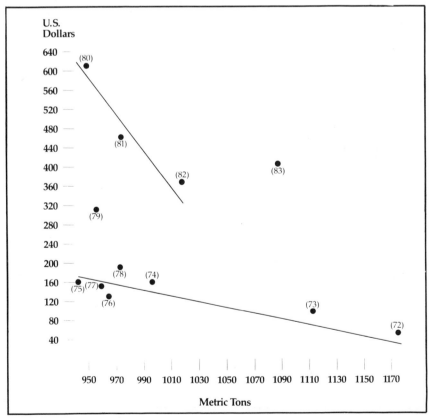

elasticities are approximately grouped around −0.5 for the 1972–78 period, and a more inelastic (or a less responsive) −0.2 for the 1980–82 period. Recent new mine production is highly inelastic; a 1 percent increase in the dollar gold price is associated with a 0.2 percent decrease in new mine production. Shifts apparently occurred in 1979, 1980, and 1983. The shift in 1979, during a large price change, contrasts with the 1973–74 episode in which supply did not change (supply changed along the same schedule in 1973–74).

Disaggregating, similarly we find unconventional, downward-sloping supply schedules for production in South Africa and elsewhere (Figures 1–2 and 1–3).

Figure 1–2

South African New Mine Production vs. Dollar Gold Price.

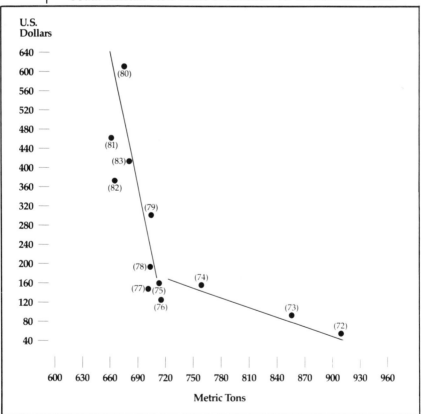

Figure 1–3
New Mine Production Outside South Africa vs. Dollar Gold Price.

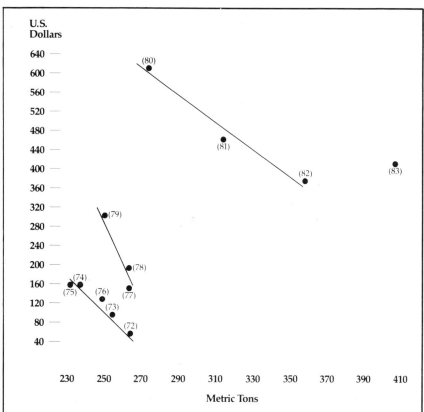

South African production was a well defined function of the dollar gold price until about 1977, when the supply schedule abruptly became almost completely inelastic. However, the still downward-sloping schedule remained quite well defined in terms of the dollar gold price with closely fitting scatter points. South African gold production has an unusual, if not unique, kinked supply schedule.[15] The scatter for new mine production outside South Africa depicts a series of downward sloping but upward shifting, less well defined sched-

[15]The standard example of a kinked downward-sloping schedule is the kinked demand curve of oligopoly theory. Downward-sloping supply schedules in freely traded markets are unusually infrequent. The kinked South African gold supply schedule is very likely a unique phenomenon.

ules (Figure 1–3). While South African production had a single unusually well defined shift, becoming almost completely price inelastic, production outside South Africa was considerably less well defined in terms of the dollar gold price. It shifted upwards in 1977, 1980, and 1983. Interestingly, neither supply schedule shifted during 1973–74, but they did shift upwards in 1977, both becoming less price elastic just prior to the next major dollar gold price increase.

The scatter diagrams suggest that unconventional downward-sloping supply schedules are characteristic of the gold mining industry. Shifts in new mine production, becoming more inelastic in recent years, have been a causal factor in the observed increased volatility of the dollar gold price.

COMMUNIST SECTOR SALES. Communist sector net sales have two, only loose fitting, downward-sloping relationships with the dollar gold price—1972–1975 and 1979–83 (Figure 1–4). A variety of shifts occur in 1976–79 and again 1981–83. The elasticities for the two groups of scatter points center around −0.3 and −0.7, tentatively suggesting an upward, but more elastic shift toward the end of the sample period. The timing of the supply shift between 1978 and the 1979–80 large dollar gold price increase (but not in 1973–74) replicates the shift in new mine production. The absence of a well defined supply relationship with the dollar gold price is not surprising. Communist sector sales, mostly from the Soviet Union, are believed principally determined by foreign exchange requirements.

OFFICIAL AGENCY SALES. The scatter diagram for official agency net sales does not suggest any meaningful supply-price relationship (Figure 1–5). Since this

Figure 1–4
Communist Sector Sales vs. Dollar Gold Price.

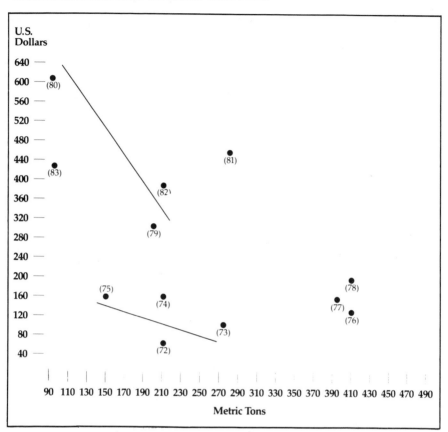

data represents the net figures from a substantial number of transactions involving diverse political and economic considerations by official agencies, this is not an unexpected result. The diagram does depict several upward-sloping, but unstable and only loosely fitting relationships. The points between 1973 and 1976 are nearly vertical, that is, virtually completely inelastic, centering around zero tonnage. The points for 1977–79 do express a well defined linear relationship with a 0.6 elasticity, but this is too short a period from which to make reliable inferences. Thereafter, the supply schedule shifts over the next several years.

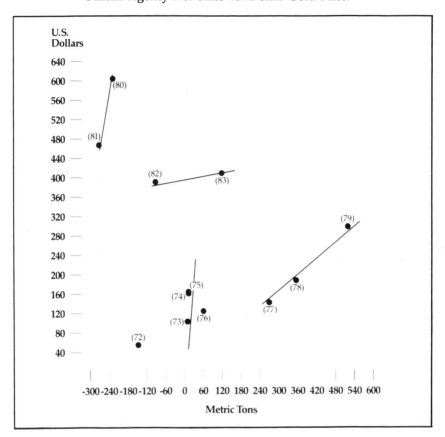

Figure 1–5
Official Agency Net Sales vs. Dollar Gold Price.

Fabricated Gold Demand

Summary

Fabricated gold demand has a conventional, well defined, linear, downward-sloping, stable relationship with the dollar gold price with a price elasticity of about −1 (Figure 1–6). A 1 percent increase in the dollar gold price will accompany a 1 percent decrease in the physical demand for fabricated gold products and vice versa. Since fabricated gold demand comprises about 80 percent of aggregate gold demand, by inference, aggregate gold demand also has −1 elasticity.

Figure 1–6
Fabricated Gold Demand vs. Dollar Gold Price.

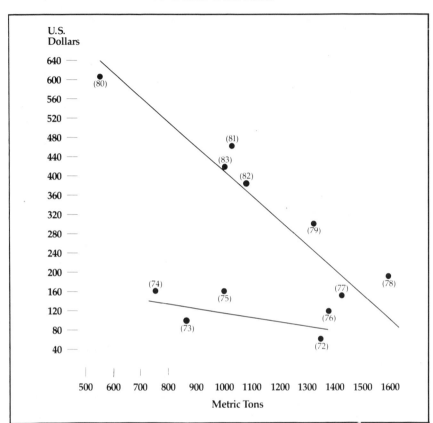

Unexpectedly, disaggregation generally finds well developed demand schedules for fabricated gold demand components in terms of the dollar gold price.

Karat jewelry, the largest component, is unusually well defined in terms of the dollar gold price with an elasticity of -0.6 in recent years. A 1 percent increase in the dollar gold price will accompany a 0.6 percent decrease in the physical demand for karat jewelry at the fabricator/manufacturer level. Karat jewelry demand is similarly well defined upon disaggregating into developed and less developed countries. The former has -1 elasticity. Changes in the dollar gold price will be offset proportionally by changes in the opposite direction in physical karat jewelry demand with karat jewelry dollar sales volume remaining unchanged at the fabricator/manufacturer level. Less developed country karat jewelry demand had price elasticities ranging between −1.4 and −0.6 in recent years. Contrary to conventional wisdom we found no outstanding differences in karat jewelry demand as between developed and less developed countries. Decumulation did occur in the latter group in 1974 and 1980, but occurred along established demand schedules.

Industrial gold demand was fairly well defined with a price elasticity of about −0.5 in recent years and also for electronic and decorative components. In recent years a 1 percent increase in the dollar gold price was associated with a 0.5 percent decrease in aggregate industrial, decorative, and electronic gold demands. However, dentistry demand, the third component of industrial gold demand, is not well defined in terms of the current dollar gold price.

Gold coin demand, associated with gold investment activities, has an unconventional, upward sloping, well defined demand schedule with an elasticity of about 1.5. A 1 percent increase in the dollar gold price is associated with a 1.5 percent increase in gold coin demand. Gold coin demand is more properly viewed as a hoarding demand. Prior to 1978, the price elasticity was 2.5; thus demand has become less responsive over time to changes in the dollar gold price.

The gold medals demand is a conventional, downward-sloping schedule with a price elasticity of about −1.4 and is similar to karat jewelry demand. Gold medals demand accounts only for about 3 percent of fabricated gold demand.

Each of the fabricated gold product demands (with the exception of dentistry) shifted upwards after 1977–78, becoming less elastic, that is, less responsive to changes in the dollar gold price. These shifts in fabricated gold demand are, at least in part, causally responsible for the observed increased dollar gold price volatility in recent years.

The well defined component demand-price relationships for fabricated gold, with both upward-and downward-sloping schedules, is a strong result and contrasts with aggregate supply and its components. For practical purposes, year-to-year variation in fabricated gold demand reflects changes in karat jewelry demand. Analytically, the gold market is demand-driven. Importantly, fabricated gold demand and its components did not shift during the major dollar gold price increases in 1973–74 and 1979–80. Those increases were causally associated with changes in gold supply, bullion demand, or factors other than the dollar gold price. Karat jewelry demand rebounded completely in 1975 to levels prior to the earlier 1973–74 dollar gold price increase. But demand remains about 40 percent below levels prior to the 1979–80 dollar gold price increase, as does aggregate fabricated gold demand itself.

Overview

Aggregate fabricated gold demand averaged about 1,100 metric tons annually over the 1972–83 period with a high of 1,595 tons in 1978 and a low of 544 tons in 1980 (Table 1–6). Demand in 1983 was about 25 percent less than in 1972 and was fairly volatile over the period. The average absolute change from one year to the next (ignoring sign) was 286 metric tons or about 22 percent of average aggregate gold demand (Table 1–7). Fabricated gold demand was about 20 percent more volatile than aggregate gold supply even though it was 15 percent smaller. Fabricated gold demand declined about 1,000 tons in just two years, from a high of 1,595 tons in 1978 to a low of 544 tons in 1980. And in only three years (1977, 1982, and 1983) was the change in aggregate fabricated demand from one year to the next less than 100 tons.

In terms of market share, karat jewelry demand accounted for 60 percent, with the balance evenly di-

Table 1–6
Fabricated and Nonfabricated Gold Demand.

		1972	1973	1974	1975	1976	1977
I	**Fabricated Gold Demand**						
	A. Official coins						
	and medals	105	74	294	272	233	194
	–coins	63	54	287	251	182	142
	–medals	42	20	7	21	51	52
	B. Industrial	240	263	215	186	216	228
	–dentistry	65	67	57	62	77	85
	–electronic	105	124	91	66	74	76
	–decorative	70	72	67	58	65	67
	C. Karat jewelry	999	508	216	516	937	1004
	D. Total Fabricated						
	Gold Demand	1345	845	724	974	1384	1426
II	**Non-Fabricated**						
	Gold Demand	– 106	547	512	130	50	206
III	**Aggregate Gold Demand**	1239	1392	1236	1104	1434	1632
	Gold Price: $U.S.	58	97	159	161	125	148

Notes: (a) Totals may not add due to rounding.
     (b) Coin and medal fabrication figures are for products actually sold to private users as
         distinct from total production for public authorities.
     (c) Data in metric tons.

Source: Consolidated Gold Fields PLC

1978	1979	1980	1981	1982	1983	Average	Range
337	324	202	219	153	196	217	74 to 337
287	291	186	192	131	165	186	54 to 291
50	33	16	27	22	31	31	7 to 52
255	265	217	219	208	208	227	186 to 265
91	87	62	64	61	53	69	57 to 91
89	99	89	90	85	97	90	66 to 124
75	79	66	65	62	58	67	58 to 79
i004	728	126	595	715	598	662	126 to 1004
1595	1317	544	1033	1076	1002	1105	544 to 1595
149	385	268	− 56	67	297	204	− 106 to 547
1744	1702	812	977	1140	1299	1309	812 to 1744
193	305	612	460	375	424	260	58 to 612

Table 1-7
Year-to-Year Changes in Gold Demand.

		1973	1974	1975	1976	1977
I	**Fabricated Gold Demand**					
	A. Official coins					
	and medals	−31	+220	−22	−39	−39
	−coins	−9	+233	−36	−69	−40
	−medals	−22	−13	+14	+30	+1
	B. Industrial	+23	−48	−29	+30	+12
	−dentistry	+2	−10	+5	+15	+8
	−electronic	+19	−33	−25	+8	+2
	−decorative	+2	−5	−9	+7	+2
	C. Karat jewelry	−491	−292	+300	+421	+67
	D. Total Fabricated					
	Gold Demand	−500	−121	+250	+410	+42
II	**Non-Fabricated**					
	Gold Demand	+653	−35	−382	−80	+156
III	**Aggregate Gold Demand**	+153	−156	−132	+330	+198
	Gold price: $U.S.	+39	+62	+2	−36	+23

Notes: (a) Totals may not add due to rounding.
      (b) Data in metric tons.

1978	1979	1980	1981	1982	1983	Average	Range
+ 143	− 13	− 122	+ 17	− 66	+ 43	69	− 122 to + 220
+ 145	+ 4	− 105	+ 6	− 61	+ 34	67	− 105 to + 233
− 2	− 17	− 17	+ 11	− 5	+ 9	13	− 22 to + 30
+ 27	+ 10	− 48	+ 2	− 11	0	22	− 48 to + 30
+ 6	− 4	− 25	+ 2	− 3	− 8	8	− 25 to + 15
+ 13	+ 10	− 10	+ 1	− 5	+ 12	13	− 33 to + 19
+ 8	+ 4	− 13	− 1	− 3	− 4	5	− 13 to + 8
0	− 276	− 602	+ 469	+ 120	− 117	287	− 602 to + 469
+ 169	− 278	− 773	+ 489	+ 43	− 74	286	− 773 to + 489
− 57	+ 236	− 117	− 324	+ 123	+ 230	218	− 382 to + 653
+ 112	− 42	− 890	+ 165	+ 163	+ 159	227	− 890 to + 330
+ 45	+ 112	+ 307	− 152	− 85	+ 49	83	− 152 to + 307

vided between industrial demand and coins/medals demand (Table 1–8). Market share was volatile, particularly during years of major gold price changes. Karat jewelry market share declined by one-half, from 60 to 31 percent in 1974, and again from 56 to 23 percent in 1980. Coins/medals market share rose temporarily in 1974 to 40 percent, and industrial demand rose to between 30 and 40 percent in 1974 and 1980. The three components of industrial gold demand—decorative, electronic, and dentistry—had approximately equal market shares. The gold medals component averaged only one-sixth of aggregate coins/medals demand or about 3 percent of aggregate fabricated gold demand. Over the sample period, gold coin demand absorbed the equivalent of about one-sixth of new mine production.

Karat jewelry was the primary determinant of the changes in aggregate fabricated gold demand from one year to the next. Over the 12-year period, the average absolute year-to-year changes were virtually identical—286 metric tons for aggregate fabricated demand and 287 tons for karat jewelry demand. The three largest increases and the three largest decreases in aggregate fabricated demand and karat jewelry demand occurred in the same year and had the same order of ranking with each other. These increases and decreases by size ranking and year are as follows:

Years	Change in aggregate fabricated demand from prior year (metric tons)	Change in karat jewelry demand from prior year (metric tons)
1981	489	469
1976	410	421
1975	250	300
1980	−773	−602
1973	−500	−491
1979	−278	−276

Indeed, only once during the 12-year period did another component other than karat jewelry demand provide a larger portion of the year-to-year change in aggregate fabricated demand. Moreover, karat jewelry demand was 40 percent more volatile than coin/medal demand and 250 percent more than industrial demand. In a real sense, variation in fabricated gold demand is largely determined by variation in karat jewelry demand.

Sensitivity to Dollar Gold Price Change

The analysis of sign changes between changes in fabricated demand and of the dollar gold price suggests a conventional, downward-sloping demand-price relationship. This contrasts with the unconventional aggregate supply schedule, also downward-sloping. Fabricated gold demand and its major component, karat jewelry, each moved opposite to changes in the dollar gold price in seven out of eight years (Tables 1–9 and 1–10). Industrial demand sign changes were coincident in five out of eight years. Coin/medals were opposite in five out of nine years. Coins were coincident in five of nine years.

Of particular interest are the sign change comparisons between fabricated gold demand components and the major dollar gold price increases. Karat jewelry did not initially respond to the 1973 increase, but did respond with a large decline (more than 50 percent) to the 1974 dollar gold price increase. Then, in 1975, it posted a large increase. A similar delayed response occurred to the 1979–80 dollar gold price increase. This delayed adjustment pattern was also observed for aggregate fabricated demand in 1980–81. A delayed response also occurred for the small medals component, suggesting a demand-price response similar to karat jewelry. Coins responded to the 1974 dollar gold price increase with a very large increase, and also increased in 1978. No large changes in industrial de-

Table 1–8
Gold Demand Market Share (in Percent).

		1972	1973	1974	1975	1976
I	**Fabricated Gold Demand Market Shares**					
	A. Official coins					
	and medals	8	9	40	27	17
	–coins	5	6	39	25	13
	–medals	3	3	1	2	4
	B. Industrial	18	31	29	19	16
	–dentistry	5	8	8	6	6
	–electronic	8	15	12	7	5
	–decorative	5	8	9	6	5
	C. Karat jewelry	74	60	31	53	68
	D. Total Fabricated Gold Demand	100	100	100	100	100
II	**Fabricated Gold Demand as Percent of Aggregate Demand**	109	61	59	88	97
III	**Non-Fabricated Gold Demand as Percent Aggregate Demand**	−9	39	41	12	3
	Gold Price: $U.S.	58	97	159	161	125

Notes: (a) Totals may not add due to rounding.
      (b) Data in metric tons.

1977	1978	1979	1980	1981	1982	1983	Average	Range
14	21	25	37	21	14	20	21	8 to 40
10	18	22	34	19	12	16	18	5 to 39
4	3	3	3	3	2	3	3	1 to 4
16	17	21	39	21	19	21	22	16 to 39
6	6	7	11	6	6	5	7	5 to 11
5	6	8	16	9	8	10	9	5 to 16
5	5	6	12	6	6	6	7	5 to 12
71	63	56	23	58	67	60	57	31 to 74
00	100	100	100	100	100	100	100	
87	91	77	67	106	94	77	84	59 to 109
13	9	23	33	− 6	6	23	16	− 9 to 41
48	193	305	612	460	375	424	260	58 to 612

Table 1–9
Sign of Year-to-Year Changes in Gold Demand.

	1973	1974	1975	1976
I Fabricated Gold Demand				
A. Official coins				
and medals	−	+ + +	−	−
−coins	−	+ + +	−	−
−medals	−	− −	+ + +	+ + +
B. Industrial	+	−	−	+
−dentistry	+	−	+	+
−electronics	+	−	−	+
−decorated	+	−	−	+
C. Karat jewelry	−	− −	+ + +	+ +
D. Total Fabricated				
Gold Demand	−	−	+	+
II Non-Fabricated Gold Demand	+ + +	−	− −	− −
III Aggregate Gold Demand	+	−	−	+
Gold Price: $U.S.	97	159	161	125
Sign of change	+ +	+ +	n.a.	−

Notes: (a) + and − denote increase or decrease in gold fabrication from one year to the
next.
(b) + + and − − denote a percentage change exceeding 50% but less than 100%
from one year to the next.
(c) + + + and − − − denote a percent change exceeding 100% from one year to
the next.
(d) n.a. denotes non applicable-less than one percent change.

1977	1978	1979	1980	1981	1982	1983
−	+ +	−	−	+	−	+
−	+ +	n.a.	−	+	−	+
+	−	−	− −	+ +	−	+
+	+	+	−	n.a.	−	n.a.
+	+	−	−	n.a.	−	−
n.a.	+	+	−	n.a.	−	+
+	+	+	−	−	−	−
+	n.a.	−	− −	+ + +	+	−
+	+	−	− −	+ +	+	−
+ + +	−	+ + +	−	− − −	+ + +	+ + +
+	+	−	− −	+	+	+
148	193	305	612	460	375	424
+	+	+ +	+ +	−	−	+

Table 1–10
**Comparison of Signs of Year-to-Year Changes in Gold Demand
with Signs of Changes in Dollar Gold Price.**

	1973	1974	1975	1976	1977	1978	1979	1980	1981	1982	1983
Increase or Decrease in Market Shares of Fabricated Gold Demand											
Official coins and medals	+	+++	–	–	–	+	+	++	–	–	+
Industrial	++	– –	–	–	n.a.	n.a.	+	++	–	–	++
Karat jewelry	–	– –	++	+	+	–	–	– –	+++	+	–
Gold Price: $U.S.	97	159	161	125	148	193	305	612	460	375	424
Increase or decrease of dollar gold price	++	++	n.a.	–	+	+	++	++	–	–	+

Notes: (a) + and − denoe increase or decrease.
(b) + + and − − denote increase or decrease larger than 50% over previous years price or market share but less than 100%.
(c) + + + denotes increase greater than 100% over previous year.
(d) n.a. denotes not applicable-less than one percent change.

Sign of Year-to-Year Changes in Market Share of Fabricated Gold Demand.

	Classification of Sign Changes			Co-incident Sign Changes		Opposite Sign Changes
	Plus	Minus	No change	Plus	Minus	
I Fabricated Gold Demand						
A. Official coins and medals	4	7	n.a.	3	2	5
–coins	4	6	1	3	2	4
–medals	5	6	n.a.	2	1	7
B. Industrial	5	4	2	4	1	3
–dentistry	5	5	1	3	1	5
–electronics	5	4	2	4	1	3
–decorative	5	6	n.a.	4	2	4
C. Karat Jewelry	5	5	1	1	n.a.	8
D. Total Fabricated Gold Demand	6	5	n.a.	2	n.a.	8
II Non-Fabricated Gold Demand	5	6	n.a.	4	2	4
III Aggregate Gold Demand	7	4	n.a.	4	n.a.	6
Gold Price: $U.S.	7	3	1	n.a.	n.a.	n.a.

Notes: (a) n.a. denotes not applicable.

mand or in any of its components occurred over the 12-year period.

Thus, comparison of sign changes suggests downward-sloping, conventional demand-price responses for karat jewelry and medals demand. The gold coin response suggests an upward-sloping demand schedule, that is, a hoarding demand.

Fabricated Gold Demand-Price Schedules

KARAT JEWELRY DEMAND. The karat jewelry scatter diagram depicts an unusually well defined downward-sloping demand schedule with an upward shift in demand in 1977 (Figure 1–7). The price elasticities are −2.5 and −0.6 for 1972–76 and 1977–83, respectively. The upward shift from an elastic to an inelastic demand schedule in 1977 implies that karat jewelry demand has been a factor in the increased volatility of the dollar gold price. Previously a 1 percent dollar gold price increase accompanied a 2.5 percent decrease in physical karat jewelry demanded. After the increase (shift) in demand, the decrease in karat jewelry was only −0.6 percent. The causes of that shift were not investigated in this study, but they likely were related to the broad-based global gains in income and employment at that time.

The conventional wisdom holds that the line between karat jewelry as adornment and as investment is blurred in the less developed countries. This implies that the price elasticities should be substantially different upon disaggregating karat jewelry demand. Since the karat jewelry data is collected by source of fabrication, rather than by location of final demand, there are some limitations in our confidence with which we can empirically distinguish between these disaggregated karat jewelry demands. Note that about two-thirds of all the privately held gold is in the form of karat jewelry. In 1980 these stocks were estimated at about

Figure 1–7
Karat Jewelry Gold Demand vs. Dollar Gold Price.

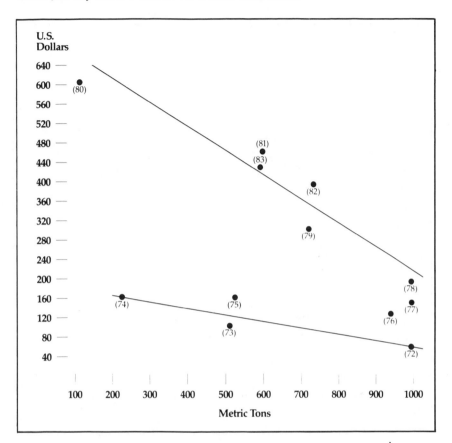

27,300 metric tons in the noncommunist world.[16] Of that amount about two-thirds were estimated to be held in the developed countries—Western Europe, North America, and Japan. Western Europe was estimated to hold almost one-half of all privately held karat jewelry stocks.

The scatter diagram for developed country karat jewelry demand depicts well defined, linear, downward sloping schedules for the 1972–76 and 1978–83 periods with an upward shift in 1977 (Figure 1–8). The price elasticities are −1.3 and −1.1, respectively.

[16]See Chapter 2, p. 88.

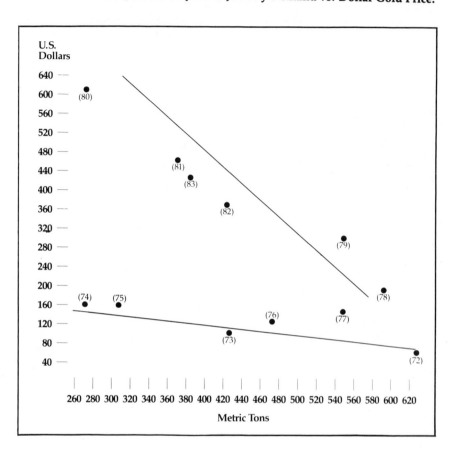

Figure 1-8
Developed Country Karat Jewelry Demand vs. Dollar Gold Price.

Karat jewelry demand in the developed countries has approximately unit elasticity. Changes in the dollar gold price will be offset by proportional changes in physical karat jewelry demand in the opposite direction; karat jewelry dollar sales will remain unchanged at the fabricator/manufacturer level. Since the shift did not appreciably change the demand-price elasticity, the increased demand for karat jewelry in developed countries was not a causal factor in a more volatile dollar gold price.

The scatter diagram for less developed country karat jewelry demand also depicts well defined, downward-sloping schedules for 1972–76 and 1977–83 with an up-

Figure 1–9
Less Developed Country Karat Jewelry Demand vs. Dollar Gold Price.

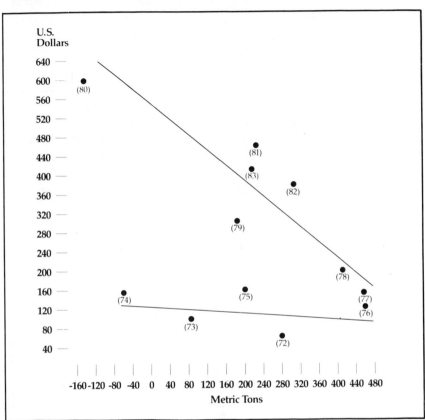

ward shift in 1977 (Figure 1–9). However, the demand-price elasticities are less closely grouped, becoming more inelastic over time. For 1972–76 the elasticities are −1.2 to −2. For 1978–83 the elasticities are generally smaller, between −1.4 and −0.6. Thus, the upward shift in developing country karat jewelry demand was a factor in increased dollar gold price volatility. Interestingly, during the years of decumulation—that is, meltdown—in 1974 and 1980, karat jewelry demand changed along existing demand schedules rather than shifting. This is important evidence suggesting karat jewelry demand is also stable in the less developed countries.

This evidence suggests that karat jewelry demand is well defined and stable, both in the aggregate and when disaggregated into developed and less developed countries. Demand shifted upwards in 1977 becoming more inelastic. However, the increased inelasticity for aggregate karat jewelry demand originated in the less developed countries. Demand-price elasticity did not appreciably change in the developed countries. The evidence suggests that karat jewelry demands are basically similar as between the developed and less developed countries, although the demand-price elasticities are different. The evidence does not

Figure 1–10
Industrial Gold Demand vs. Dollar Gold Price.

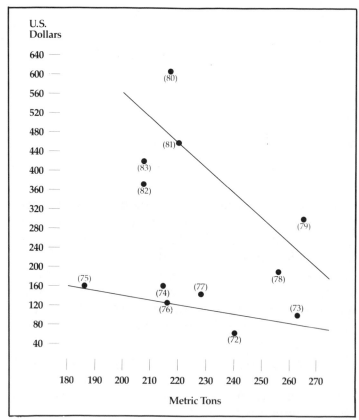

Figure 1–11
Electronic Gold Demand vs. Dollar Gold Price.

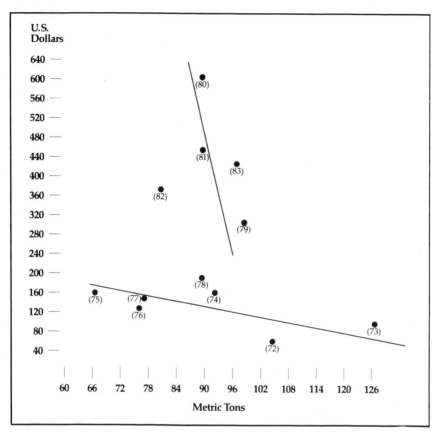

support the conventional wisdom which holds that karat jewelry demands are substantially different between developed and less developed countries.

INDUSTRIAL GOLD DEMAND. Aggregate industrial gold demand had a conventional downward-sloping, fairly well defined, linear demand schedule with a price elasticity of about −0.5 (Figure 1–10). Shifts occurred after 1977. Electronic and decorative gold demands were similarly behaved, with shifts in 1977, and elasticities of between −0.6 to −0.9, and −0.3, respectively (Figures 1–11 and 1–12). In recent years a 1-percent increase in the dollar gold price was associated with about a 0.5-percent decrease in both aggregate industrial, electronic, and decorative gold de-

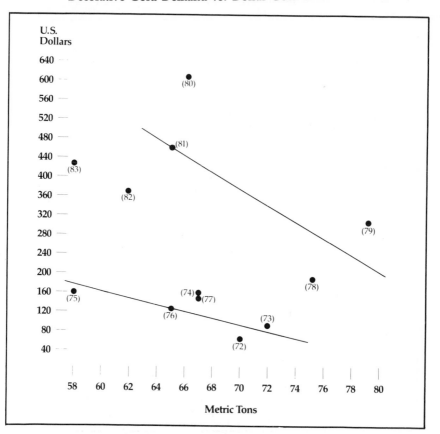

Figure 1–12
Decorative Gold Demand vs. Dollar Gold Price.

mand. In contrast, dentistry gold demand was quite unstable in terms of the current dollar gold price (Figure 1–13). It changed direction, with a downward slope in 1973–75 and −0.2 elasticity, then shifted to an upward slope in 1976–78, and shifted again in 1979–1980 with an elasticity of about 0.5. Other factors determine dentistry gold demand.

GOLD COIN AND MEDALS DEMAND. The gold coin scatter diagram depicts a well defined, linear, upward-sloping schedule for 1972–78, with upward shifts in 1979 and 1980, and then another schedule for 1981–83 (Figure 1–14). The elasticities are about 2.5 and 1.5, respectively. Gold coin demand has been less elastic following the increase in the dollar gold price since 1978.

Figure 1–13
Dentistry Gold Demand vs. Dollar Gold Price.

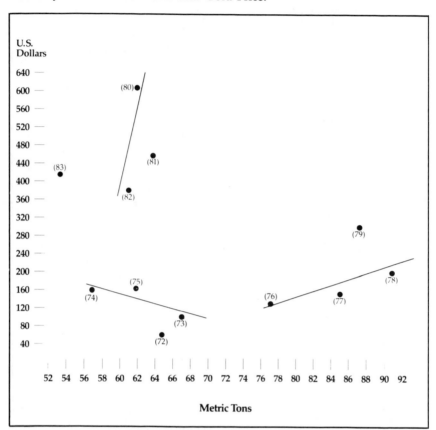

Previously a 1-percent dollar gold price increase induced a 2.5-percent increase in the physical quantity of gold coin demanded. Recently, the quantity increase has been only 1.5 percent. The shift to a less elastic gold coin demand has been a factor in a more volatile dollar gold price.

The gold medals scatter diagram depicts a conventional, well defined, downward-sloping schedule for 1972–75, followed by upward shifts, and then another schedule for 1979–83 (Figure 1–15). The demand-price elasticities are −2.5 and −1.4, respectively. The less elastic gold medals demand has been a factor in a more volatile dollar gold price. Prior to the U.S. government medallion programs in the 1980s, medals were largely demanded by less developed countries.

Figure 1–14
Gold Coin Demand vs. Dollar Gold Price.

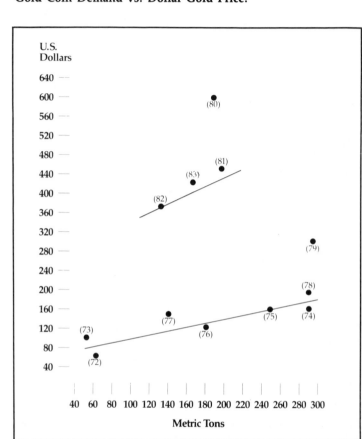

The aggregate gold coin and medals demand scatter diagram has similar characteristics to gold coin demand scatter, owing to the large weighting of gold coins (Figure 1–16). The elasticities are 2.7 for the earlier period and 1.8 for the latter period.

Gold coin and medals demand, aggregating 20-percent market share of fabricated gold demand, is often considered as one category. But the scatter diagrams depict quite different demand-price responses,

Figure 1–15
Gold Medals Demand vs. Dollar Gold Price.

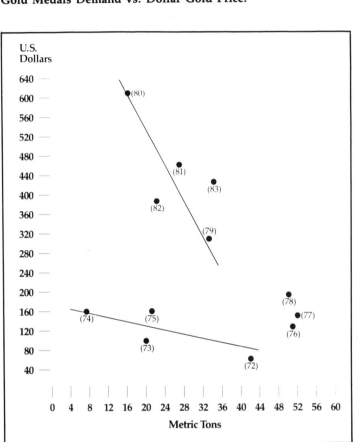

confirming the sign change comparisons. Gold coin demand was positively related to the dollar gold price, suggesting a hoarding demand. Gold medals demand, only one-sixth the size of gold coin demand, had a conventional, downward-sloping demand-price schedule similar to karat jewelry demand. Gold medals are often viewed as karat jewelry equivalents in less developed countries.

Figure 1–16
Gold Coin and Medals Demand vs. Dollar Gold Price.

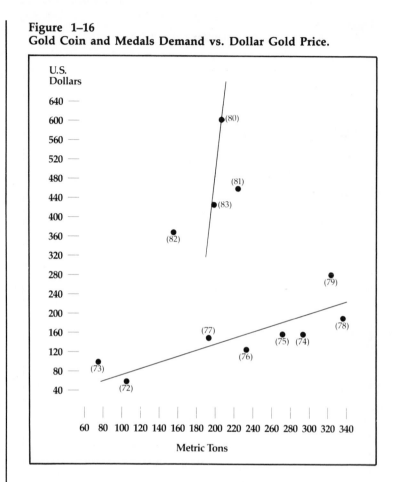

Nonfabricated or Gold Bullion Demand

Summary

Nonfabricated or gold bullion demand was unusually volatile over the sample period (Figure 1–17). It was similar to gold coin demand in that it was positively associated with changes in the dollar gold price. Thus the two demands most closely associated with gold investment activities are more properly

viewed as hoarding demands. Large increases in gold
bullion demand occurred during each year of a major
dollar gold price. Gold bullion demand absorbed the
equivalent of about two full years of new mine production over the 12-year period, that is, about one-sixth of
new mine production was added to private bullion
stocks.

The evidence is consistent with the view that
changes in gold bullion demand were a causal factor in
the large dollar gold price increases. Generally,
nonfabricated or gold bullion demand added to privately held, above-ground stocks each year during the

Figure 1–17
Nonfabricated Gold Demand vs. Dollar Gold Price.

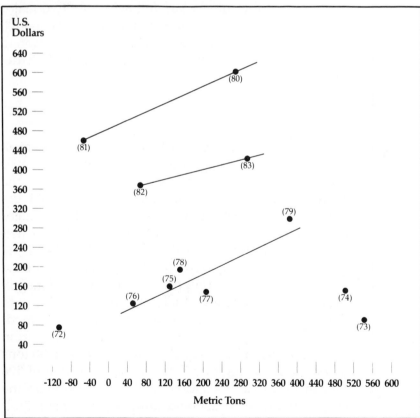

sample period. Moreover, large dollar gold price increases did not induce dishoarding from previously accumulated gold stocks in 1973–74 and 1979–80. Nor did significant dishoarding occur in 1981 when the dollar gold price decreased 25 percent.

Because gold bullion demand data was derived as a residual by subtracting fabricated demand from aggregate supply, our findings are subject to qualification. However, the basic features of our gold bullion analysis are internally consistent. Large gold bullion demand increases accompanied each of the major dollar gold price increases. And moderate increases of 156 metric tons in 1977, and 230 tons in 1983 accompanied moderate 15 percent increases in the dollar gold price. Also, the average increase in gold bullion demand over each of the three years following the two major dollar gold price increases was about the same—100 tons. Casual inspection does not provide any reason to reject our findings with respect to gold bullion demand because of data inconsistency.

Overview

Nonfabricated or gold bullion demand is the most volatile demand component. It averaged 204 metric tons or 16 percent of aggregate gold demand over the 12-year period (Table 1–6). Nonfabricated gold demand was especially large during each of the major dollar gold price increases—547, 512, 385, and 268 metric tons, respectively, in the years 1973, 1974, 1979, and 1980. Excluding these four large demands, the average falls to 92 tons, roughly the same order of magnitude as any of the individual industrial fabricated gold demand components. Gold bullion demand was moderately negative in two years—that is, drawdown from above-ground stocks—by 106 tons in 1972 and 56 tons in 1981. The swing of 653 tons from a decline of 106 tons in 1972 to an increase of 547 tons in 1973 was the largest for any gold demand component (Table 1–7). It rivals in size the swing of net official agency activities on the supply side in the years 1979–80 when aggregate gold supply decreased by almost 50 percent.

Nonfabricated gold demand market share was volatile, ranging as high as 40 percent in 1973–74, and 33 percent in 1979–80 (Table 1–8). The absolute average change in nonfabricated gold demand from year to year of 204 metric tons was as large as average nonfabricated gold demand itself. Nonfabricated gold demand was four times as volatile as fabricated gold demand. Excluding the large dollar gold price years, nonfabricated demand market share was only about 7 percent. Thus, on average, gold bullion demand was only a small proportion of aggregate gold demand; this was also true for the other activity associated with gold investment, gold coin demand.

Sensitivity to Dollar Gold Price Change

The sign of changes in nonfabricated or bullion gold demand were coincident with the sign of changes in the dollar gold price in six of ten years (Tables 1–9 and 1–10). Large changes in nonfabricated gold bullion demand occurred eight times, but there was no clear pattern with respect to the large dollar gold price increases. Gold bullion demand increased in 1973 and 1979, but also in 1977, 1982, and 1983. Comparison of sign changes implies an unconventional, upward-sloping demand schedule for gold bullion, similar in direction to the relationship observed for gold coins.

Nonfabricated Gold Demand-Price Schedule

The scatter diagram for gold bullion demand depicts a series of unconventional upward shifting schedules (Figure 1–17). The relationship is approximately linear for the 1975–79 period with an elasticity of about 2.0. However, the shifts for the other points cover only two or three years; the approximate elasticities are 4 to 5—a highly elastic price response. The dated scatter diagram for gold bullion demand clearly illustrates the unstable nature of this demand component in terms of the dollar gold price over the sample period. Given the residual nature of data for gold bullion demand, some portion of the volatile behavior depicted in the scatter diagram may reflect errors and omissions, and/or changes in the inventory of gold product fabricators and manufacturers.

Data Notes

The data used in this study was obtained from *Gold 1983* and *Gold 1984*, published by Consolidated Gold Fields PLC, London. The relevant data are reproduced in Tables 1–1 and 1–6. Data from these tables, in turn, were used in constructing Tables 1–2 through 1–5, Tables 1–7 through 1–11, and Figures 1–1 through 1–17.

On the supply side, new mine production figures refer to aggregate newly mined gold production brought to market within the noncommunist sector. Communist sector sales refers to net aggregate gold bullion sales from the communist sector to the noncommunist sector. Such sales come from newly mined production, mainly within the Soviet Union, and/or changes in communist sector official stocks. Official agency activities refer to the net aggregate sales (or purchases) from noncommunist sector central banks and government directed institutions, such as IMF.

Fabricated gold product data was collected by country of processing, not by location of final demand, and is net of scrap recycling. Gold coins are officially designated coins actually sold, differing from production by the change in inventory. Gold medals refers to medals, medallions, and fake coins. Industrial gold fabrication is disaggregated into karat jewelry, electronic, and decorative categories where the decorative classification includes all nonelectronic, industrial gold fabricated products excluding dentistry.

Nonfabricated or gold bullion refers to the net change in privately held bullion stocks in all forms within the noncommunist sector. Data for this classification was obtained as the residual by subtracting aggregate fabricated gold data from aggregate gold supply. As such, this residual may include changes in inventories of gold fabricators/manufacturers, goods in transit, loss, leakage, the inevitable errors and omissions, and nonreported bullion or fabricated product trade between communist and noncommunist sectors.

The data has been collected systematically on a net basis—that is, net sales from the communist sector—new mine production, net sales (purchases) from official agencies, and net fabricated gold products (total fabrication net of recycled materials). Thus, for our purposes, we do not need to consider changes in inventory or recycled materials. Also note that all demand and supply gold data is in metric tons.

The dollar gold price is the yearly average of daily average London fixings of the U.S. dollar gold price per troy ounce.

Note that for the purposes of data gathering the universe is explicitly divided between communist and noncommunist sectors. For the indigenous noncommunist private sector there are two sources of new gold supply coming to market—new mine production, and net sales by official agencies, that is, central banks and multinational investment agencies. Net purchases by the official agencies are reported as negative sales. However, only net sales by the communist sector to the noncommunist sector are reported. This includes the net balance from communist sector new mine production, mainly from the Soviet Union, and changes, if any, in communist sector official agency stocks. In the data collection, no distinction is made between changes in communist sector official stocks and gold obtained from new mine production. Also note that fabricated gold data applies only to the noncommunist sector. Neither fabrication data nor changes in privately held bullion within the communist sector are reported, nor is data on aggregate gold demand or supply. We need assume that there is no trade between communist and noncommunist sectors in fabricated products, nor trade in bullion between the sectors by private parties. The situation is similar to that in studying just one country, and lumping trade with the rest of the world together in one net account. In our study the communist sector is treated as a rest of the world gold net account. Since the trade in fabricated gold products between sectors and nonreported gold with the communist sector is ordinarily considered moderate, this data classification should not affect the analysis.

2
Above-Ground Stocks of Gold: Amounts and Distribution

Fundamental to the analysis of any market is supply and demand. In the case of gold, owing to its indestructibility and high value, virtually all of the gold ever mined has been preserved and could conceivably find its way back to the market, directly as bullion, or indirectly as scrap to be refined. It is therefore useful to have a notion of the amount, form, and distribution of the existing stock of above-ground gold.

This study undertakes that analysis. It was conducted by Economic Consulting Services, Inc., employing a team of experts headed by Tom Wolfe, a former U.S. Treasury official and acknowledged expert on gold. It was commissioned by the Chamber of Mines of South Africa, a private association of the major mining interests of the country.

One interesting conclusion that emerges from this study is that there is a potential imbalance developing between supply and demand—growing demands and firm ownership against stable supplies. Consolidated Gold Fields PLC in its annual analysis of supply and demand for gold drew the same general conclusions based on recent developments and well established trends.

EUGENE J. SHERMAN
Vice President, Economist
October, 1982

Folklore and myth have conjured up visions of fabulous hoards of gold. Over the millennia legend and reality have become confused so that even today naive but widely accepted estimates of available gold far exceed actual supplies.

Reliable statistical sources have become available in recent times. Estimates of private stocks of gold can be constructed from these within a framework of the overall historical supply and its distribution. The procedure used in this study is to begin with a known (or reliable) figure for historical gold production, delete official stocks and various component uses for which there are reasonable estimates, arrive at an irreducible residual of bullion and coin, and distribute this total among the world markets by using whatever reliable information is available. A summary of the quantitative results is shown in Table 2–1.

In estimating the amount and distribution of private stocks of gold, two basic assumptions have been made.

1. Virtually all the private stocks of bullion and coin have been largely accumulated subsequent to the end of World War II since most of the world's gold has been produced since that time. There was very little incentive for individuals to hold gold in bullion form prior to the 1960s, and only small amounts were acquired for private investment prior to then.

2. There is very little chance that large, concentrated, privately held stocks of gold have been accumulated since World War II outside of countries where gold ownership and trade is free of governmental restriction. Where governmental restrictions on gold ownership and/or trade apply, private holdings tend to be small and diffused among a great many individuals. Even today most of the IMF member countries restrict ownership and trade in gold by their nationals. Gold buyers, legal or illegal, wanting to hold large amounts, where possible, purchase and store their holdings in politically and economically secure free market locations. Historically, Switzerland and Great Britain have met this standard most closely. In recent years the United States, West Germany, and Japan have qualified as preferred depositories. The largest build-up of stocks has probably taken place in these countries.

The free markets where the accumulation of private gold stocks since World War II has occurred include:

1. The U.S. and Canada in the Western Hemisphere.
2. Switzerland, the United Kingdom, West Germany and the Benelux countries in Europe.
3. Most of the Arab countries in the Middle East.
4. Japan, Singapore, and Hong Kong in the Far East.

Estimating Procedures

Production

Mining production establishes the theoretical limit to the amount of gold that exists in all forms. The U.S. Gold Commission in its report to the Congress estimates the total amount of gold produced from prehistory through 1980 to be approximately 90,000 tons (2.9

World Production, Distribution, and Stocks of Gold, 1800-1980
(Metric Tons)

For Decade Ending	(1) Cumulative World Mine Production	(2) Increment in World Mine Production	(3) Monetary Stock	(4) Increment in Monetary Stock	(5) Official Reserves	(6) Increment in Official Reserves
1800	3,515.4					
1810	3,697.4	182.0	1,203.4			
1820	3,816.2	118.8	1,297.4	94.0		
1830	3,961.7	145.5	1,399.1	101.7		
1840	4,166.1	204.4	1,449.1	50.0		
1850	4,698.6	532.5	1,691.8	242.7		
1860	6,706.7	2,008.1	3,184.8	1,493.0		
1870	8,607.2	1,900.5	4,089.6	904.8		
1880	10,367.0	1,759.8	4,729.4	639.8	1,505.4	
1890	11,996.3	1,629.3	5,295.8	566.4		
1900	15,156.8	3,160.5	7,274.7	1,978.9	3,732.5	
1910	20,899.2	5,742.4	10,636.1	3,361.4	6,320.4	2,587.9
1920	27,318.5	6,419.3	14,475.6	3,839.5	10,917.6	4,597.2
1930	33,109.2	5,790.7	18,299.5	3,823.9	16,469.7	5,552.1
1940	42,927.8	9,818.6			26,059.1	9,589.4
1950	51,814.0	8,886.2			33,570.8	7,511.7
1960	61,593.8	9,779.8			37,950.2	4,379.4
1970	75,600.0	14,006.2			38,311.0	360.8
1980	88,847.9	13,247.9			37,471.2	−839.8

e = ECS estimate.
Source: By Column:
(1) Statistical Compendium of The Report to the Congress of the Commission on the Role of Gold in the Domestic and International Monetary Systems (Gold Commission Report), March 1982, Table SC-6, pp. 195-196. Includes Soviet mine production.
(2) Calculated from (1).
(3) Monetary gold stock includes both official gold reserves and bank-and nonbank holdings of gold coins.
    1810-1910: Statistical Compendium of the Gold Commission Report, Table SC-7, p. 198.
    1920-1930: League of Nations, Interim Report of the Gold Delegation of the Financial Committee (Geneva, 1930) Table B, pp. 82-84 (converted from monetary pounds to ounces by dividing by 4.2287 pounds per fine ounce).
(4) Calculated from (3).
(5) These figures represent physical gold, in the form of bullion or coin, held either at home or abroad by central banks and governments and international organizations. All the estimates include Soviet reserves.
    1880-1900: Estimates from Short-Term Capital Movements Under the Pre-1914 Gold Standard, by Arthur I. Bloomfield, Princeton Studies in International Finance, No. 11, 1963, p. 15. Estimates are actually given for 1880 and 1903. Our 1900 figure (120.0 million ounces) is estimated from Bloomfield's 1903 figure of $2.6 billion (125.8 million ounces).
    1910: Estimate from Key Currencies and Gold: 1900-1913, by Peter H. Lindert, Princeton Studies in International Finance, No. 24, 1969, p. 25.
    1920-1980: Estimates from Statistical Compendium of the Gold Commission Report, Table SC-8, p. 199, compiled from Banking and Monetary Statistics, 1914-1941, 1941-1970. Board of Governors of the Federal Reserve System, pp. 544-48 and pp. 913-22, from International Financial Statistics, IMF; and Gold Statistics and Analysis, Dec. 1981/Jan. 1982, J. Aron & Co.
    The Federal Reserve series was used for all years except 1980 for which the IMF estimate was used. Soviet reserves were not reported from 1918 to 1921, but they were probably minimal as of 1920 as gold was sold to finance the war effort. Reported Soviet reserves in 1922 were only $2.6 million (125,786 troy oz). The last time Soviet reserves were reported was September 1935. This figure ($838.3 million − 24 million ounces) was included as an estimate in the 1940 total. From 1950-1980, J. Aron's estimates of Soviet reserves were added to the Gold Commission statistics to reach a total.
(6) Calculated from (5).

(7) Cumulative Absorption in Fabricated Products	(8) Increment in Absorption in Fabricated Products	(9) Residual Coin and Bullion in Private Hands (1)-(5)-(7)	(10) Increment in Residual	(11) Accumulation of Gold in Karat Jewelry Since 1900	(12) Increment in Jewelry Holdings	(13) Percentage Change in Real Gold Price From Beginning to End of Decade
2,493.9						− 1.51
2,518.8	24.9					+ 23.47
2,562.7	43.9					+ 16.46
2,717.0	154.3					+ 2.16
3,006.8	289.8					+ 6.63
3,521.9	515.1					− 4.68
4,517.6	995.7					− 20.75
5,637.6	1,120.0	3,224.0				+ 17.27
6,700.5	1,062.9					+ 22.08
7,882.1	1,181.6	3,542.2		141.2		+ 0.34
10,263.1	2,381.0	4,315.7	773.5	2,227.4	2,086.2	− 20.39
12,842.9	2,579.8	3,558.0	− 757.7	4,451.3	2,223.9	− 54.46
14,809.6	1,966.7	1,829.9	−1,728.1	6,655.4	2,204.1	+ 78.75
15,450.4	640.8	1,418.3	− 411.6	7,090.2	434.8	+ 86.45
16,485.8	1,035.4	1,757.4	339.1	8,200.9	1,110.7	− 50.49
21,441.7	4,955.9	2,201.9	444.5	12,376.7	4,175.8	− 13.81
32,060.7	10,619.0	5,228.3	3,026.4	20,745.3	8,368.6	− 11.74
41,485.2	9,424.5	9,891.5	4,663.2	27,351.2	6,605.9	+601.81

Net absorption of gold in all fabricated products.
1810-1930: Cumulative figures derived as difference between cumulative production in (1) and monetary stocks in (3). Increments calculated from these figures.
1940-1950: Estimates of increments from Annual Reports of the Director of the Mint, U.S. Treasury Department, various years. Increments then added to update cumulative total.
1960-1980: Increments from Gold Statistics and Analysis, Dec. 1981/Jan. 1982, J. Aron & Co.; figures for jewelry and industrial demand from 1950-1968 include coins and medallions, so estimates of official gold coinage for these years from Gold Coins, Federal Coin & Currency, Inc., Switzerland, 1973 were subtracted. Increments added to update cumulative total.
Calculated from (7).
Residual = Cumulative World Mine Production (1) minus Official Reserves (5) minus Cumulative Absorption in Fabricated Products (7). This column represents the theoretical maximum amount of gold coin and bullion held by private individuals and banks.
Calculated from (9).
This is a subset of column (7), absorption in fabricated products. It represents holdings of karat jewelry in private hands which are considered potentially accessible to the market.
Calculated from (11).
Calculated from Statistical Compendium of the Gold Commission Report, Table SC-16, pp. 219-223, in which the real price of gold is calculated using the United States wholesale price index, with 1967 = 100.

billion ounces). The important point is that gold has been produced in large quantity only in very recent times. Over 95 percent of all world gold production has occurred since 1850 and more than half since the end of World War II. In recent years annual gold production (including the Soviet Union) has been relatively stable at about 1,260 tons.

Official Gold Reserves

During the century after gold was first produced in quantity in 1850, the monetary role of gold was preeminent, and most of the world's gold output was absorbed in official reserves. Of the estimated 52,000 tons of gold historically produced up to 1950, 65 percent, or 34,000 tons, was held in vaults of central banks—mainly in the United States. From 1880 until 1950, official gold stocks rose by more than 32,000 tons or 77 percent of all gold produced during that period (Table 2–2).

After 1950, governments ceased to be the dominant buyer in the gold market. During the period 1950–1980, official gold reserves rose by 4,000 tons, only about 10 percent of total gold production, with virtually all of the increase occurring prior to 1960. But the shift between the government and private offtake

Table 2–2
Gold Supply and Demand, 1880–1980* (Metric Tons).

	1880-1900	1900-1920	1920-1950	1950-1980	1880-1980
Mining Production	4,800	12,150	24,500	37,050	78,500
Distribution of Newly Mined Gold:					
Increase in Official Stocks	2,250	7,200	22,650	3,900	36,000
Use in Fabricated Products	2,250	4,950	3,650	25,000	35,850
Increase in Private Holdings	300	0	-1,800	8,150	6,650

*Exact figures, rounded to nearest 50.

of gold after 1950 in absolute terms is even more striking. During the 30 years prior to 1950 the offtake of gold for official reserves and fabricated products was substantially greater than total mining production. Consequently, bullion and coin in private stocks actually declined. By contrast, during the 30 years after 1950, the bullion and coin in private stocks rose by an estimated 8,000 tons, about 20 percent of total mining production over that period.

Gold in official reserves at the end of 1980 totaled 37,471 tons.

Stocks in Fabricated Gold Products

Until recent historical times, the greater part of world gold production was fabricated into jewelry and other decorative objects. This was the principal form in which gold was held as wealth. By 1930, when the role of gold as circulating money was near its end, the gold content in karat jewelry held worldwide was an estimated 6,700 tons, more than three times the estimated amount of privately held gold bullion and coin.

From 1930 to 1950, with a higher real price, gold jewelry production declined to the lowest level since the mid-19th century. During those 20 years only 1,500 tons were added to the stock of jewelry worldwide. Over that period private holdings of gold bullion and coin also showed little change with nearly all gold production ending up in official reserves. After 1950 with rising real income and a favorable gold price, the absorption of jewelry by the public increased rapidly. By 1980 holdings of gold in jewelry worldwide had risen to an estimated 27,000 tons.

Private Stocks of Bullion and Coins

While jewelry has been the traditional form in which gold is owned by the public, since the end of World

War II there has been a substantial rise in public holdings of bullion and coin. Prior to that time it made very
little sense in areas of reasonable political stability to
hold gold as an investment or store of value. For more
than a century gold was circulating money with a fixed
nominal value, and, as such, its usefulness as an
inflation hedge was moot.

When the function of gold as circulating money
ended in the early 1930s, a substantial increase in the
government support price in a time of general
deflation made gold even less attractive for public
holding—particularly in the form of coin. So by 1950
there was little or no increase in private stocks of gold
from the relatively small quantity held by the public 20
years earlier.

It seems evident, therefore, that various estimates
prior to 1960 of large stocks of gold privately held in
certain areas, to the extent they have any validity, almost certainly refer to holdings of gold jewelry. Prior
to the 1960s, the weight of evidence indicates that
there were no very large private stocks of gold in any
other form. In regions where high real income made
accumulation of wealth practical, there was no strong
incentive to acquire gold in nonjewelry form. Moreover, until recently, the residual remaining after the
offtake of gold for official stocks and fabricated products left no margin for a substantial build-up in private
holdings of bullion and coin.

In the 1950s the pattern of gold supply and demand
began to change radically. Despite a declining real
gold price, mining production rose steadily. Although
the offtake for fabricated products also showed a substantial increase, the sharp decline in the growth of
official reserves left a large margin for private accumulation of bullion and coin. From 1960 through 1980,
world private stocks of gold bullion and coin increased
by over 7,000 tons, bringing the total within a probable
range of 9,000 to 11,000 tons.

Distribution of Private Gold Stocks Between Bullion and Coin

It is highly probable that the greater part of private gold holdings (apart from jewelry) is in the form of coin. From early historical times until the gold standard ended in the early 1930s, about 15,000 tons of gold were minted into gold coins. About 90 percent of this total was by Great Britain, the U.S., and France. Only minor amounts of gold coins were produced from the early 1930s until the late 1960s when bullion coins came on the scene.

Over time a portion of this total became lost and effectively disappeared from private stocks. This long-term attrition is estimated at 1,500 metric tons.[1] The larger problem is estimating the unknown but large portion of gold coins that were melted back into bullion bars during the 1930s and 1940s when the value of the gold content substantially exceeded the face value of the coins.

How large was this meltdown? Fortunately there are good clues in U.S. Treasury data. From 1933 through 1953 the Treasury acquired 6,100 tons of gold bars derived from coin, about 40 percent of all coins minted

---

[1]The estimates for this loss were constructed as follows. Coin weight and mintage figures published in *Gold Coins,* Federal Coin and Currency, Switzerland, 1973, were used to derive decade-by-decade figures for official gold coin production from 1800 to 1930. The per-decade loss was calculated as 2 percent of the coin stock for the period, defined as the sum of the beginning stock and half of the coin production of the decade. (Assuming straight-line coin production from the beginning to the end of the decade, half of the decade increment represents the average new stock for the whole ten-year period to which a loss estimate should be applied.) The estimated decade coin loss rate of 2 percent was based on the *annual* karat jewelry loss rate of 0.23 percent. That figure was established in another study of jewelry. The loss figure was then subtracted from the sum total of coin production of the decade and the beginning stock. The cumulative loss figure of approximately 1,500 metric tons was then calculated as the sum of the losses for each decade.

prior to World War II. Interestingly enough, the Treasury acquired and melted a smaller percentage of existing U.S. coins (35 percent) than of foreign coins (45 percent). There is an obvious reason for this. In the 1930s American coin holders had only two options—either sell the gold in the coins to the Treasury for $20.67 an ounce or continue to hold the coins illegally. Many chose the second option. The refineries in effect enforced this Hobson's choice.

By contrast, holders of gold coins in other countries (mainly Sovereigns and Napoleons) were free to cash in on the premium of the gold content over the nominal value of the previously circulating coinage. So the percentage of British, French, and other gold coins melted down in the 1930s and 1940s was probably much larger than that of U.S. coins. As already noted, a substantial part of this meltdown ended up in U.S. official reserves. The amount of melted coins in this period that was not acquired by the U.S. Treasury is estimated at about 3,000 tons. This brought the total amount of gold coins in existence at the end of World War II to an estimated 4,500 tons—taking account of loss and normal attrition over the past century.

Gold coin production since World War II—primarily bullion coins—totals about 2,500 tons. Thus, the combined amount of gold coins is around 7,000 tons. From this figure an allowance of 1,000 tons of coins still in central bank reserves leaves a final estimate of roughly 6,000 tons of gold in coins held by the public worldwide at the end of 1980 (see Table 2–3). Generally speaking, gold in coins tends to be held by relatively firm holders. Therefore, coins are not ordinarily sold in large amounts and are not a significant supply factor in the market.

A reasonable estimate for private stocks of gold in bullion form worldwide would be in the range of 3,000 to 5,000 tons, taking into account other supply and use factors. The total would be higher (a) if the use of gold in fabricated products is overestimated, (b) if the meltdown of gold coins in the 1930s and 1940s was larger than had been thought, or (c) if central banks hold a larger portion of their reserves in coins than calculated here.

In any event, it is highly probable that most of the existing private holdings of gold bullion have been accumulated during the last 20 years. The first large build-up in bullion stocks occurred in the late 1960s largely through price-fixing operations of the London pool. Because the gold market was geographically limited, and restrictions on gold trade were still extensive,

Table 2–3
Production, Melting, and Stocks of Official Gold Coins (Metric Tons).

Pre-W.W. II Coin Production	
France	1,866
U.S.	6,809
Great Britain	4,902
Others	+1,423
Total	15,000
Coins, Returned and Melted:	
(1933–1950)	
U.S. Treasury	
U.S. Coins	2,400
Others	+3,600
Subtotal	6,000
Others	+3,000
Total	9,000
Loss and Normal Attrition	1,500
Coins in Existence—end of W.W. II	4,500
Post-W.W. II Coin Production	+2,500
Coins in Existence—1980	7,000
Coins in Central Bank Reserves—1980	−1,000
Coins Held by Public—1980	6,000

Source: Report of the Director of the Mint, various years, Bureau of the Mint, U.S. Department of Treasury; *Gold Statistics and Analysis,* Dec. 1981/Jan. 1982, J. Aron & Co.; *Gold 1981,* Consolidated Gold Fields Limited.

the greater part of the rise in private stocks of bullion remained in the traditional European trading centers.

When the second surge in private stocks of gold bullion developed in the middle and late 1970s, the world market had greatly changed. Restrictions on U.S. buying and trade in gold were gone, wealth in the Middle East had vastly increased, and more sophisticated markets had developed in the Far East. As a result the build-up in gold bullion stocks in the 1970s was not only larger than a decade earlier but was also more widely dispersed among the regional markets of the world.

The recent pattern of diversified world demand for gold bullion (and coins as well) is likely to continue in the 1980s. Stocks should grow in all the expanding free regional markets—the U.S., Japan, Hong Kong, the Middle East, and Western Europe. More rapid intermarket communication and more standardized trading procedures will link those markets more closely through efficient arbitrage operations in gold and currencies. So there is a paradox in the changing monetary role of gold in the world. While its formal role in official international monetary operations has diminished, the function of gold as a form of international currency in the private sector is likely to expand in the decade ahead.

The Geographical Distribution of Private Stocks of Bullion and Coin

The U.S. Market

Since the end of legal restrictions on the private holding of gold, the U.S. has become perhaps the largest of the world investment markets. From 1974 through 1981 the build-up of private stocks of gold bullion and coin in the U.S. market was an estimated 1,213 tons—about 640 tons in gold coins (see Table 2–4).

Table 2–4
Increase in Private Gold Stocks in the U.S. (Metric Tons).

Pre-1974	1400-1600[1] Bullion[2]	Coins	Total
1974	42[3]	98[4]	140
1975	43	52	95
1976	70	41	111
1977	134	50	184
1978	140	116	256
1979	136	87	223
1980	−22	106	84
1981	33	87	120
Total (1974-81)	576	637	1,213

1/ Mostly U.S. gold coins acquired before 1934, but not returned to U.S. Treasury.
2/ Bullion includes increases/decreases in private holdings of bullion and stocks in exchange depositories.
3/ Gold acquired by dealers in December 1974 to meet expected demand by individuals
   following the end of ownership restrictions.
4/ Coins acquired under an administrative easing of gold regulations prior to the total end
   of restraints.
Source: U.S. Department of the Treasury, Office of Gold Market Activities, and U.S.
   Bureau of Mines, Mineral Industry Surveys, various issues.

The estimate of 576 tons of gold bullion bars in the U.S. may be somewhat high. It is a residual from the total supply and demand components—including figures by the Bureau of Mines—which probably slightly understates industrial consumption. But the total of gold bullion bars in the U.S. can reasonably be placed in a range of 500 to 600 tons—not all of which, of course, is American owned.

The annual increment in gold investment stocks in the U.S. has since 1974 ranged from a low of 84 tons in 1980 to a high of 256 tons in 1978. The increase in the gold coin component, however, has remained fairly stable, averaging close to 80 tons a year.

Western Europe

FRANCE. France is popularly considered to have the largest gold hoard in Europe and possibly in the world. Various estimates of French gold holdings range up to 6,000 tons—mostly acquired prior to 1948.

However, nearly all the prevailing estimates of French private gold holdings of bullion and coin are excessive and inconsistent with estimated amounts in existence derived from other sources. The greater part of the estimated world total of 6,000 tons of gold coins existing in 1948 consisted of U.S. coins, most of which were probably American owned. The addition to the world total since then consists almost entirely of bullion coins which the French have not been able to legally acquire. A reasonable maximum of current French private holdings of gold coins would seem to be in order of 1,000 tons (more than the estimated existing amount of Napoleons).

In 1946 very little gold bullion was privately held within France. Coins were the practical way to satisfy hoarding needs. Since then there has obviously been a considerable build-up of bullion holdings, mainly in the 1967–68 surge, with a further increase from smuggling in recent years. Nevertheless it is difficult to see how the total post-war build-up could be much over 500 tons—which would be a substantial portion of the world increase in private bullion holdings.

Adding the gold coin and bullion estimates gives a figure for total current private holdings of gold (excluding jewelry) within France of about 1,500 tons. Using the accepted ratio, perhaps 15 percent of this total, or 250 tons, is held in banks. While these estimates are considerably smaller than most others, they are more rational in the context of the latest available world data.

THE U.K., SWITZERLAND, AND WEST GERMANY. London, Zurich, and Frankfurt are the major gold trading centers of Western Europe, and it is in these markets that most of the private gold stocks would be expected to be held. The principal world gold dealers can trade gold held in any market; so the physical distribution of gold stocks among the major free trading centers is of less significance than the overall amount and its ownership.

Domestic hoarding of gold in the European trading centers is quite low, mostly in coin form. In the 1970s the VAT discouraged local investment in gold bullion and more recently gold coins as well. So the bulk of gold stocks in the European trading centers is owned, directly or indirectly, by interests outside the country of deposit.

There are no explicit figures on gold stocks in any of the European trading centers. Totals have to be pieced together from various estimates of gold accumulation since the end of World War II. One widely quoted estimate of total European bullion hoards, except France, put the figure in 1968 at 500 tons, which seems somewhat low.[2] In 1967 and 1968 alone, an estimated 2,000 tons of gold bullion moved into world private stocks, mostly through the London market. Additional smaller surges occurred in 1973–74 and again in 1978–80. A considerable portion of these totals have been redistributed to other markets, notably the U.S. and the Far East. Nevertheless it seems likely that private bullion stocks in London, Zurich, and Frankfurt had risen to a range of 1,500–2,000 tons by 1981.

Other Europe

Gold in limited quantities is held in physical form in other countries in Europe, such as Austria, which produces and hoards coins; Greece, where the favorite hoarding instrument is also gold coins; and, to a lesser extent in the Benelux countries, Portugal, and Spain. Scandinavian countries neither absorb nor hold significant amounts of gold. Perhaps a hundred tons of bullion would be a reasonable maximum for the "other Europe" category. Holdings of gold coins in these areas would be significantly larger.

[2]*Gold—A Worldwide Survey* (London: Economic Intelligence Unit, Charter Consolidated, 1969).

Middle East

This area has been an important center of gold trade as well as significant gold accumulation. Beirut was historically the main distribution point. Jeddah, Kuwait, and Dubai have more recently assumed increased importance. Gold stocks in the Middle East take all forms including small bars, coins, and high-karat jewelry. In recent years Iran, Turkey, and the rising middle class in the Gulf states have accumulated significant amounts of gold. But a good deal of the private gold holdings of the very wealthy class is held as part of diversified portfoiios abroad rather than locally.

India

Gold buying is deeply rooted in the Indian religion, social customs, and economic attitudes. Charter Consolidated estimated the private gold stocks in all forms in India to be approximately 3,500 tons in 1968. Using this as a base, the total now would be well over 4,000 tons. The great bulk of this is in old jewelry and other types of gold that do not have ready access to the market.

India prohibits the import and export of gold bullion and coins. Timothy Green estimates the amount of gold smuggled through Dubai to the Indian subcontinent was at least 1,700 tons between 1960 and 1983. (*The New World of Gold*, Timothy Green, 1984). It accounts for a steady accumulation of gold stocks in spite of legal restrictions.

Other Asia

The major distribution and depository centers for gold in Asia have been Hong Kong, Singapore, and, recently, Japan. Significant accumulation of gold bullion has also occurred in Indonesia, Taiwan, Korea, and Thailand. Bullion holdings in the Far East probably now exceed 700 tons—including a large recent build-up in Japan.

Rest of the World

Other areas in Africa and Latin America have not developed a pattern of heavy local investment in gold apart from jewelry. Government restrictions on the impact and acquisition of gold are widespread, and the opportunity to acquire gold bullion and coin in these areas is extremely limited.

Summary of Investment Stocks

Privately held stocks of gold bullion and coin held throughout the world at the end of 1980 are estimated to be 9,000 to 11,000 tons. The estimated distribution of the bullion component of this total among the principal world markets is indicated in Table 2–5. Statistical detail of the geographical distribution of coins is simply unavailable and impossible to estimate with any reasonable confidence. This is so because of the long history of gold coins and the ease with which they can be transported and hidden.

Table 2–5
Distribution of Main Investment Stocks of Gold Bullion, 1980 (Metric Tons).

United States	500- 600
France	500
Switzerland, United Kingdom and West Germany	1,500-2,000
Asia[1]	700
Other Europe	100
Other[2]	200- 500
Total	3,000-5,000

[1] Includes Japan, Hong Kong, Singapore, Indonesia, Taiwan, Korea and Thailand.
[2] Primarily the Middle East.

Jewelry

Most of the world's privately held gold is in the form
of jewelry. The total amount of gold in jewelry at the
end of 1980 is estimated to be over 27,300 tons. The
distribution of this total by region is indicated in Table
2–6. Of course, a good deal of this tonnage, especially
in the "Other" category is high karat jewelry in North
Africa, the Middle East, India, and the Far East, where
it is regarded as a form of investment. In those parts of
the world, the lines of distinction between gold as investment and gold as adornment are blurred.

Table 2–6
**Estimated "Free World" Stocks of Karat Gold Jewelry, 1980
(Metric Tons).**

United States	4,284
Japan	1,381
Western Europe	12,356
Other	9,330
Total	27,351

Sources:
   1900-29 Interim Report of the Gold Delegation of the Financial Committee,
       League of Nations
   1930-49 Reports of the Director of the Mint, U.S. Treasury
   1950-67 Gold Statistics and Analysis, J. Aron and Company
   1968-80 Consolidated Gold Fields PLC
Various adjustments were made to allow for other industrial uses, losses, etc.

Secondary Recovery from Scrap

The absolute level of industrial gold offtake deter-
mines the volume of new scrap generated and the rate
of new contributions to the supply theoretically recov-
erable from the stock of old or "obsolete" gold-
containing materials. The volume of this secondary
gold actually recovered and recycled, however, is
determined—apart from price—by changes in the pattern of gold use by industry, technological developments, and the proximity and sophistication of secondary gold trading and processing/refining in the

major scrap-generating areas. There is no evidence to suggest that the current rate of new scrap recovery will be influenced materially by factors other than the gold content of the fabricated items and the level of output.

The major factor in the secondary recovery of gold has been the supply from old karat jewelry. This source accounted for virtually all of the large variance in supply refined from old scrap between 1979 and 1980, as well as much of the net dishoarding of jewelry holdings recorded in much of the developing world (see Table 2–7). Apparently, the largest single factor determining the variability in total supply from scrap is the willingness of individuals holding karat jewelry to sell their holdings as scrap at some price. That supply is generally price-responsive in every major region of the world. However, the older the jewelry, the more it takes on antique as well as "heirloom" value, and, therefore, the less likely it is to be sold for melt.

Update on Above-Ground Stocks: Year-End 1984 Estimates

The estimated total of all above-ground stocks of gold increased by 2,915 tons over the past two years to an accumulated total of around 94,300 tons. The increment was accounted for by newly mined gold from the noncommunist world (2,261 tons) and the communist bloc (654 tons).

Central banks and government-controlled investment institutions represented the largest holders of gold reserves at 38,435 tons. However, official gold reserves of the free world dropped 227 tons over the 1983–84 period to 35,826 tons. This decline reflects distress sales from debt-ridden countries and a lack of interest by official institutions (some of which were known to be buyers of gold), for the most part in adding gold to portfolios.

Table 2–7
Changes in Holdings of Karat Jewelry (Metric Tons).

Industrial Market Economies:	1970	1971	1972	1973	1974	1975	1976	1977	1978	1979	1980
Italy	160.5	174.3	313.0	98.2	50.0	76.0	177.0	209.0	235.0	227.0	87.0
United States	97.8	125.8	127.3	102.0	61.1	58.7	72.8	79.5	83.4	79.5	57.8
Japan	34.5	34.5	40.0	45.0	39.9	38.6	40.1	38.5	56.7	53.5	26.3
Germany	47.6	47.1	45.4	38.0	25.0	27.0	36.0	44.0	47.0	45.5	28.5
France	25.7	30.8	29.4	22.4	14.6	17.9	24.5	26.2	25.3	24.4	11.7
Switzerland	23.0	23.0	22.0	16.0	13.5	8.2	10.9	15.5	17.7	15.3	12.2
United Kingdom & Ireland	14.7	15.5	18.0	20.3	15.8	18.3	19.6	24.0	22.0	21.7	9.1
Australia	6.9	7.1	7.1	4.7	4.1	3.7	4.4	3.0	2.7	2.1	3.0
Belgium	4.2	4.8	5.5	6.5	5.5	6.0	6.6	7.4	6.1	5.0	1.5
Canada	5.9	6.7	9.0	9.7	9.4	9.2	12.2	17.7	20.3	17.0	7.0
Netherlands	2.9	3.4	3.4	2.4	1.4	1.7	2.4	3.0	2.2	1.8	0.6
Austria	6.1	6.8	6.6	4.1	2.5	2.0	3.5	3.6	2.9	2.6	0.7
Sweden	2.0	2.7	2.7	2.3	1.8	1.8	1.8	2.1	1.7	1.3	0.8
Denmark	3.6	3.1	4.1	2.6	0.9	0.9	1.7	2.0	1.4	1.1	0.3
Finland	2.2	1.9	2.0	1.8	1.2	1.1	1.4	1.6	1.6	1.4	0.6
Norway	1.3	1.3	1.0	0.5	0.5	0.5	0.8	0.8	0.7	0.8	0.3
Subtotal	438.9	488.8	636.5	376.5	247.2	271.6	415.7	477.9	526.7	500.0	247.4

	1970	1971	1972	1973	1974	1975	1976	1977	1978	1979	1980
Industrial Market Economies:											
Middle-Income Countries:											
Spain	53.0	55.0	58.0	45.2	22.5	37.8	45.5	49.7	51.5	37.7	11.4
Greece	11.0	12.0	13.5	13.5	7.0	9.5	8.3	11.0	14.0	10.0	4.0
Portugal	11.0	13.9	12.3	8.9	4.4	2.9	5.8	5.5	4.5	4.0	1.3
Yugoslavia	—	—	—	0.3	3.0	3.0	4.0	4.5	4.5	4.5	5.9
Brazil	29.0	30.0	19.0	12.0	10.0	13.0	16.2	20.4	29.0	33.0	14.0
Mexico	21.0	20.0	15.5	7.8	5.0	6.1	10.5	7.9	9.3	7.4	3.0
Venezuela	5.0	4.9	4.2	0.3	-1.0	0.3	1.5	1.8	3.4	2.8	1.3
Colombia	2.8	2.9	1.7	1.9	0.8	1.2	1.0	2.0	2.0	1.9	0.4
Peru	4.2	3.7	3.0	1.4	1.3	1.2	1.2	0.8	0.8	0.5	0.4
Chile	0.6	1.3	0.8	0.8	—	—	—	0.1	0.4	0.3	-4.0
Argentina	16.5	12.0	0.5	—	-2.0	-10.0	-10.0	-8.0	-5.0	-2.0	—
Other Latin America[1]	2.2	2.1	2.0	—	-0.5	0.5	1.5	4.9	5.2	3.7	-3.0
Central America & Caribbean	3.5	4.3	2.2	1.0	12.0	41.4	100.7	80.0	86.0	10.0	—
Turkey	32.0	23.0	13.1	3.0	5.0	25.0	53.0	64.0	30.0	-4.0	-18.0
Iran	13.0	14.0	11.0	7.0	-23.0	6.0	25.5	21.0	20.5	12.5	-70.0
Egypt	6.5	7.0	3.5	-6.0	2.9	2.9	4.0	5.6	7.4	7.5	-5.0
Israel	5.0	5.0	4.0	3.0	1.0	2.0	2.0	2.0	2.0	3.0	4.0
Lebanon	3.0	4.0	3.0	-2.0							-1.0

	1970	1971	1972	1973	1974	1975	1976	1977	1978	1979	1980
Saudi Arabia & Yemen[2]	2.5	2.5	2.0	-2.0	-1.0	8.0	33.0	34.5	30.0	7.5	2.0
Iraq, Syria & Jordan[2]	7.5	7.0	3.5	-18.0	-23.0	10.0	15.0	17.0	21.1	6.1	-5.0
Arabian Gulf States[3]	5.0	9.1	4.1	-12.0	-9.0	9.0	13.0	17.2	16.0	13.7	2.6
Cyprus & Malta[2]	0.8	0.8	0.6	0.6	0.2	0.2	0.7	1.0	1.3	1.1	0.3
Hong Kong	10.0	11.0	-13.0	10.0	-1.0	0.5	7.5	8.0	11.0	14.0	3.0
Thailand	12.0	8.0	-10.0	-24.0	-15.0	5.0	12.0	10.0	10.0	5.0	—
Singapore	5.0	5.0	4.2	4.2	0.5	3.0	6.3	8.5	9.0	7.0	-2.0
Taiwan[3]	4.0	4.5	2.0	5.0	—	6.0	6.5	6.5	7.0	5.0	-1.0
Malaysia	6.5	6.0	5.0	2.0	0.3	4.0	7.1	6.0	6.8	5.5	2.0
Philippines	5.0	6.0	2.0	2.0	-3.0	0.8	2.5	3.7	4.0	2.8	0.5
South Korea	6.0	6.0	4.0	3.0	—	1.5	2.0	2.0	3.0	2.5	0.5
Morocco	23.0	25.0	12.0	9.0	5.4	12.0	25.0	22.0	21.7	16.0	1.0
Algeria	3.0	5.0	2.5	1.5	1.0	1.5	2.0	2.0	1.8	1.2	—
South Africa	3.2	3.5	3.2	3.0	2.8	1.4	2.0	2.0	2.0	1.4	1.0
Tunisia	2.0	2.0	1.5	—	—	1.0	1.5	1.5	1.0	1.7	0.2
Subtotal	314.8	316.5	220.9	82.4	6.6	206.7	406.8	415.1	411.2	223.3	-54.6

	1970	1971	1972	1973	1974	1975	1976	1977	1978	1979	1980
Low-Income Countries:											
India	215.0	175.0	107.2	60.5	14.0	25.0	32.9	39.5	44.0	10.0	-9.0
Pakistan & Afghanistan	30.0	25.0	1.0	4.0	-0.5	5.5	20.0	15.0	5.0	2.0	-2.5
Sri Lanka	4.0	6.0	3.0	2.0	-1.0	-0.5	2.0	1.5	0.5	0.3	-0.5
Bangladesh & Nepal	—	—	-3.0	-3.0	-6.5	-3.5	-2.0	1.0	3.0	0.3	-1.0
Indonesia	30.0	25.0	10.0	2.5	-15.0	15.0	35.0	30.0	-3.0	-8.0	-55.0
Vietnam 4/	10.0	8.0	3.5	-6.0	-5.0	-5.0	-0.2	—	—	-3.0	-8.0
Burma, Laos & Kampuchea	7.0	6.0	-1.0	-3.0	-14.0	-2.0	-0.1	-0.5	—	—	—
Subtotal	296.0	245.0	134.7	57.0	-28.0	34.5	87.6	86.5	49.5	1.6	-76.0
Capital-Surplus Oil Exporters:											
Kuwait 5/	—	—	—	—	—	—	9.0	5.6	13.3	9.0	1.0
Libya	7.5	4.2	2.0	1.4	1.2	3.7	5.6	4.5	4.0	1.4	1.7
Subtotal	7.5	4.2	2.0	1.4	1.2	3.7	14.6	10.1	17.3	10.4	2.7
Other Africa 6/	9.0	9.0	5.0	1.0	-2.0	6.0	10.0	5.0	2.5	1.7	—
Total	**1,066.2**	**1,063.5**	**999.1**	**518.3**	**225.0**	**522.5**	**934.7**	**1,002.6**	**1,007.2**	**737.0**	**119.5**

1/ Beginning in 1974, Other Latin America and Central America and Caribbean are combined.
2/ Iraq and Saudi Arabia should actually be included in the Capital-Surplus Oil Exporters category; but their figures are not given separately.
3/ These countries are not included in the World Bank listing.
4/ Beginning in 1978, Vietnam and Burma, Laos, and Kampuchea are combined.
5/ Prior to 1976, data for Kuwait is combined with that of the Arabian Gulf States.
6/ No more detailed breakdown given by Consgold. Includes low- and middle-income countries.

Source: Gold 1981. Consolidated Gold Fields Limited; categorization of countries is based on World Bank definitions.

In contrast, the communist sector, primarily the Soviet Union, stepped up its pace of accumulation somewhat (356 tons) to close to 2,610 tons. Russian gold reserves are now estimated to be at about 2,600 tons, with China accounting for the difference. Whether it was really the Russian intention to increase its stockpile of gold or reluctance to sell more than it did owing to market conditions is uncertain. The situation is difficult to fathom owing to Russia's secretive market behavior and the resulting uncertainties of available data. On the whole, official institutions still hold an estimated 41 percent of all of the known gold that has been mined over time. The status of gold as a financial unit, a reserve and a "stateless currency" remains intact. This statement is buttressed by the fact that gold represented 48 percent of free world total reserves ($758 billion). At year-end 1984, the free world gold reserves were valued at $363 billion, based on an approximate current market value of $315 per ounce, while the dollar value of nongold reserves was $395 billion.

Gold held in karat jewelry increased in proportion slightly faster over the past two years and in 1984 accounted for over 32 percent of all of the above-ground stocks. The increase was attributed to comparatively stronger less developed country karat jewelry demand, resulting in large jewelry accumulation as the price declined, especially in India and the Far East.

Coin and bullion in private hands for investment purposes remained at 12 percent of the known above-ground total at year-end 1984. Here, the general lack of interest in gold within the international investment community was offset by active bar hoarding in the Far and Middle East. This suggests that investors in these regions were especially keen to increase demand at lower prices in contrast to the historic pattern in Europe and the United States, where lower prices seemed to discourage investment accumulation. It also showed that gold as a financial asset and an appropriate part of a balanced portfolio is finding its way into "virgin territory"—namely, countries like Japan—in sluggish market conditions.

The residual item includes industrial gold demand, unrecoverable gold, lost gold, and amounts that cannot be accounted for. The absolute amount in this category increased over the past two years to 13,925 tons, while the relative proportion remained at 15 percent of the total. The sharp rise in the use of gold for electronic purposes in Japan and the U.S. contributed in large measure to the overall increased amount.

Figure 2–1 shows the broad categories and proportions of estimated above-ground stocks. These figures are based first on the data contained in our October

Figure 2–1
Estimated Above-Ground Stocks of Gold (Metric Tons, 1984).

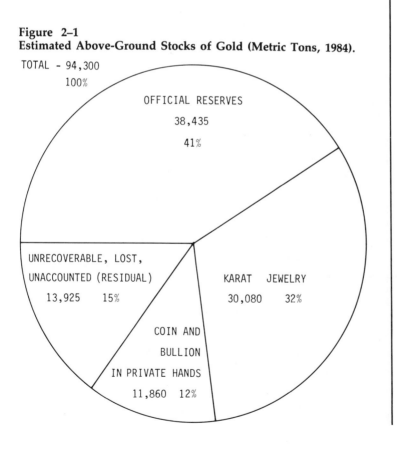

TOTAL - 94,300
100%

OFFICIAL RESERVES
38,435
41%

UNRECOVERABLE, LOST, UNACCOUNTED (RESIDUAL)
13,925   15%

KARAT   JEWELRY
30,080   32%

COIN AND BULLION IN PRIVATE HANDS
11,860   12%

1982 publication entitled *Above-Ground Stocks of Gold— Amounts and Distribution.* We have updated and adjusted those figures for annual changes as reported by Consolidated Gold Fields. The communist bloc gold reserves figures are based on J. Aron estimates. Reserve figures are drawn from the bulletin of the International Monetary Fund. The calculations for the 1983–84 figures were undertaken by the International Gold Corporation, Ltd., Japan.

ITSUO TOSHIMA
Investment Division Manager
Japan
June 1985

II
The Determinants of the Gold Price

A mysticism has surrounded gold, leading to a folk tale that gold is different and cannot be analyzed as one would another commodity or phenomenon. Furthermore, given its dual role as an historic monetary asset and a commodity used for adornment and industrial purposes, there were presumed to be too many complexities to permit rigorous economic analysis.

In fact, the analysis presented in the first article in this section demonstrates that the gold markets can be systematically studied.

For this purpose, International Gold Corporation, assisted by Hudson Strategy Group, has developed a gold pricing model that explains the gold price and changes in it from month to month in terms of the following five independent variables, namely:

1. World liquidity.
2. U.S. trade-weighted exchange rate.

3. Eurodollar rate.

4. Unanticipated inflation.

5. Hudson Institute's political tension index.

The reduced form model utilized in the study explains 99 percent of the variation of the gold price over the period January 1972 to March 1984; it also demonstrates, particularly, that variables 1 and 2 are the major determinants.

However, this monetary aspect of gold had not come into full play until the end of the 1960s, because the official price of gold had been fixed at $35 an ounce for many years prior to 1968. The second article, "Gold: The Transition from Commodity to Currency Form: 1968–73," examines the interesting period of transition during which gold transformed itself from a commodity to a form of money. It provides an historical perspective for the contention embodied in "A Gold Pricing Model."

Both of the works in this part were written by Mr. Eugene J. Sherman.

3
A Gold Pricing Model: 1985 Update

The gold pricing model explained in this chapter monitors gold price movements on a regular basis. The model relies on a straightforward single-equation methodology that treats gold as "stateless currency." This analysis provides evidence that "gold markets are not mysterious, but can be understood using basic tools of economic analysis."

Enhancements, as well as data revisions and extensions, are incorporated in the results presented in this chapter for the period January 1972 through March 1984. The enhanced gold pricing model, estimated over new data, reaffirms our earlier findings. The updated equation explains 99 percent of the monthly gold price variation with a high degree of statistical confidence after adjusting for serial correlation. Several potential conceptual and statistical problems were noted in earlier studies. The adjustments made, the reasoning behind the choice of variables, and the choice of estimation techniques are all spelled out in the following pages. Despite our efforts, the results continue to display statistical problems of multicollinearity and serial correlation.[1]

We believe that this model is more useful as a means of explaining gold price changes than as a forecasting tool. Nevertheless, the model can be used to project probable gold prices under different economic scenarios. Three alternative projections are provided in the final section of the chapter. However, any projection must be viewed with caution since its accuracy depends on good assumptions about future values of other models' variables and stability of the model's estimated relationships. Even though gold price estimates from this model track market behavior very closely over the sample period, we still do not have sufficient confidence in the stability of the model or in the continuity of past market behavior patterns to assign high confidence to price projections. Nevertheless, we believe a regularly revised and updated model that substantially explains recent price behavior can be used in the context of other information about gold markets to derive a sense of "appropriate" price trends over time.

As in the previous studies, this update draws heavily on analysis undertaken by Hudson Strategy Group, an affiliate of the Hudson Institute. Special appreciation is extended to Jimmy W. Wheeler, who spearheaded the econometric work and the series of working drafts, and his assistant, Adrienne Kearney. However, the origination of the concept, the approach, and the ultimate responsibility for the end result are Mr. Sherman's.

January, 1985

---

[1]Multicollinearity results from two explanatory variables moving together in ways that the computer program cannot sort out. Serial correlation occurs in time series analyses when the errors associated with observations in a given time period influence future time periods.

Model Enhancements, Statistical Problems, and Analytical Issues[2]

The simple reduced form model utilized in this chapter is based on a detailed review of theory and empirical evidence, based on previous studies. Broad consistency of the model with both a financial market and a commodity market view of the formation of gold prices, combined with good statistical results, support this reduced form approach. However, since all the variables used to explain gold prices are simultaneously determined in a very complex world economy, they can interact in ways that produce bias in the statistical analysis.[3] The analysis performed here is based on data series from January 1972 through March 1984.

The Dollar Exchange Rate: An Unresolved Problem

The concept of trade-weighted exchange rates was developed to help explain relative competitiveness among nations in a period of floating exchange rates. Typically, they are constructed using bilateral exchange rates weighted by trade shares for the country in question. Most of the regularly reported series, such as the Federal Reserve Board series used in the "gold pricing model" are of this form.[4]

Some concern had been expressed in previous studies that bilateral trade weighting, while appropriate for measuring changes in competiveness, may be much less appropriate for measuring opportunity costs perceived by gold investors. There is some theoretical

[2]Much of this section is drawn from previous reports.

[3]Bias is a systematic error in one or more of the estimated regression coefficients.

[4]These weights may be modified in the process of computing the exchange rate index. For example, the IMF-MERM series modifies the trade weights with model-generated price elasticities.

justification for this concern. Investors are generally concerned only with exchange rates among a small handful of major currencies, and almost certainly not in proportion to any particular bilateral trade pattern. In practice, however, most regularly reported trade-weighted exchange rate series exclude all but the most important countries from their calculations. For example, the Federal Reserve Board series used in this model is based only on the "Group of Ten" plus Switzerland, and excludes such an important trade partner as Mexico. Even with a small group of major countries as the base, bilateral trade weights probably remain inappropriate for approximating the perceptions of investors.

The question remains, of course, what are more appropriate weights? The only regularly reported series using alternative weights that we have found is the SDR rate computed by the IMF. The SDR is a composite basket currency weighted by total trade shares (modified by other considerations), and is heavily dominated by the U.S. dollar. The importance of the dollar in the basket sharply reduces the value of the dollar-SDR exchange rate in measuring perceived opportunity cost.

To date, we have been unable to locate a regularly reported dollar exchange rate index using weights that are more appropriate for investors. One alternative would be to construct such a series especially for the gold pricing model. However, debate and analysis of the theoretical basis for alternative weighting schemes left many issues unresolved. Thus the decision was made to continue use of the Federal Reserve Board series.

World Liquidity

The world liquidity variable used in past versions of the model was constructed from three separate series.

The first was the industrial component of the M-1 index calculated by the International Monetary Fund (reported on a monthly basis). The second component was the net Eurocurrency market size estimated by Morgan Guaranty Trust Company (reported quarterly in U.S. dollars). The third was a world quasi-money index constructed by Hudson Institute from a geometric mean of monthly quasi-money indices for fourteen major industrial countries.

The new model contains one important revision in the calculation of world liquidity. Net Eurocurrency market size is no longer estimated by the Morgan Guaranty Trust Company. Consequently, gross Eurocurrency market size, which does not adjust for interbank deposits, is now being used. Net and gross Eurocurrency market size have moved together in a reasonably consistent fashion over time; however, gross is much larger. Since net Eurocurrency market size is the theoretically correct concept, the gross index was weighed only by the net share in the base year in the calculation of world liquidity. This data revision does not dramatically change the world liquidity variable or the regression results reported later.

Rather than the global M-1 index of previous versions of the model, the industrial country component of that series is used. It is a more appropriate index for gold investors and its coverage is consistent with the other components of the world liquidity series. Moreover, excluding the developing countries eliminates potential sources of upward bias in world liquidity as a proxy for future inflation. Of course, the IMF uses geometric weighting to reduce upward bias in its calculations. But elimination of these countries is preferable for the purposes of this analysis. In addition, industrial country data is available sooner and with fewer inaccuracies than developing country data.

The coverage of the quasi-money index has been expanded to include fourteen industrial countries.[5]

Real Interest Rates and Unanticipated Inflation

In earlier versions of the model, a moving average of the IMF world inflation series was subtracted from the 90-day Eurodollar rate to estimate the real Eurodollar rate, and from current values of itself to estimate unanticipated inflation. The inclusion of developing countries in this total produced a high average inflation data series. This resulted in a measure of the real interest rate that was predominantly negative over time. Besides an increase in the measured inflation average, developing country data accuracy and biases are important concerns.

As important as the accuracy and bias concerns is the question about the appropriateness of including developing country consumer price inflation in the average under any circumstances. The real interest rate variable in the gold pricing model attempts facing investors. Most developing countries' currencies are convertible only to a limited extent on international

---

[5]This is based on the ten largest countries plus four other countries that report data quarterly to the OECD. Although dropped as a variable here, previous versions of the model used the total Gross Domestic Product of the big seven industrial countries as a proxy for world output (including the United States, Canada, France, West Germany, Italy, Japan, and the United Kingdom). Since these seven countries accounted for 84 percent of OECD output (in 1981), this total served as a good first approximation. We have expanded this total to include more countries. Of the next three largest countries (Spain, Australia, and the Netherlands), neither Spain nor the Netherlands reported quarterly GDP to the OECD. We were able to acquire quarterly GDP estimates for Spain from Banco de Espana; for the Netherlands, quarterly GDP was calculated from an interpolation of annual data. Four other countries currently report quarterly GDP to the OECD (Greece, Sweden, Austria, and Finland). It was decided to include them in the new total. Greece began reporting quarterly data to the OECD only in 1974. Data from 1970 to 1974 were interpolated from annual data. The enhanced world GDP series, now covering 14 advanced industrial countries, accounts for 94 percent of OECD output.

markets. As a result, borrowing on private markets must be compared to other sources of scarce foreign exchange (exports). Thus, in developing countries, the most appropriate price series for calculating opportunity costs in international markets is probably some composite of export prices, rather than domestic prices. These prices, in turn, tend to reflect industrial country demand. Therefore, to improve the quality of the data, and also to make the calculation more appropriate in terms of true opportunity costs, it was decided to use only the industrial country component of the IMF's world inflation series for calculating real interest rates in the January 1984 update.[6] This practice is followed here.

Political Tension Index

One goal of these studies was to determine if it was possible to systematically include political events in an economic analysis of gold prices. A political tension index that measured cumulative changes in underlying

[6]Use of consumer prices is less appropriate than a broader-based measure such as the GDP deflator, even in industrial countries. These data are not available on a monthly basis. However, behavior patterns of GDP deflators and consumer price indices are close enough in the industrial countries to minimize distortion to calculated real interest rates.

Use of a real interest rate series calculated by subtracting a weighted average of past inflation rates from current market interest rates offers theoretical deficiencies. A theoretically correct measure of real interest rates must be based on anticipated inflation rates. If anticipated future rates differ substantially from the historical weighted average, errors may creep in. We make the relatively simplistic assumption that expectations of future prices are sticky relative to recent experience and only slowly adapt to new conditions. This is less true today than in the past, since individuals in most countries have become sensitive to expectations about changes in inflation rates. However, even in the U.S., with the broadest and deepest financial markets among the industrial countries, inflationary expectations are an important element in the persistence of high market rates of interest relative to current inflation. This suggests that, even with heightened sensitivity, recent experience dominates expectations, and thus represents a reasonable assumption for our analysis.

international tension on a monthly basis was developed.

The development of the international political tension index entailed three steps:

1. The listing of salient events.
2. The weighting of those events in terms of their impact on the level of international political tension.
3. Totaling the weights of the individual events to derive a month-by-month cumulative level of international political tension.

First, salient political, economic, military, and other events likely to have an impact upon the level of global political tension were identified and listed on a monthly basis. Among the types of international events singled out were international military conflicts; instances of domestic political violence, unrest, and instability; other domestic political changes, such as the death of a particularly important leader; and a mixture of other global political and economic events ranging from a breakdown of the SALT talks to the proposed merger of Egypt and Libya.

Second, the impact of an individual event on the level of international tension was evaluated. Beginning with a determination of whether that event raised or lowered international tension, the impact of each event was then assessed in terms of six different dimensions of international tension. These dimensions were:

1. The risk of superpower confrontation.
2. Threat to Soviet or U.S. security.
3. Consequences for other important global political patterns or relationships.
4. Economic importance and impact on the international economic system.
5. Impact on regional political and military alignments.

6. Impact on a country's regional alignment or domestic policies.

7. The level of bloodshed involved.

For each event, it was then determined whether it had a high, moderate, limited, or neutral weight on each of these seven dimensions (scaled ± 3, 2, 1, and 0). The determination was made utilizing the judgment of a senior international political analyst in consultation with other experts. Though subjective, Hudson Institute's experience has proved the value of such methods in forecasting and ranking actions in similar areas. It is especially useful for taking into account subtle nuances between different types of events, and sorting out events whose significance might be greater than indicated by more rigidly applied quantitative data.

After weighing, the weights were summed to produce the monthly cumulative level of international tension, shown in Table 3–1.

It was found that the index indeed may be useful for explaining some otherwise inexplicable short-term gold price variations. However, this month-to-month consistency does not hold up very well in averages. Referring back to the table, no consistent relationship between annual gold price growth and average tension, or frequency of high tension events during the year was found. Other forces dominate the longer-period relationship.

The New Sample Period

The new data are drawn from a period (April 1983 through March 1984) that shows some of the following characteristics:

1. World liquidity growth fluctuated somewhat around a rising trend, although the trend growth is slower than most of the earlier sample period.

Table 3–1
Hudson Institute Political Tension Index: 1971–84.

	1971	1972	1973	1974	1975	1976
January	50	20	25	39	26	22
February	36	19	38	29	42	29
March	54	28	19	23	55	24
April	45	29	16	31	49	33
May	27	50	27	38	41	31
June	17	19	30	22	47	33
July	49	14	32	36	35	34
August	41	10	28	34	30	52
September	25	30	30	25	27	11
October	33	23	62	29	27	25
November	37	22	48	15	32	28
December	35	28	26	28	47	31
Average	37.4	24.3	31.8	29.1	38.2	29.4
High	54	50	62	39	55	52
Low	17	10	16	15	26	11
Number of Months With An Index Of*						
45 & Over	4	1	2	0	4	1
50 & Over	2	1	1	0	1	1
55 & Over	0	0	1	0	1	0
Gold Price Growth**	14	43	67	63	1	−22

* For a list of events in the high tension months (index of 50 and over), see Appendix.
** Annual Average over previous year's average.

1977	1978	1979	1980	1981	1982	1983	1984	
23	32	43	77	42	35	41	32	
25	32	62	42	27	36	46	41	
26	25	14	52	41	29	48	37	
35	13	23	40	33	40	37		
23	28	8	58	43	42	41		
23	26	8	42	37	40	39		
28	27	36	35	34	37	35		
36	16	28	46	40	38	44		
17	30	45	36	28	41	52		
27	43	39	35	30	42	56		
32	48	45	54	26	63	40		
21	39	40	77	31	26	37		
26.3	29.9	32.6	49.5	34.3	39.1	43	37	34.4
36	48	62	77	43	63	56	37	52.4
17	13	8	35	26	26	35	32	20.5
0	1	3	6	0	1	4	0	27
0	0	1	5	0	1	2	0	15
0	0	1	3	0	1	1	0	8
18	31	58	101	− 25	− 18	13	− 0.1	

2. World GDP growth, after bottoming out in early 1983, rose consistently thereafter.

3. Political tension continued at the moderately high average that has characterized the period 1982–84.

4. The dollar exchange rate continued the rising trend set in 1982, going from 117.7 in January 1983 to 135.1 in January 1984; the rate then declined to the end of the sample period.

5. Nominal Eurodollar rates fluctuated between 8.96 and 10.4, with a rising trend in early 1984. Real Eurodollar rates rose sharply in the first half of 1983, and have fluctuated around 5.0 through the first quarter of 1984.

6. Average world inflation fell from April 1983 to September 1983, on average, and began to rise slightly from that point on.

7. Gold prices fell abruptly in early 1983 and have drifted somewhat erratically downward thereafter.

Empirical Results of the Revised Gold Pricing Model

The gold pricing model as modified and estimated using revised data over the new longer sample period, contains five independent variables:

1. *Log World Liquidity:* World liquidity is used here as a measure of expected future nominal income, both real and inflationary components. Multicollinearity problems continue to plague attempts to sort out the effects of liquidity growth to support economic activity at constant prices from that causing true inflationary pressure.

2. *Log U.S. Trade-Weighted Exchange Rate:* This variable serves two functions, both influencing gold prices in the same direction. The first is statistical in nature: Since gold prices are quoted in terms of U.S.

dollars, and we are viewing gold as a stateless currency, a change in the U.S. dollar exchange rate vis-a-vis the rest of the world will necessarily alter the value of gold in these other currencies. As a result, market transactions will occur to adjust the market price of gold to reflect the relative price of dollars to other currencies. The exchange rate also tends to summarize a variety of relative macroeconomic conditions among the major countries in ways that are not picked up by other variables in this simple model, and thus tends to reflect the perceived value of dollar assets as opposed to other assets. The series, published by the Federal Reserve Board, is the U.S. exchange rate weighted by bilateral trade with the Group of Ten plus Switzerland on a monthly average basis.

3. *Real Eurodollar Rate:* This variable shows the opportunity cost of holding gold, a noninterest earning asset, versus other financial assets. An increase in the real interest rate decreases the desirability of gold and thus should depress its price. It is defined as the nominal Eurodollar rate, less a moving average of industrial country/consumer price inflation. The nominal rate is the monthly average of 90-day maturity Eurodollars reported by the Federal Reserve Board.

4. *Unanticipated Inflation:* Inflation above or below the anticipated level suggests that individual portfolios were somewhat out of line at the beginning of the period. This encourages a portfolio shift toward assets such as gold if unanticipated inflation is positive and toward interest earning assets if unanticipated inflation is negative. The series is computed as the current rate of inflation less a weighted 18-month moving average.

5. *Log Political Tension Index:* This variable reflects gold's role as a precautionary asset in times of turmoil. An increase in global tensions will increase gold prices as individuals attempt to shift out of

riskier countries or locations and into more highly mobile and almost untraceable assets such as gold.

The procedure followed was similar to that used in earlier studies. First, a multiple regression of the five independent variables on the logarithm of gold prices was performed. The ordinary least squares results of this regression are:

Log Gold Price = 3.133 + 1.595 (Log World Liquidity Lagged One Month)

(3.52) (24.23)

−1.519 (Log U.S. Exchange Rate
(−8.61)

+0.001 (Real Eurodollar Rate Lagged One Month)

(0.19)

+0.054 (Unanticipated Inflation)
(1.67)

+0.20 (Log Tension Index)
(3.99)

R^2 = .899 SEE = 0.224 MDV = 5.350 D-W = 0.256

Values in parentheses are t-values. Explanations of the various statistics are provided in the Notes on page 114.

This regression displays several problems, despite a high R^2. Most importantly, the low Durbin-Watson (D-W) statistic suggests positive serial correlation. An interactive Cochrane-Orcutt regression procedure to adjust for serial correlation was performed on this same set of variables. The results from this regression, which is the same formulation as provided in January 1984, are:

Log Gold Price = 7.212 + 0.848 (Log World Liquidity
                                                    Lagged One Month)
                     (30.44)   (2.06)

                      − 1.303   (Log U.S. Exchange Rate)
                      (−4.59)

                      − 0.017   (Real Eurodollar Rate
                                                    Lagged One Month)
                      (−3.26)

                      + 0.050   (Unanticipated Inflation)
                       (2.03)

                      − 0.002   (Log Tension Index)
                      (−0.15)

R^2 = 0.991   SEE = 0.066   MDV = 5.360   D-W = 1.546

Values in parentheses are t-values.

The above Cochrane-Orcutt result is better than that provided by ordinary least squares, though it too has some problems.

The results from the regression adjusted for serial correlation are quite strong. Nevertheless, the magnitude and significance of individual coefficients and goodness of fit have altered enough to support our previous concerns about changing market structure and the stability of the model over time. The principal measure of goodness of fit, R^2, indicates that the adjusted equation explains 99 percent of the variation of the gold price over the same period.[7] The standard of error of the estimate (SEE) is less than 2 percent of the

[7]The dependent variable in terms of natural logarithms; transforming the results to the anti-log form and recalculating the R^2 will yield approximately the same value.

mean of the dependent variable (MDV), a strong result. The Durbin-Watson statistic indicates that some serial correlation may remain even after adjustment.

Regression Results: Explanatory Notes

t-Statistic   A measure of the statistical significance of the estimated coefficient. Critical values for 90-percent, 95-percent, and 99-percent confidence intervals are 1.658, 1.98, and 2.617 respectively with 120 degrees of freedom, and 1.645, 1.960, and 2.576 respectively at infinity. The regressions reported have in excess of 140 degrees of freedom.

R^2 A descriptive measure of the goodness fit of the regression: the proportion of the total variation in log gold price explained by the regression. Generally the closer R^2 is to 1.00 the better. But, the value is sensitive to the kind of data being used and care must be used in interpretation.

SEE   Standard error of the estimate (or standard error of the regression). A summary measure of the size of the prediction errors within the sample period. It has the same units as the dependent variable.

MDV   Mean of the dependent variable. Useful for comparing the value of SEE.

D-W   Durbin-Watson, a test statistic for serial correlation. A value near 2 suggests no serial correlation. Critical values of the ambiguous range for this regression for positive serial correlation are 1.51 and 1.72. A D-W value between 0 and 1.51 implies positive serial correlation, between 1.72 and 2, no serial correlation.

The reported regression produces estimates that are in line with expectations and previous results. Real World GDP, which previous versions used as one of the independent variables, was dropped from the reported results. Multicollinearity forced us to combine the real output and excess liquidity variables used in previous reports into a world liquidity variable. In this reduced-form equation, all the variables are in fact interdependent and the result of complex economic processes. The logic behind two variables was to try to sort out the effect of real and monetary activity on gold prices, even though the magnitude and sign of the coefficients were expected to be similar. By aggregating them into a world liquidity variable, the interpretation changes to expected nominal world income—including both real and inflation components. This world liquidity variable provided a statistically significant coefficient near unity, as expected.

Ordinary least squares estimates produce highly significant results from the political tension index and counterintuitive results for the real interest rate (a positive sign)—after adjustment for serial correlation political tension becomes insignificant and real interest rates become significantly negative. Despite its loss of significance we will retain the tension index as theoretically correct.

It is important to state a caution: Adjustment for serial correlation is a mechanical procedure that can introduce new statistical problems while attempting to correct for another. We prefer and use the adjusted form based on a judgment that the potential gains exceed the potential costs, especially if the results are going to be used for projections.

Indeed, an argument can be made that, if forecasting is the main interest, a major simplification is possible. Since world liquidity and the exchange rate explain most of the variation in the gold price, it was felt a regression excluding the other variables could forecast almost as well. The Cochrane-Orcutt version is as follows:

Log Gold Price = 7.597 + 0.818 (Log World Liquidity
                 (37.98)   (2.17) Lagged One Month)

                       – 1.372   (Log U.S. Exchange Rate
                      (–4.83)

$R^2 = 0.990$ SEE = 0.069   MDV = 5.36   D-W = 1.413

Values in parentheses are t-values.

This equation's projected gold prices differed from the full model by some 6 to 11 percent. This was considered too wide a range of error to provide confidence

Figure 3–1
Predicted vs. Actual Gold Price: 1972–84

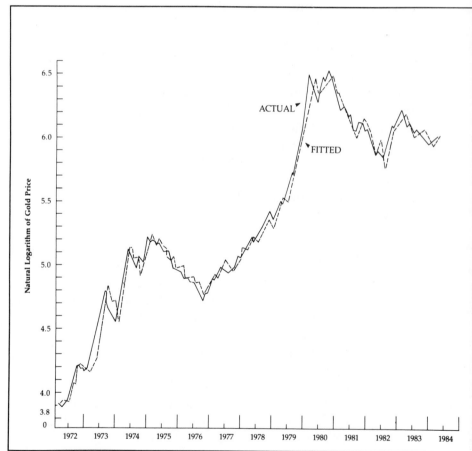

in the validity of the abbreviated version, especially in view of the concerns over the full structure, already expressed.

Actual gold prices (in logarithmic form) are plotted against estimated prices from the full model in Figure 3–1. It is clear from this chart that the strong cyclical pattern of the errors has been significantly reduced. This can be attributed mainly to a better adjustment for serial correlation.

Projections

Table 3–2 presents gold price projections under three scenarios. The assumptions for each gold price scenario are discussed below.

The projections provided here are not an attempt to predict the future. Rather, they provide a range of gold prices consistent with "not unreasonable" projections of the main independent variables for the next several years.

The three scenarios bracket a reasonable range of plausible outcomes. Extreme scenarios are not reported. The first scenario, "most probable," is characterized by an initially sluggish economy, limited monetary stimulus, a cyclical (not structural) decline in the U.S. dollar followed by cyclical economic upturn. In

Table 3–2
Gold Price Projections: 1985–87 (U.S. Dollars).

Scenario	1985		1986		1987	
	June	Dec.	June	Dec.	June	Dec.
I. Most Probable	395	440	460	460	460	475
II. Rapid Liquidity Growth, Weak Dollar	455	570	560	550	530	545
III. Strong Stable Dollar	345	355	365	380	390	405

the second scenario, monetary authorities promote rapid liquidity growth, accompanied by a sharp decline in the dollar and accelerating inflation. The third scenario is most characterized by a strong, stable dollar and a modest, stable rate of world liquidity growth.

In the first two scenarios, the rate of world liquidity growth rises then falls. In the first, it is assumed to increase from a 9.5 percent rate in 1984 to a 10.5 percent rate in the second half of 1985 and the first half of 1986, followed by a gradual diminution back to 9.7 percent in the second half of 1987. The second scenario displays a more dramatic cycle, rising from 9.5 percent to 11.5 percent in the second half of 1985, declining gradually back to 9.5 percent by the second half of 1987. In the third scenario it is assumed that monetary authorities hold liquidity growth at a stable rate of 9.5 percent throughout.

The U.S. trade-weighted exchange rate is fixed at 150 in the third scenario to characterize a strong, stable dollar. This is sharply contrasted in scenario II, which has the exchange rate falling to a low of 110 by December 1985 and then rising back to 125 by December 1987. Scenario I is similar, but less extreme; the dollar is assumed to bottom out in December 1985 at 130, hold steady for six months, and then rise to 140 by June 1987.

The real Eurodollar rate moves in opposite directions in scenarios I and II. In scenario I it declines from 4.0 percent in June 1985 to 3.0 percent in December 1986, where it stays through December 1987.

In scenario II, it starts at a level of 3.0 percent, falls to 2.5 percent in December 1985 and grows to a high of 4.0 percent by June 1987. There is no fluctuation of the Eurodollar rate in the third scenario, which holds steady at a rate of 5.0 percent throughout.

Unanticipated inflation follows with a lag behind liquidity growth in scenarios I and II, with scenario II having the larger changes. Scenario III holds unanticipated inflation at zero. Political tension is fixed at 35 in all scenarios.

For those persons interested in constructing their own projections, we provide the values for the final observation in our sample period—March 1984—along with two statistics needed to correctly adjust the projections.

Gold Price	394.50
World Liquidity Lagged One Month	397.857
Exchange Rate	128.07
Real Eurodollar Rate Lagged One Month	4.992
Unanticipated Inflation	0.330
Political Tension	37.0
Final RHO[8]	0.9759792
Residual 1984:03[9]	0.088424

Projections must use the following procedure:

1. Calculate projections for each of the independent variables for the appropriate time period.
2. Compute a projection based on the equation reported in the text, with one adjustment. This adjustment is to add to the result (still in logarithm form) or to the constant term in advance the value of RHO^n X (residual 1984:03) where n equals the number of months between March, 1984 and the projection period.

---

[8]The estimated serial correlation coefficient from the Cochrane-Orcutt estimation: Reported here for its use in projecting gold prices from the regression results.

[9]The unconditional residual between log actual gold price and the prediction based on the coefficients from the Cochrane-Orcutt procedure but without incorporating the serial correlation adjustment. Reported here for its use in projecting gold prices from the regression results.

4

Gold: The Transition from Commodity to Currency Form: 1968–73

Is gold primarily a commodity or a defacto currency? Did the gold price explosion of the 1970s represent a once-and-for-all adjustment to a free market after decades of control? Or did the adjustment take place promptly, with the explosive price increases of the 1973–74 and 1978–80 periods merely "currency" and investment responses to the events of the times?

This chapter sets out to answer those questions. Additionally, it provides detailed charts of price behavior for the key adjustment periods, which many readers should find useful for reference purposes.

EUGENE J. SHERMAN
Vice President, Economist
International Investment Manager
June, 1984

Premises

What are the key determinants of the price of gold? Some view gold primarily as a commodity and look to the general trend of commodity prices, either individually or in an index, as a guide and major influence on the gold price. Others look upon gold as a monetary form and look to general influences on inflation as the determinant. We fall into the latter camp and argue that gold is a form of unofficial money that people use worldwide as a means of storing value, as an investment, and, on rare occasion, for purposes of exchange. On the grounds that gold is a form of money, it can be analyzed by applying monetary theory. This is what we have attempted to do in "The Gold Pricing Model."

Clearly, gold remains a metal with many industrial applications, most importantly jewelry. Thus it still retains its character as a commodity. However, variations in price are explicable primarily by variations in investor demand. Investors, in turn, are motivated to invest or liquidate gold on the basis of their expectations of inflation. Inflationary expectations are heavily influenced by rates of growth of money supply. Internationally, the major alternative currency to home country currencies is the U.S. dollar. Thus variations in the dollar also have an important influence on the gold price, since gold is another alternative currency form. These two factors in combination—the rate of growth of money supply and variation in the dollar— are the major components of our gold pricing model, and are the major determinants of the gold price.

This was not always the case. Gold was held at stable prices by central banks for most years in this century until 1968. It was a commodity with a fixed price. Even after a free market was established, gold did not move immediately in response to money supply and dollar exchange rates. In fact, it remained relatively stable. As the charts show, the gold price did not start to move significantly upward until the middle of 1971.

The purpose of this study is to examine the period of transition during which gold became the preferred hedge against inflation. Our contention is that the commodity character of gold gradually was subordinated to its unofficial monetary and investment role. Furthermore, the adjustment from an artificially suppressed price to the free market was completed by the middle of 1969. Thereafter, as the world became more inflation-prone, gold broke away from the commodity market to become primarily a monetary alternative.

Summary and Conclusions

The charts in Figures 4–1 and 4–2, on commodity prices and gold prices, pretty well tell the story. Commodity prices moved up and back within a range of about 12 percent for the 10 years ending about mid-1972. Thereafter commodity prices soared, found a much wider trading range, 1973 through 1978, and then soared again. Gold behaved differently. It was quite stable through mid-1971 and then started a slow uptrend which gathered momentum through 1974. It lost almost 50 percent of value from the end of 1974 into September of 1976. Thereafter it developed a major, accelerating uptrend. Obviously, the gold pattern differed substantially from the commodity pattern.

The transition of gold to primarily a money and investment form was several years in the making. Major changes were underway in 1968, and these continued over the next several years. The United States was involved in a war in Southeast Asia that it would not or could not win. Owing to the Vietnam experience and other sociological change, society was in transition during those years as well. Students and blacks revolted over the war and civil rights matters, and the Watergate episode undermined the public's confidence in government. There developed a general disenchantment with institutions of authority. Inter-

Figure 4–1
Futures Price Index (Monthly High, Low, & Close of Nearest
Future, 1962–83).

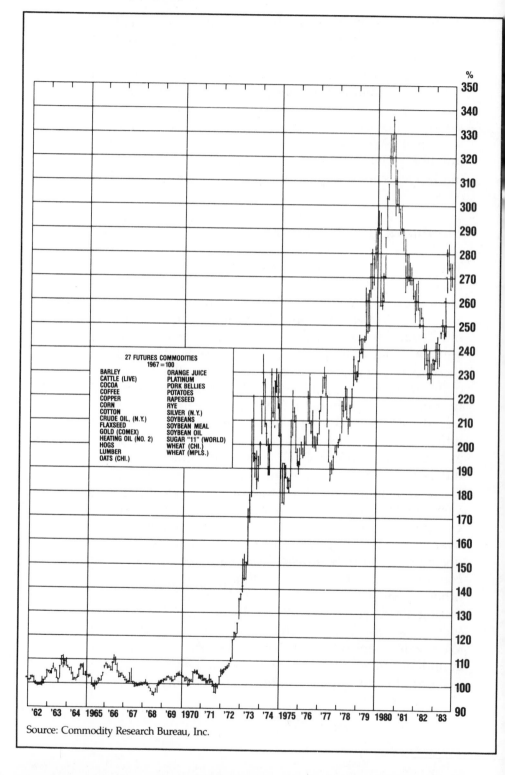

27 FUTURES COMMODITIES
1967 = 100

BARLEY	ORANGE JUICE
CATTLE (LIVE)	PLATINUM
COCOA	PORK BELLIES
COFFEE	POTATOES
COPPER	RAPESEED
CORN	RYE
COTTON	SILVER (N.Y.)
CRUDE OIL, (N.Y.)	SOYBEANS
FLAXSEED	SOYBEAN MEAL
GOLD (COMEX)	SOYBEAN OIL
HEATING OIL (NO. 2)	SUGAR "11" (WORLD)
HOGS	WHEAT (CHI.)
LUMBER	WHEAT (MPLS.)
OATS (CHI.)	

Source: Commodity Research Bureau, Inc.

Figure 4–2
Gold (Monthly High, Low, & Close of Nearest Future, 1968–83).
Comex, N.Y.

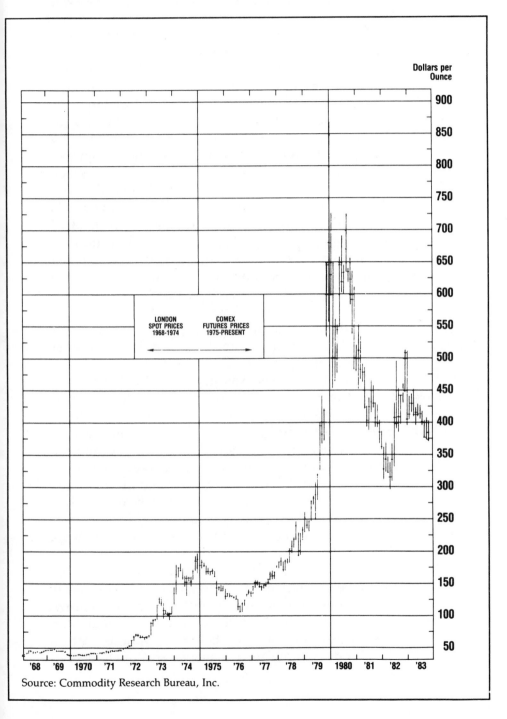

Source: Commodity Research Bureau, Inc.

nationally, similar things were happening as post-war-generation young adults objected to the status quo and brought on sociological and political changes. There was substantial intermittent turbulence in the Middle East and other areas of the world. But, perhaps most important, the inflation trend got under way. Inflation was virtually nonexistent in the United States in the early 1960s. However, as an outgrowth of the Vietnam War and excessive fiscal and monetary policies in the latter part of the 1960s into the 1970s, inflation spiraled upward and was never substantially checked. Wage-price controls were attempted in 1971 into the early part of 1973 which, when it was all over, proved to be counterproductive. Not only did inflation accelerate, it led to inflationary expectations, so that decision makers at every level acted on the assumption that inflation would continue unabated into the indefinite future. This led to self-fulfilling prophecies.

As a result of all of these political and economic forces, the markets moved to adjust to the realities of life. In the process it forced changes in the international monetary system. The gold pool was broken in 1968 and the market was permitted to find its own level. The United States severed its link to gold in 1971, and exchange rates were permitted to float freely in 1973. Those and other market developments were not the cause of the economic turbulence but the corrective mechanism in response to market forces in an inflationary world. The gold market and the gold price were responding to these forces and were merely a part of the adjustment process. By 1973 gold was reflecting all of the economic events that were taking place at the time.

And it was a litany of economic setbacks and failures: The industrialized countries were in the midst of an inflationary boom with commodity prices soaring. The first oil price shock took place late in that year. There was a series of crop failures in various parts of the world, creating food scarcities and upward pressure on food prices. Foreign exchange rates were floating and the dollar was weakening. Interest rates were in the process of deregulation in the United States, so that fixed income markets, both short- and long-term, were fluctuating over much wider ranges. Financial innovation seemed to be insulating business and the financial markets from the disciplining effects of monetary policy and earlier imposed constraints. Monetarism was established as the guiding theory to monetary policy, but was honored in the breach as monetary expansion was excessive. As a result, inflationary expectations progressively intensified. No wonder that investors worldwide (it was still illegal to hold monetary gold in the United States) sought refuge in an inflation hedge, "created" a new currency, and investment form, and chased the gold price to ever higher levels.

Annual Chronology

1968

The international gold pool was broken in the early part of March. From 1961 through this point, the United States and six European central banks maintained a pool that bought and sold gold at the fixed price of $35 an ounce to stabilize it. From 1961 into the early part of 1966, the pool had been a net purchaser of gold. But thereafter it became a net seller. By the time of the crisis in just 10 trading days, an estimated 900 tons of gold were sold in the London market. That represented a 20- to 30-fold increase over the normal amounts. The participants in the pool agreed to allow the free market to find its own level, but to exchange gold among themselves at the still fixed price of $35 an ounce. The crisis had developed out of growing scarcities of newly mined gold, rising inflation, and a substantially worsening U.S. balance of payments deficit.

Investors and speculators had come to the conclusion (1) that these basic trends would not be reversed, (2) that inevitably major new adjustments to the international financial system would have to be made, and (3) that these would include a major adjustment to the gold price.

The year was also characterized by a great deal of turbulence and tension. On the international front Czechoslovakia sought major liberalization and freedom from Soviet Union domination, which led to a Soviet invasion of the country to put down the developing revolution. The U.S. ship *Pueblo* with its 83-man crew was seized in January. The North Vietnamese undertook an offensive at the time of Tet which demonstrated the difficulty the United States would have in realizing its objectives in Southeast Asia. There were continuing clashes in the Middle East between Israel and various Arab neighbors, especially Jordan. There was unrest in North Korea in April. Students rioted in France and nearly brought the country to civil war.

On the domestic front President Johnson declared that he would not run for re-election. Martin Luther King, the civil rights leader, was assassinated. This assassination led to a series of antiwar and race riots in April and May, in many cases led by students, but carrying on to other members of the public. There were also major protests by the poor. This was highlighted by a march on Washington in May. Robert Kennedy, a candidate for the Democratic nomination, was assassinated in June.

In the U.S. economy the balance of payments deficit grew substantially worse with a $3.57 billion deficit for the year 1967 and a fourth quarter deficit alone of $1.8 billion. Furthermore, it appeared that the situation would worsen. The U.S. economy was reasonably strong with 5-percent real growth and 3.8-percent inflation in 1968 over 1967. Congress passed a tax increase measure, designed to help finance the Vietnam War, that took effect in mid-July. By historic standards, monetary policy was relatively accommodating and money supply grew rapidly in 1967 and 1968.

As the chart in Figure 4–3 shows, the price of gold moved up relatively rapidly during the initial stages of the free market, declined from the middle of May into the middle of July, and then moved erratically higher through the end of the year.

Figure 4–3
Gold: 1968 Daily Spot Prices, London Final Afternoon Quote.

Source: Commodity Research Bureau, Inc.

1969

International turbulence was not quite as great in 1969 as in the prior year. However, the war in Vietnam continued with varying degrees of intensity. A new element of unrest developed in March of that year when there were border clashes between the Soviet Union and the Chinese. The Middle East remained an area of tension as there were on and off border conflicts between Israel and its neighbors. In April North Korea downed a U.S. reconnaissance plane over international waters.

On the domestic front student riots continued, at-

Figure 4–4
Gold: 1969 Daily Spot Prices, London Final Afternoon Quote.

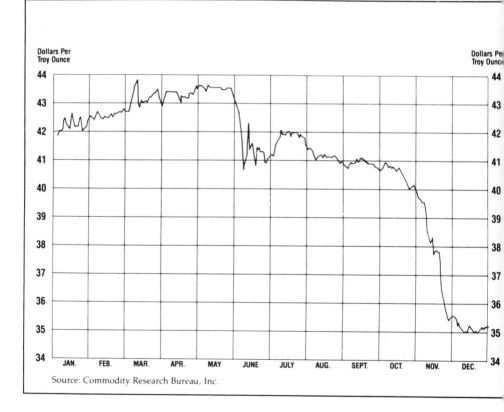

Source: Commodity Research Bureau, Inc.

tributable to both race relations and antiwar protests. The new administration imposed some fiscal and monetary restraints, which became progressively sharper. Monetary growth slowed substantially as the year advanced. Inflation for the year was still historically high at that point at 4.7 percent, but by the latter part of the year it was visibly slowing. The economy also gradually slowed down throughout the course of the year, headed toward recession. Money supply slowed and interest rates moved upward. Nominal interest rates were considered high with Treasury bills near 7¾ percent, commercial paper at 8⅞ percent, and Eurodollars at close to 11 percent by year end. Corporate bonds were at around 7¾ percent at that time. With inflation slowing this meant that real interest rates were quite high and rising.

The rising trend in the gold price that was evident in December of 1968 continued through May of 1969. Thereafter there were declines and, by late 1969, sharp declines, back to the $35 an ounce price level. It would appear that by this time the gold market was responding to economic and political forces current at the time. Evidently the adjustment process to the free market was completed. High real interest rates and slowing monetary growth seemed sufficient to bring the gold price down.

1970

Internationally, fighting continued on and off in the Middle East. New hostilities developed along the Cambodian border and fighting in Vietnam was heavy from time to time. A Middle East cease fire was accepted in July and took effect in August. However, Palestinians and Jordanians fought each other in September. Gamal Abdel Nasser, President of Egypt, died in September of that year and within 10 days Anwar Sadat succeeded him.

Domestically social protests continued primarily on campuses as students opposed the Vietnam war. In perhaps the most famous event, four students were shot in war protests at Kent State University in May. In the economy, the Federal Reserve shifted to a monetarist approach. The economy was in recession with GNP losing 0.4 percent from the prior year. Nevertheless inflation remained relatively high at 5.3 percent. Both of these results represented substantial disappointment over the policies that had been employed to cope with the phenomena of recession and inflation. In June, Penn Central went bankrupt when it could not meet its commercial paper maturities. This created a great deal of turbulence in the financial market and brought on a reversal of monetary policies

Figure 4–5
Gold: 1970 Daily Spot Prices, London Final Afternoon Quote.

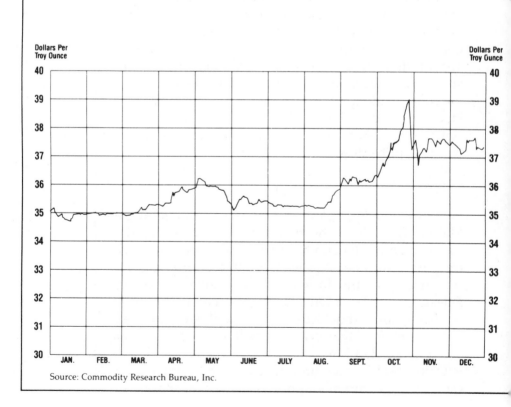

Source: Commodity Research Bureau, Inc.

away from restraint. Money supply accelerated and interest rates declined.

The gold market in 1970 remained fairly stable until September. It moved up rather sharply in October, fell back again, and then stabilized at a new higher level in November and December. The sharp jump was probably in response to the events in the Middle East with the death of Nasser and the conflict between the Palestinians and Jordanians, and the easing of monetary policy and declines in interest rates.

1971

Internationally, President Sadat consolidated his strength, ousted his opponents, and signed a treaty of friendship and cooperation with the Soviet Union. The Middle East was quieter as the cease fire seemed to hold. Bangladesh was created as an outgrowth of an India-Pakistan war.

Domestically, antiwar demonstrations continued on and off culminating in mass arrests during demonstrations in the spring in Washington. As part of the growing antiwar sentiment the Pentagon Papers were released. This probably added growing negative attitudes regarding the U.S. involvement in the Vietnam War.

On the economic front there was a foreign exchange crisis in Europe in May leading to a number of European countries floating their currencies. The U.S. economy began a modest recovery but inflation remained relatively high, especially in the light of the most recent recession and early stage of expansion. In the second quarter the inflation was generally running at a 4-percent annual rate. Despite the recovery, unemployment remained relatively high and stable at around 6 percent with little evidence of diminution in the near term. To cope with the dual problem of rising inflation and high unemployment with unsatisfactory economic expansion, President Nixon imposed wage/

133

Figure 4–6
Gold: 1971 Daily Spot Prices, London Final Afternoon Quote.

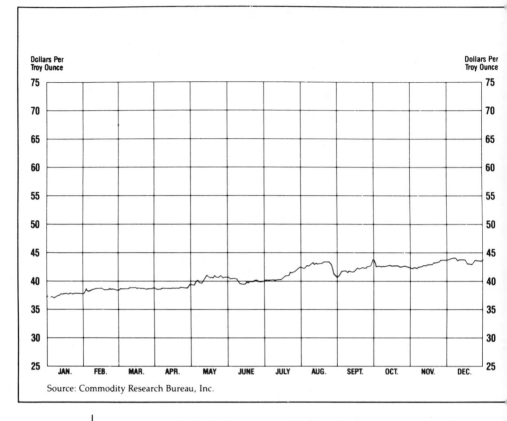

Source: Commodity Research Bureau, Inc.

price controls in August of 1971. At the same time he severed the link of the dollar from gold and declared that the U.S. would no longer meet its international obligations with gold. All currencies were free to float independent of the dollar. At the time interest rates were on the rise and inflationary expectations were worsening again, even though economic pressures were not yet creating new inflationary conditions. The policy brought on a period of euphoria with people thinking that this would break the spiral of inflation. By December substantial foreign exchange adjustments had been made and new fixed rates were established for most currencies in the famous Smithsonian Agreements concluded in the middle of December. Gold was officially devalued by the U.S. by 8.57 percent and the price fixed at $38 an ounce. Monetary policy turned restrictive in the second half of the year after having been very expansionary in the first half.

Despite all of these major changes, especially the so-called new economic plan introduced in August, the gold price remained relatively stable over the course of the year and traded within the range of $37 to $44 an ounce.

1972

The Vietnam war continued in 1972 and, in fact intensified with the United States mining Vietnamese

Figure 4–7
Gold: 1972 Daily Spot Prices, London Final Afternoon Quote.

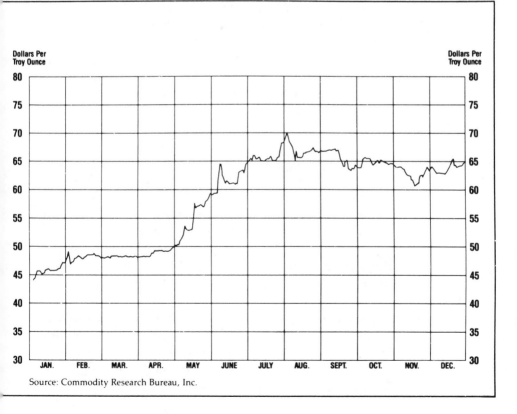

Source: Commodity Research Bureau, Inc.

harbors. Nevertheless, President Nixon visited both the Soviet Union and the People's Republic of China, the latter being a historic event. President Nixon won re-election by a landslide. The U.S. economy gathered momentum over the course of the year with real GNP rising 6.5 percent. Inflation was artificially suppressed by controls so that the GNP deflator rose by only 3 percent. However, monetary policy turned expansionary again with interest rates declining by the fourth quarter and money supply growing rapidly.

From relative stability in 1971, the gold price started to move higher, and broke new ground in the early part of 1972. The price stabilized in the latter part of February through the early part of April but then rose sharply, reaching a temporary high point of $70, or double the old official price, in the early part of August. Coincidently monetary policy both within the United States and on a worldwide basis turned aggressively expansionary in 1972, with world money supply growing at a post-war high rate up to that point. Perhaps stimulated by this monetary expansion, world economic activity started to expand also.

1973

Internationally the major political event of the year was the war in the Middle East, which took place in October. There had been hostilities all year long leading to it. This led shortly thereafter to the oil embargo by first the Arab oil exporters and then the entire Organization of Petroleum Exporting Countries. When the embargo was ended, prices were doubled. Earlier in the year, U.S. involvement in Vietnam started to wind down and the troops were withdrawn.

Domestically the major political event was the unfolding of all of the events associated with the Watergate situation. This created an atmosphere of political uncertainty in that the President himself was seen as culpable.

In the economy, both the U.S. and the other industrialized countries were in the midst of an inflation-driven boom. Most price controls were removed and prices jumped sharply higher. GNP for the year rose 6 percent, but by the end of the year was slowing. However, inflation rose 5 percent, but by the end of the year was accelerating. It was during this period, especially as inflation accelerated against weakening economic growth, that inflationary expectations really started to take hold. These inflationary expectations were exacerbated by a series of harvest disappointments and crop failures, and the oil shock.

Figure 4–8
Gold: 1973 Daily Spot Prices, London Final Afternoon Quote.

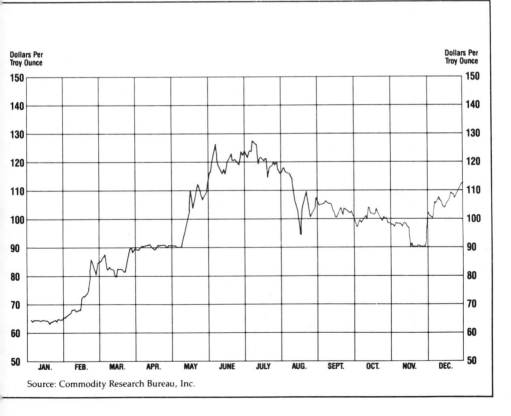

Source: Commodity Research Bureau, Inc.

The gold market started to move sharply higher again in February of 1973. The second devaluation in 14 months took place in February against a background of a massive flows of funds out of the dollar. This one was 10 percent to $42.22. New currency parties were set. But two weeks later, in early March, a new currency crisis led to general currency floating. It became apparent that no new international financial system could be agreed upon. So the finance ministers and central bankers agreed to disagree—in other words they decided to let the markets determine exchange relationships. Investors responded by seeking gold. The gold price rose intermittently into early July and actually moved above $126 an ounce. By then the market adjustment had taken place and the gold price started to settle lower.

III
The Role of Gold in a Large Portfolio

Having examined the gold market in terms of micro- and macroeconomic theories, our attention now shifts to the analysis of gold as investment vehicle.

Mr. Sherman was instrumental in applying modern portfolio theory to gold and shedding light on the role of gold in a large portfolio. In his pioneering work, "Gold—A Conservative Prudent Investment for Diversified Portfolios" (October 1980), he proved through statistical analysis of gold price volatility that gold provides an escape from the U.S. financial environment. There, he demonstrated that gold, when held in modest proportions of a large balanced portfolio, reduces volatility while enhancing overall returns.

This original study has been enlarged to incorporate the results of portfolio simulations and updated for periods ending 1981, 1982, and 1983.

This part contains the latest in the series entitled "The Application of Modern Portfolio Theory to Gold 1974–1983" and a part of "Gold—A Conservative Prudent Investment for Diversified Portfolios." While the discussion in this part is based on figures in U.S. dollars, we will approach the issue in an international perspective in the next chapter, appraising and comparing the performance in six major currencies.

5
The Application of Modern Portfolio Theory to Gold: 1974–83

Investor Philosophy in the 1980s

The 1980s, called "the age of uncertainties," is characterized by strong preference on the part of investors to transfer risk, diversify assets, and hedge against inflation. New investment vehicles and techniques, which were not considered as prudent investments or were not yet fully developed, are now incorporated into portfolios and portfolio management practices. The reasoning is as follows. As we entered the 1970s, investment managers believed they could anticipate the future and undertake investments based on a long-term view. Econometric models were coming on stream that purported to predict economic developments or a series of scenarios based on anticipated assumptions. It was believed that, by anticipating the right assumptions and applying those to the econometric models, one could get an accurate reading of the future. Portfolio practices evolved out of this basic assumption. Other investment techniques were developed based on growth assumptions, price earnings multiples as variations of them, earnings predictions, price volatility, and so on.

Actual practice demonstrated that the models sometimes didn't work at all, regardless of the accuracy of the assumptions. More importantly, the events of the 1970s demonstrated that political, social, and natural developments frequently cannot be predicted at all. Thus, regardless of the sophistication of the model or the investment management technique, investment commitments still retain varying degrees of risk.

In the latter 1980s, investment managers and their superiors—boards of directors, chief executive officers, and the like—have their sense of certainty tempered by the events of the 1970s and early 1980s. This is likely to be the case even if the amplitude of variation lessens, because policies are made on the assumption of wide swings that typified markets in the 1970s and early 1980s. Even though market swings represent opportunity, they are widely viewed as hazards to be avoided. Accordingly, investment practices of the 1980s are characterized by risk aversion. This should take at least three forms: (1) hedging in various markets, (2) diversification across industry and, more importantly, across currency lines, and (3) use of new vehicles that represent claims on secure assets, such as land, precious metals, and other items of accepted and lasting value.

Conclusions

Gold continues to be a useful diversifier in large, balanced portfolios. It has low correlation against stocks and bonds and reduces volatility when held in modest proportions while enhancing overall returns. These conclusions are the result of the statistical analysis contained here. Moreover, similar conclusions were drawn as a result of three earlier studies for periods ending 1980, 1981, and 1982. Especially noteworthy is the fact that gold continued to demonstrate these qualities despite the three years ending 1983, which was a period of sharply declining inflation rates and variable but generally declining gold prices. Thus, while gold is generally perceived as an inflation hedge, it continues to perform ahead of inflation during periods that include reducing inflation. It therefore has very useful properties for a balanced portfolio throughout the cycle, not just during the stage of the cycle in which inflation is accelerating.

Understandably, some caution is required in assessing the full implications from any set of portfolio simulations over the past 10 years, no matter how carefully constructed. This tumultuous period witnessed the largest gold price acceleration and deceleration in the twentieth century, both in absolute and relative terms. It was a period of unprecedented peacetime inflation, adoption of floating exchange rates for the major currencies including gold, and unusual volatility, innovation and reform as well as disruption in domestic and international financial markets.

For the period as a whole, gold outperformed stocks and bonds; compounded annual rates of return were 13, 11 and 6 percent annualized, respectively. However, this does not hold true for some subperiods. For example, over the past 5 years stocks outperformed both gold and bonds by very substantial margins. And gold actually declined at a 15-percent rate after adjustment for inflation between 1980–83. Thus there is broad diversity within the 10-year period with which to undertake meaningful portfolio simulations.

Inflation decelerated from 12.2 percent in 1974 to 4.8 percent in 1976, accelerated to 13.2 percent in 1979, and subsequently decelerated to 3.9 percent in 1983.

Thus, the 1974–83 period covers a cycle and a half of inflation with one upswing sandwiched between two downswings. Simulations in this investment environment are unlikely to significantly upwardly bias the results in favor of gold in risk adjusted terms. And the 5-year 1979–83 period, dominated by a decelerating inflation environment, provides a reasonable assessment of the potential near-term costs of maintaining moderate gold diversification even during periods unfavorable to gold investment, such as in times of falling prices.

Our own work has been independently corroborated by other analyses, and is now reaffirmed for 1983 by this study. This would appear once again to validate our assertion that gold seems to have some statistical dominance in the capital markets. This is at variance with conventional notions of efficiency in U.S. capital markets, suggesting that the market may not be as efficient as frequently presumed. It would appear that the market has failed to fully price gold (or gold mining shares, for that matter), to take into account the benefits of favorable performance and low volatility. A probable explanation for this apparent inefficiency is the presence of institutional rigidities. These have interfered with what would otherwise be capital market efficiency, which would result in full and "appropriate" pricing. Those rigidities could be the result of traditional American reluctance to use gold as an investment for fiduciary-type accounts.

Statistical Measures

Beta

To determine whether or not gold is appropriate for a conservatively managed portfolio, we applied conventional tests of the price of gold in relation to a number of standard measures of market performance and volatility. The usual measure of volatility is the beta. A beta with a value of 1.0 would suggest that the investment under consideration performs the same as the standard investment and provides no greater and no lesser variability. A positive beta in excess of 1.0 would suggest a more aggressive investment than the standard and therefore more volatility; a positive beta between 0.0 and 1.0 would suggest a less aggressive performance—less volatility. A negative beta indicates an opposite performance relative to the basic measure of investment; a lower value than minus 1.0 implies smaller volatility in the opposite direction; greater than minus 1.0 indicates more volatility in an opposite direction.

Correlation

The correlation indicates how close the variation of the investment under consideration is to the variation in the basic investment. A correlation of 1.0 or close to it would suggest that variation in the selected investment is entirely—95 percent, or whatever—consistent with variations in the basic investment. A zero correlation or close to it would suggest no relationship. A minus 1.0 correlation or close to it would suggest that variations in the measure under review are identical to variations in the basic measure, but in the opposite direction. The correlation is expressed here as R^2, which is stated in percentage terms. Thus an R^2 of 16.26 means that .1626, or 16.26 percent, of the variation in gold can be explained by variation in the S&P 500.

Alpha

The alpha represents timing performance. The presumption is that, by timing purchases and sales, the investor can outperform the standard measure with a similar beta. The alpha presumably measures the continuous differential over the beta as a result of judicious market timing. A high positive value suggests that good market timing can substantially improve portfolio performance.

Standard Error

There are also standard errors of the beta and the alpha. The lower the value on these, the greater the confidence in the consistency of the beta and alpha themselves. In other words, the standard error should be added to or subtracted from the beta or the alpha to derive the range over which the statistics provide confidence. It is a measure of possible divergence of the estimates from the true value.

Past research on portfolios supports the contention that a beta has excellent predictive value. Alphas are less stable, since they reflect market timing that, of course, is uncertain. Even though they have no predictive value, however, they are useful in measuring past performance. In all cases, betas, alphas, and R^2 reflect only the performance of the past 60 months, ending December 1983. They are suggestive, but not forecasts, of future performance.

The Results of Statistical Analysis of Gold Price Variability

We used the following measures:

1. Afternoon London gold fixings, end of month.
2. Salomon Brothers index of high-grade corporate bonds, end of month, as a proxy for long-term interest rates.
3. Standard & Poor's 500 monthly stock index, end of month, as a proxy for stock prices.

We can summarize our findings with regard to gold as follows:

1. Where the standard measure of investment was long-term interest rates:

   a. The beta for gold shows that gold is much less volatile.

   b. The alpha for gold shows that there are good rewards for good market timing.

   c. The correlation is virtually nil, indicating that gold moves totally independently from long-term interest rates. This means that gold provides an escape from long-term interest rates within the U.S. and the factors that influence them.

   d. The standard error of the beta is small, providing reasonable confidence on the results of the beta. The standard error of the alpha is fairly high in absolute terms but not relative to the alpha, suggesting that improved results owing to timing in gold are a reasonable bet.

2. Where the independent variable was the Standard & Poor's 500:

   a. The beta was lower than unity, indicating that there was less volatility in gold than in stocks.

   b. The alpha was low, suggesting that active trading is a lost cause.

   c. The correlation was low, indicating that there is very little relationship in the variations of the price of gold to the price of stocks. This conforms the implication of the low beta.

In summary, we can say that gold provides an escape from the U.S. financial environment—long-term interest rates and stocks. Furthermore, the price of gold reduces volatility in a portfolio of stocks and bonds, and gives high returns for good market timing.

Table 5–1
Summary of Results of Statistical Analysis of Gold Price Volatility in Comparison to Price Volatility of Various Standard Investments.

GOLD versus	BETA	STD. ERROR OF BETA	ADJUSTED R²	ALPHA	STD. ERROR OF ALPHA
High-Grade Corporate Bonds	0.04	0.06	0.73	7.20	2.09
Standard & Poor's 500	0.90	0.27	16.26	0.30	4.20

NOTE: Each figure is based on 60 months of data ending December 31, 1983

Summary of Portfolio Simulations

Our statistical analysis indicates that gold reduces volatility in a portfolio of stocks or bonds. Volatility reduction is one of the objectives of a portfolio manager. The other, of course, is performance, or rate of return. Over the ten-year period ending 1983, gold performed rather well, providing compounded annual rates of return over 13 percent on a buy-and-hold basis, and well over 18 percent on a period-averaging basis. Over the five years ending 1983, the rate of return on gold was lower—just over 11 percent on a buy-and-hold basis and slightly higher on a period-averaging basis.[1] That performance was clearly superior to the inflation rates for similar periods and to compounded annual rates of returns on bonds. However, the stock market outperformed gold by a considerable margin for the five-year period ending 1983, although it underperformed gold by a significant margin for the ten-year period. It should also be noted that the compounded annual rate of return for gold over 11 percent for the five-year period is rather good when compared to the sharp decline in inflation that took place in the

---

[1]These data are drawn from our study, "The Performance of Gold Versus Stock, Bonds, and Money Markets in Six Countries 1968–83," chapter 6 in this book.

Table 5–2
Compounded Annual Rates of Return for Gold, Stocks, Bonds, and Consumer Price Index.

Year	Annual Growth Rates, Year End (Buy and Hold Basis)			
	Gold	Stocks	Bonds	C.P.I.
1974	66.2%	-26.4%	-3.1%	12.2%
1975	-24.8	37.2	14.7	7.0
1976	-4.1	23.7	18.7	4.8
1977	22.6	-7.2	1.7	6.8
1978	37.0	6.7	-0.1	9.1
1979	131.9	18.6	-4.2	13.2
1980	12.5	32.4	-2.6	12.5
1981	-32.2	-4.9	-1.0	8.8
1982	14.2	21.5	43.8	4.2
1983	-16.5	22.4	3.7	3.9
1974–79	29.3	6.6	4.3	8.8
1979–83	11.0	17.3	6.6	8.4
1974–83	13.0	10.6	6.3	8.2

last three of those five years. Thus gold provided considerably higher rates of return than bonds for the five-year period despite the poor performance of gold in the last three. This is important evidence that gold has at least as important diversifying and performance roles to play in a portfolio as do bonds during declining inflation periods as well as during accelerating periods.

Ten-Year Portfolios

For the ten-year period ending 1983, the rates of return on all portfolios rose as gold was added to the portfolio. Volatility was reduced and held relatively low for both the portfolios with five- and ten-percent proportions in gold. Higher proportions added to the overall volatility. The reward/variability ratios (which may also be looked upon as risk adjusted returns)

149

showed optimum performance at ten-percent proportions in gold. However, these were only marginally superior to the portfolios with five-percent proportions. Thus, once again, five- to ten-percent proportions in gold seem optimal in large, well balanced portfolios with long-term investment objectives. The differences in the mixes within the portfolios among varying proportions of bonds and stocks were marginal.

Five-Year Portfolios

Gold underperformed stocks in terms of rate of return for the five-year period ending 1983, but outperformed both bonds and inflation by wide margins for the same period. Had one known this in advance he would have excluded bonds and gold from his portfolio and concentrated in stocks. However, that would have represented considerable risk and might have been considered imprudent. Thus diversification.

The rates of return for the overall portfolios with five-percent proportion in gold were only slightly below the portfolios which excluded gold altogether. The volatility of the portfolios with five-percent gold was higher than those portfolios without gold. Thus, the reward/variability ratios (or risk-adjusted returns) were lower than the zero proportions in gold, but the degree of loss in performance was moderate considering the poor performance of gold over the past three years. The inclusion of bonds at all gold proportions worsened returns of the portfolios considerably more than did gold, and added to the volatility as well. Thus gold provided good qualities of diversification for both enhancement of return and suppression of volatility.

However, in a forced choice between bonds or gold, bonds provided a better reward/variability ratio owing to their lower volatility, which more than compensated for lower returns. For the five-year period the optimum proportion in gold would have been zero or five percent. Performance deteriorated sharply after the five-percent proportion. In other words, rates of return declined sharply and volatility rose as the proportion shifted to 10, 15, and 20 percent in gold.

Methodology and Terms Used in Simulations

A series of simulations have been compared to three-base portfolios.

1. 100% S&P 500.
2. 90% S&P 500; 10-percent bonds.
3. 80% S&P 500; 20-percent bonds.

Each base portfolio was diversified into increasing percentages of gold in 5-percent increments from 5 to 20 percent. In each case, the money invested in gold was drawn from the S&P portion; once the initial investment was made, there was no rebalancing or suppression of results. In other words, profits and losses were allowed to accumulate. Interest and dividend income was presumed to be reinvested in their respective categories.

Obviously, gold had no income, which put it at a disadvantage against income-producing assets. Since the study concentrated on total rate of return, however, the price performance of gold dominated the results and overpowered the other investment alternatives. It was presumed that the portfolios were initiated on either January 1, 1974 or January 1, 1979 and ran in all cases through December 31, 1983. Returns were calculated on a monthly basis.

It was further presumed that the portfolios began their periods with $100 million of cash, appropriately invested by category. Note that, by carrying the analysis through year-end 1983, the extreme price volatility that took place in 1979–82 was captured. Even so, the results in terms of variability when gold was included were favorable.

Data

Data are described under 1, 2, and 3 on page 146.

Terms

Total Return. Total dollar return with income reinvested where appropriate. Percentage per annum is compounded annual rate of return.

Buy/Hold. Results based on end-of-period pricing. It is assumed that assets were bought and held for the duration of the simulation period.

Period Average. The cumulative rate of return from the start of each year to the end of every subsequent year averaged for the entire period. This measure diminishes the significance of the particular starting and ending dates. For this reason, it is typically more valid than the buy/hold measure.

Relative Volatility. The standard deviation of the simulated portfolio relative to the standard deviation of the base portfolio set at 100 percent. The higher the value, the greater the variability relative to the base portfolio. Values in excess of 100 indicate greater volatility; values less than 100 indicate less volatility, one of the major objectives.

Beta. Measures systematic variability and sensitivity to a market. Would not effectively capture residual variability of an overall portfolio.

R^2. A measure that explains the proportion of movement in one variable by the changes observed in another variable. In this study the improved returns in the portfolio can be explained by the presence and addition of gold.

Annualized Standard Deviation. Measures average absolute variation of the portfolio calculated in annual
terms. This measure is necessary for calculating the
reward/variability ratio.

Reward/Variability Ratio. The annual compounded rate
of return divided by the annualized standard deviation of returns of that portfolio. This ratio ranks each
portfolio according to the amount of return produced per unit of variation. The higher the value,
the higher the rate of return per unit of variation
and, therefore, the more desirable the results.

Figure 5–1
Rate of Return vs. Proportion in Gold 1974–1983.

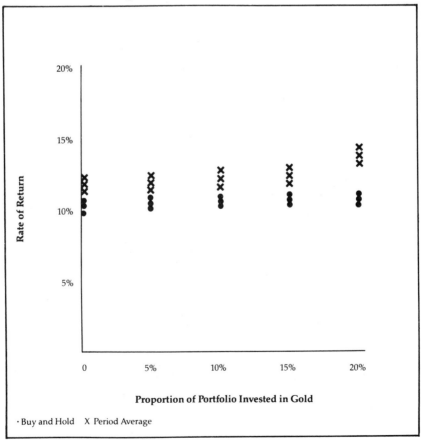

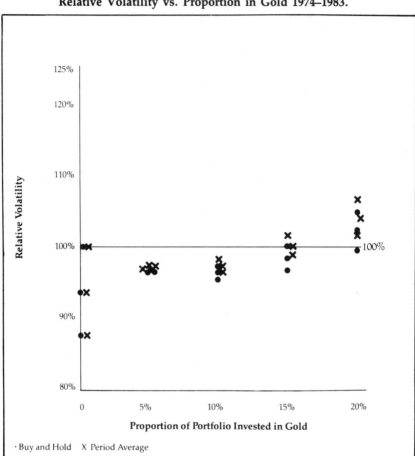

Figure 5–2
Relative Volatility vs. Proportion in Gold 1974–1983.

Figure 5–3
Reward/Variability Ratio vs. Proportion in Gold 1974–1983.

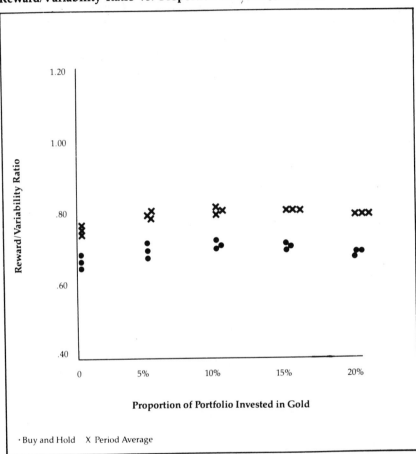

Table 5–3
Portfolio Simulation Results, Period: 1974–1983.

PROPORTIONS IN			BASE PORTFOLIO		TOTAL RETURN		RELATIVE VOLATILITY	
Gold	S&P 500	Bonds	S&P 500	Bonds	Buy/Hold	Period Avg.	Buy/Hold	Period Avg.
0	100	0	100	0	10.62%	12.27%	100.0%	100.0%
0	90	10	100	0	10.26	11.63	93.5	93.6
0	80	20	100	0	9.89	10.99	87.5	87.8
5	95	0	100	0	10.76	12.48	96.4	96.9
5	85	10	90	10	10.40	11.86	96.7	97.1
5	75	20	80	20	10.03	11.25	96.6	97.1
10	90	0	100	0	10.89	12.72	95.6	96.8
10	80	10	90	10	10.53	12.12	96.6	97.5
10	70	20	80	20	10.17	11.53	97.2	98.2
15	85	0	100	0	11.01	12.99	96.8	98.6
15	75	10	90	10	10.66	12.41	98.6	100.1
15	65	20	80	20	10.31	11.84	100.2	101.6
20	80	0	100	0	11.14	13.27	99.5	101.7
20	70	10	90	10	10.79	12.71	102.3	104.1
20	60	20	80	20	10.44	12.16	104.8	106.6

BETA		R²		ANNUALIZED STANDARD DEVIATION		REWARD/ VARIABILITY RATIO	
Buy/Hold	Period Avg.	Buy/Hold	Period Avg.	Buy/Hold	Period Avg.	Buy/Hold	Period Avg.
1.00	1.00	NOT APPLICABLE		16.33%	16.33%	.65	.75
.93	.93	NOT APPLICABLE		15.27	15.29	.67	.76
.87	.87	NOT APPLICABLE		14.29	14.33	.69	.77
.95	.95	10.4	16.0%	15.74	15.83	.68	.79
.95	.95	11.4	16.6	14.76	14.85	.70	.80
.94	.95	12.4	17.0	13.87	13.92	.72	.81
.90	.90	21.9	25.8	15.61	15.80	.70	.80
.90	.90	24.2	27.3	14.74	14.91	.71	.81
.89	.90	26.4	28.8	13.95	14.07	.73	.82
.85	.86	34.9	36.3	15.81	16.09	.70	.81
.85	.86	38.0	38.6	15.06	15.30	.71	.81
.84	.85	41.2	40.9	14.38	14.56	.72	.81
.81	.81	47.4	46.5	16.25	16.60	.68	.80
.81	.81	51.0	49.4	15.62	15.91	.69	.80
.80	.80	54.6	52.4	15.05	15.28	.69	.80

Table 5–4
Portfolio Values and Component Percentages: 1974–1983
(Initial Market Value $100.0 million).

PORTFOLIO MIX			Gold	S&P500	Bonds	Total
Gold	S&P 500	Bonds				
0	100	0	$ 0.0 (0.0%)	$100.0 (100.0%)	$ 0.0 (0.0%)	$100.0 (100.0%)
			0.0 (0.0)	274.4 (100.0)	0.0 (0.0)	274.4 (100.0)
0	90	10	0.0 (0.0)	90.0 (90.0)	10.0 (10.0)	100.0 (100.0)
			0.0 (0.0)	246.9 (93.0)	18.6 (07.0)	265.5 (100.0)
0	80	20	0.0 (0.0)	80.0 (80.0)	20.0 (20.0)	100.0 (100.0)
			0.0 (0.0)	219.5 (85.5)	37.3 (14.5)	256.8 (100.0)
5	95	0	5.0 (5.0)	95.0 (95.0)	0.0 (0.0)	100.0 (100.0)
			17.0 (6.1)	260.7 (93.9)	0.0 (0.0)	277.7 (100.0)
5	85	10	5.0 (5.0)	85.0 (85.0)	10.0 (10.0)	100.0 (100.0)
			17.0 (6.3)	233.2 (86.8)	18.6 (6.9)	268.8 (100.0)
5	75	20	5.0 (5.0)	75.0 (75.0)	20.0 (20.0)	100.0 (100.0)
			17.0 (6.5)	205.8 (79.1)	37.3 (14.3)	260.1 (100.0)
10	90	0	10.0 (10.0)	90.0 (90.0)	0.0 (0.0)	100.0 (100.0)
			34.0 (12.1)	246.9 (87.9)	0.0 (0.0)	280.9 (100.0)
10	80	10	10.0 (10.0)	80.0 (80.0)	10.0 (10.0)	100.0 (100.0)
			34.0 (12.5)	219.5 (80.7)	18.6 (6.8)	272.1 (100.0)
10	70	20	10.0 (10.0)	70.0 (70.0)	20.0 (20.0)	100.0 (100.0)
			34.0 (12.9)	192.1 (72.9)	37.3 (14.2)	263.4 (100.0)
15	85	0	15.0 (15.0)	85.0 (85.0)	0.0 (0.0)	100.0 (100.0)
			51.0 (17.9)	233.2 (82.1)	0.0 (0.0)	284.2 (100.0)
15	75	10	15.0 (15.0)	75.0 (75.0)	10.0 (10.0)	100.0 (100.0)
			51.0 (18.5)	205.8 (74.7)	18.6 (6.8)	275.4 (100.0)
15	65	20	15.0 (15.0)	65.0 (65.0)	20.0 (20.0)	100.0 (100.0)
			51.0 (19.1)	178.3 (66.9)	37.3 (14.0)	266.6 (100.0)
20	80	0	20.0 (20.0)	80.0 (80.0)	0.0 (0.0)	100.0 (100.0)
			68.0 (23.7)	219.5 (76.3)	0.0 (0.0)	287.5 (100.0)
20	70	10	20.0 (20.0)	70.0 (70.0)	10.0 (10.0)	100.0 (100.0)
			68.0 (24.4)	192.1 (68.9)	18.6 (6.7)	278.7 (100.0)
20	60	20	20.0 (20.0)	60.0 (60.0)	20.0 (20.0)	100.0 (100.0)
			68.0 (25.2)	164.6 (61.0)	37.3 (13.8)	269.9 (100.0)

Figure 5–4
Rate of Return vs. Proportion in Gold 1979–1983.

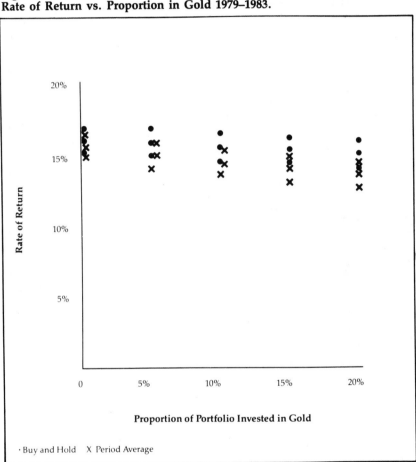

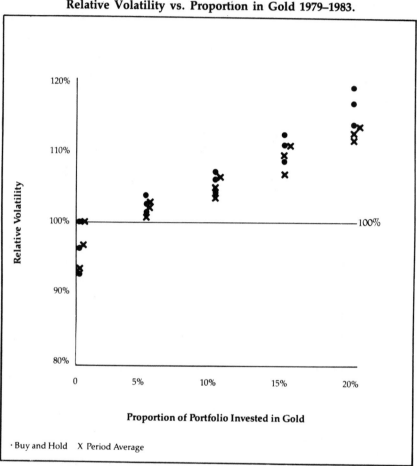

Figure 5–5
Relative Volatility vs. Proportion in Gold 1979–1983.

· Buy and Hold   X Period Average

Figure 5–6
Reward/Variability Ratio vs. Proportion in Gold 1979–1983.

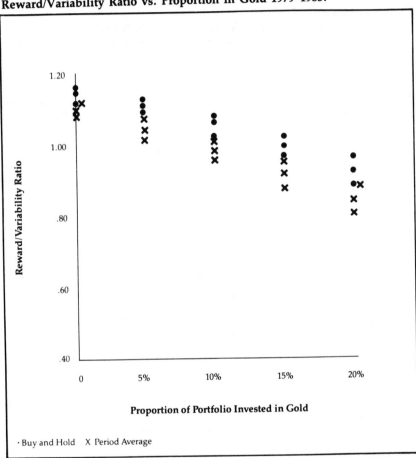

Table 5–5
Portfolio Simulation Results, Period: 1979–1983.

PROPORTIONS IN			BASE PORTFOLIO		TOTAL RETURN		RELATIVE VOLATILITY	
Gold	S&P 500	Bonds	S&P 500	Bonds	Buy/Hold	Period Avg.	Buy/Hold	Period Avg.
0	100	0	100	0	17.31%	16.62%	100.0%	100.0%
0	90	10	100	0	16.42	15.85	96.2	96.5
0	80	20	100	0	15.50	15.07	92.8	93.4
5	95	0	100	0	17.03	16.06	101.2	100.8
5	85	10	90	10	16.13	15.27	102.5	102.1
5	75	20	80	20	15.20	14.47	103.2	102.8
10	90	0	100	0	16.74	15.55	104.1	103.2
10	80	10	90	10	15.83	14.74	105.9	104.9
10	70	20	80	20	14.90	13.92	106.9	106.1
15	85	0	100	0	16.45	15.08	108.4	106.8
15	75	10	90	10	15.54	14.26	110.7	109.1
15	65	20	80	20	14.59	13.42	112.4	110.8
20	80	0	100	0	16.16	14.66	113.7	111.3
20	70	10	90	10	15.24	13.82	116.7	114.3
20	60	20	80	20	14.28	12.96	119.0	116.6

BETA		R^2		ANNUALIZED STANDARD DEVIATION		REWARD/ VARIABILITY RATIO	
Buy/Hold	Period Avg.	Buy/Hold	Period Avg.	Buy/Hold	Period Avg.	Buy/Hold	Period Avg.
1.00	1.00	NOT APPLICABLE		14.88%	14.88%	1.16	1.12
.96	.96	NOT APPLICABLE		14.31	14.36	1.15	1.10
.92	.92	NOT APPLICABLE		13.81	13.89	1.12	1.08
1.00	1.00	28.0	32.1%	15.05	14.99	1.13	1.07
1.01	1.01	28.0	32.3	14.50	14.67	1.11	1.04
1.01	1.01	27.7	32.2	14.00	14.28	1.09	1.01
1.00	1.00	40.3	42.6	15.49	15.35	1.08	1.01
1.01	1.01	41.0	43.4	14.98	15.07	1.06	.98
1.01	1.01	41.4	44.0	14.51	14.73	1.02	.95
1.00	.99	51.7	52.6	16.13	15.89	1.02	.95
1.01	1.00	53.0	54.0	15.66	15.67	.99	.91
1.01	1.01	54.0	55.1	15.25	15.39	.96	.87
1.00	.99	61.7	61.7	16.92	16.56	.96	.88
1.01	1.00	63.3	63.4	16.51	16.41	.92	.84
1.00	1.00	64.6	64.7	16.15	16.20	.88	.80

Table 5–6
Portfolio Values and Component Percentages: 1979–1983
(Initial Market Value $100.0 million).

PORTFOLIO MIX			Gold	S&P500	Bonds	Total
Gold	S&P 500	Bonds				
0	100	0	$ 0.0 (0.0%)	$100.0 (100.0%)	$ 0.0 (0.0%)	$100.0 (100.0%)
			0.0 (0.0)	222.2 (100.0)	0.0 (0.0)	222.2 (100.0)
0	90	10	0.0 (0.0)	90.0 (90.0)	10.0 (10.0)	100.0 (100.0)
			0.0 (0.0)	199.9 (93.4)	13.9 (6.5)	213.8 (100.0)
0	80	20	0.0 (0.0)	80.0 (80.0)	20.0 (20.0)	100.0 (100.0)
			0.0 (0.0)	177.7 (86.5)	27.8 (13.5)	205.5 (100.0)
5	95	0	5.0 (5.0)	95.0 (95.0)	0.0 (0.0)	100.0 (100.0)
			8.4 (3.8)	211.1 (96.2)	0.0 (0.0)	219.5 (100.0)
5	85	10	5.0 (5.0)	85.0 (85.0)	10.0 (10.0)	100.0 (100.0)
			8.4 (4.0)	188.8 (89.4)	13.9 (6.6)	211.1 (100.0)
5	75	20	5.0 (5.0)	75.0 (75.0)	20.0 (20.0)	100.0 (100.0)
			8.4 (4.1)	166.6 (82.2)	27.8 (13.7)	202.8 (100.0)
10	90	0	10.0 (10.0)	90.0 (90.0)	0.0 (0.0)	100.0 (100.0)
			16.9 (7.8)	199.9 (92.2)	0.0 (0.0)	216.8 (100.0)
10	80	10	10.0 (10.0)	80.0 (80.0)	10.0 (10.0)	100.0 (100.0)
			16.9 (8.1)	177.7 (85.2)	13.9 (6.7)	208.5 (100.0)
10	70	20	10.0 (10.0)	70.0 (70.0)	20.0 (20.0)	100.0 (100.0)
			16.9 (8.4)	155.5 (77.7)	27.8 (13.9)	200.2 (100.0)
15	85	0	15.0 (15.0)	85.0 (85.0)	0.0 (0.0)	100.0 (100.0)
			25.3 (11.8)	188.8 (88.2)	0.0 (0.0)	214.1 (100.0)
15	75	10	15.0 (15.0)	75.0 (75.0)	10.0 (10.0)	100.0 (100.0)
			25.3 (12.3)	166.6 (81.0)	13.9 (6.7)	205.8 (100.0)
15	65	20	15.0 (15.0)	65.0 (65.0)	20.0 (20.0)	100.0 (100.0)
			25.3 (12.8)	144.4 (73.1)	27.8 (14.1)	197.5 (100.0)
20	80	0	20.0 (20.0)	80.0 (80.0)	0.0 (0.0)	100.0 (100.0)
			33.8 (16.0)	177.7 (84.0)	0.0 (0.0)	211.5 (100.0)
20	70	10	20.0 (20.0)	70.0 (70.0)	10.0 (10.0)	100.0 (100.0)
			33.8 (16.6)	155.5 (76.6)	13.9 (6.8)	203.2 (100.0)
20	60	20	20.0 (20.0)	60.0 (60.0)	20.0 (20.0)	100.0 (100.0)
			33.8 (17.3)	133.3 (68.4)	27.8 (14.3)	194.9 (100.0)

The Prudent Man Rule and Its Evolution

Gold and the Prudent Man Rule

Having examined the theoretical and empirical evidence regarding the role of gold in a diversified portfolio, it now seems appropriate to review the question of prudent money management and the prudent man rule as it applies to portfolio management. Most institutional investors are bound to follow the prudent man rule in pursuance of their responsibilities.

A developing body of legal opinion recognizes that the prudent man rule must be examined within the context of the times and circumstances. Prudent management and prudent investments in the late 1950s and early 1960s are not necessarily the same as prudent management and investment in the 1980s—the times have indeed changed. Central banks are in the process of diversifying assets across the currency lines and valuing gold in market terms, at least in part, on the basis of prudent reserve management. Indeed, they are applying modern portfolio theory for this purpose, arguing that currency diversification reduces the volatility of their assets. The Federal Reserve, the International Monetary Fund, and others have taken note and are seeming to help smooth the way toward such diversification.

The Employee Retirement Income Security Act (ERISA) was enacted by Congress in 1974 to serve as a comprehensive regulatory act over private employee benefit plans. The act required that

a fiduciary shall discharge his duties with respect to a plan solely in the interest of the participants and beneficiaries and–

(A) for the exclusive purpose of:

   (i) providing benefits to participants and their beneficiaries; and

   (ii) defraying reasonable expenses of administering the plan;

(B) with the care, skill, prudence and diligence under the circumstances then prevailing that a prudent man acting in a like capacity and familiar with such matters would use in the conduct of an enterprise of a like character and with like aims;

(C) by diversifying the investments of the plan so as to minimize the risk of large losses, unless under the circumstances it is clearly prudent not to do so; and

(D) in accordance with the documents and instruments governing the plan insofar as such documents and instruments are consistent with the provisions of (ERISA).

This law overrules any state laws relating to employee benefit plans.

An important issue that has since arisen is the interpretation of prudent investment activities. Since the enactment, government regulations interpreting this rule have clearly indicated that the rule is intended to provide broad flexibility and that fiduciaries are not confined to the more traditional, income-producing investments. The Department of Labor, which is charged with administering the fiduciary responsibility provisions of ERISA, stated in a June 1979 ruling that it does not intend to adopt a "legal list" of permissible investments. The Department believes that the common law of trusts should not be applied mechanically to employee benefit plans; rather, the prudent man rule should be applied on a flexible basis. Among the reasons are the mingling of principal and income and the need to pay beneficiaries out of the combined pool of assets.

Accordingly, the Department of Labor made two important changes.

First, it rejected the single investment doctrine as the basis for determining compliance with the prudent man standard of fiduciary responsibility. The current regulations take a broader view of fiduciary prudence. This represents a liberalization from the prior restraints of the prudent man rule. Prior to the change, the prudence of any investment had been judged without reference to the other investments of the portfolio or overall portfolio performance. Many courts had focused solely on the possibility of capital loss as the measure of investment risk. As a result, trustees occasionally found themselves in positions of having their investment decisions attacked by a beneficiary over a single investment that had suffered losses, even though the fund as a whole had performed well.

The second change was to provide that an investment now made by fiduciaries need not provide a stream of income. Prior to this second change, fiduciaries were usually required to provide this income and to protect capital as well. The earlier standard grew out of common law theory that sought to resolve the fundamental conflict between interests of the income beneficiary and those of the remainderman of the common law trust.

Based on this, an investment plan may require assets that do not produce current income, but have significant growth potential, provided that the underlying trust instrument does not prohibit such an investment.

Gold is such an investment. The extent to which any such investment may be made depends upon the circumstances of the employee benefit plan, long-term investment strategy, liquidity needs, diversification, payout schedule, and a variety of other factors including economic conditions. As a result, some pension funds are now using gold as an investment since the focus is now on the overall portfolio, and the need for diversification and risk reduction is widely recognized and accepted.

The Status of States Regarding Gold

Presently, 33 states in the U.S. legally allow gold investment purchase; the status of one additional state is apparently unclear. The form is usually gold mining shares under restricted circumstances. Many states have basket clauses under which the purchase of gold is permitted. In those cases, provision is made that, depending on the state, 5 to 15 percent of the fund can be used for "opportunities." Bullion might possibly be purchased under this clause. In a number of states, the authority to invest in gold is at the discretion of the funds manager or the investment board. These managers frequently guide themselves by the prudent man rule. This frequently is interpreted to proscribe investment in gold bullion or futures and, in some cases, even stock.

Commentary

Clearly, the interpretation of the prudent man rule, when applied to a large, ongoing fund (as against an individual trust), is under evolution. At the federal level and among private investment funds, the prudent man rule has been liberalized to include concern over capital preservation and to consider the role of the asset in the context of the overall portfolio. For the ongoing fund, the total rate of return, rather than yield, seems to be the guiding principle.

In an environment of long-term inflation, frequently, capital appreciation is a compensation for the eroding effects of inflation on principal. Conceivably, inflation rates may exceed by significant amounts the inflation assumptions upon which employer contributions are based. If the inflation assumptions used by the actuary, however reasonable at the time, prove to be low in actual practice, the employer may have to make additional contributions to the plan in future years so as to meet the plan's obligations. As a result, investments that keep pace with inflation, and therefore protect the overall base of the plan, could be considered prudent. In fact, in an inflationary environment, failure to undertake investments that keep pace with inflation could be actively considered to be imprudent.

State and local retirement funds and other type institutional investments do not fall under ERISA or Department of Labor interpretations. Nevertheless, the same rationale applies in the case of a state. Failure of the fund managers to invest the retirement funds in assets that keep pace with inflation risks either compounding taxpayer liabilities to fund the retirement benefits out of current taxes, or imposing a severe financial squeeze on the retirement beneficiaries.

By extension, this rationale can be applied to almost all institutional portfolios.

IV
Gold in Relation to Major Currencies

This part puts the analysis of Chapter 5 in an international perspective, comparing the relative performance of gold, stocks, bonds, and money markets across six major countries: the U.S., Canada, U.K., Germany, Switzerland, and Japan.

Chapter 6 confirms gold's superior returns compared to other financial assets over the 16 years ending 1983 across six countries. It also demonstrates that gold has an important diversification role in multicurrency portfolios, given substantial differences in gold's rates of return across the various countries. Of equal interest are the differential responses of gold to accelerating and decelerating inflation.

All of this reinforces the notion that perhaps the capital markets in six currencies are not fully efficient in the values assigned to gold. If there were reasonable efficiency, gold would not consistently outperform other instruments in six currencies over long periods.

6
Performance of Gold Vs. Stocks, Bonds, and Money Markets in Six Countries: 1968–83

This study updates an earlier analysis of gold versus stocks, bonds, and money markets in six countries. Interestingly, the new data extends and deepens the analysis, revealing new dimensions. Given the longer time frame of available data, we were able to both confirm our earlier period findings and develop new insights by subdividing the data into different periods. Overall, this study demonstrates that gold has unique properties as a multicurrency investment, and serves as an excellent diversifier both within and across currency lines.

The body of the work and extended analysis were undertaken by Dr. Peter I. Berman, former Second Vice President/Investments.

Once again, InterSec Research Corp. of Stamford, Connecticut undertook the statistical work. This is a registered investment advisor with substantial experience and considerable expertise in the field of international diversification, serving as consultants in the area. James P. Waterman, Vice President, was the specialist and consultant on this project. While InterSec's data banks and computer capabilities were used, the responsibilities for the project and its findings rest with the Gold-Economics Service of International Gold Corporation.

EUGENE J. SHERMAN
Vice President, Economist
March, 1984

Purpose

As a matter of long-term practice, investment managers abroad have been diversifying their portfolios in foreign currencies and investments, particularly within the United States. Increasingly, American investment managers have tended to follow this pattern of diversification—investing offshore. The rationale frequently applied is modern portfolio theory.

This study extends the analysis of Chapter 5 to six major countries, comparing the relative performance of gold, stocks, bonds, and money markets denominated in local currencies. Annual data for 16 years, 1968–83, is employed.

Of particular interest is the comparison of the relative performance of gold, stocks, bonds, and money markets across six countries under two quite dissimilar inflation environments of equal sample length: accelerating inflation (1977–80) and decelerating inflation (1980–83). Gold is sometimes thought, incorrectly, of interest only during accelerating inflation. But, as the comparisons of the two alternative inflation environments make clear, the differential responses of gold to accelerating and decelerating inflation are just as complex as for other financial instruments.

The insights on the relative performance of gold across six countries during periods when gold was both appreciating and depreciating in value should broaden our understanding of its role in modern portfolio management, especially for the growing numbers of international portfolio managers.

Summary

Our finding that returns on gold are generally uncorrelated to returns on stocks, bonds, and money markets denominated in local currencies across six countries continues to find support with the addition of two more years of data through 1983. Gold outperforms all other instruments in all countries except for stocks in Japan. Gold returned 12.9 percent; stocks returned 15.5 percent.

Examining the relative performance of gold and other financial assets across two contrasting periods of accelerating and decelerating inflation for six major countries amply illustrates the complexity of the differential financial market response to changing inflation environments. The adjustment of the gold price in local currency to inflation is as complex and variable as the adjustments by other financial assets. Simple rules of thumb do not apply to gold and inflation. Some specific findings, presented in detail in Tables 6–62 and 6–63, are as follows:

1. Gold appreciated strongly in both real and nominal terms during accelerating inflation and moderately lost purchasing power during decelerating inflation. Overall, for the combined period, 1977–83, gold appreciated 9.7 percent in real terms on average, 16.5 percent nominal. During accelerating inflation, gold appreciated on average

38 percent nominally, 31 percent real. During decelerating inflation, gold depreciated 5 percent nominally, 11 percent real.

2. The local gold price appreciated fairly uniformly across all six countries during accelerating inflation despite broadly varying inflation—3 percent in Switzerland to 13 percent in the U.K. No other asset showed this relatively uniform appreciation. Just the reverse occurred during decelerating inflation—substantial variability in gold depreciation despite broad uniformity in inflation across countries. In real terms, gold declined at 13 to 15 percent rates in the U.S., Canada, and Japan, but only 1 percent in Germany. In nominal terms, gold remained unchanged in Switzerland, rose about 3 percent in the U.K. and Germany, but declined 6 to 8 percent in Canada, the U.S., and Japan. This phenomenon is interesting in its own right and illustrates the complexity of the differential response of gold returns to changing inflation environments.

3. During accelerating inflation, gold outperformed stocks, bonds, and money markets in each country. On average, gold bested stocks by 26 percent, bonds by 34 percent, and money markets by 31 percent. Variability across countries was striking. Gold outperformed stocks, generally the highest-yielding alternative, by about 8:1 in both Germany and Switzerland, but by less than 2:1 in Canada and the U.K.

4. During decelerating inflation, stocks, bonds, and money markets bested gold in each country—roughly 25 percent for stocks and 15 percent for bonds and money markets. Again, it is the cross country variability that commands notice. Money markets bested gold by nearly 20 percent in the U.S. and Canada, but by only 5–6 percent in Germany and Switzerland. Stocks bested gold by

almost 35 percent in Canada, but by only 9 percent in Switzerland.

5. Interestingly, stocks outperformed bonds and money markets by roughly the same proportion, on average 2:1, during both accelerating and decelerating inflation. The proportions were fairly consistent during decelerating inflation, as inflation differentials across countries tended to converge. Variability was substantial during accelerating inflation—stocks outperforming bonds by 10:1 in Canada and the U.S., but holding about even with bonds and money markets in Germany and Switzerland.

6. Generally stocks, bonds, and money markets earned only small or negative real returns during accelerating inflation. Only gold earned consistently strong real returns. Money markets barely kept abreast; bonds fell three percentage points behind. Excluding moderately strong gains in Canada and the U.K., stocks gained only about 1.5 percent on average. The picture reversed dramatically during decelerating inflation with stocks, bonds, and money markets earning healthy inflation premiums—well above long established historical norms. For the entire period, only stocks earned a high real return—averaging over 7 percent.

7. Surprisingly, real returns of stocks, bonds, and money markets were poorest for the United States—the country with the broadest and best developed financial markets. The discrepancy was most pronounced during accelerating inflation where, with only the one exception of Switzerland, the real returns on stocks, bonds, and money markets were inferior to every other country. Interestingly, again with the exception of Switzerland, this tended to also occur during decelerating inflation. That real returns should be well below par in both the United States (a high inflation country) and

Switzerland (the low inflation country) during both accelerating and decelerating inflation periods, underscores the need for a multicurrency investment strategy.

8. Rates of return on alternative financial instruments were distinctly more variable during accelerating inflation—illustrating the complex financial market adjustments to an unusual environment. By contrast, during decelerating inflation, variability between instruments and countries was far less pronounced. Based on this experience, we can expect portfolio managers to pay greater attention to gold during a renewed period of accelerating inflation. The present historically high real returns on stocks, bonds, and money markets may diminish gold's potential appreciation in real terms should inflation reaccelerate. But the summary comparisons presented here suggest excellent chances for attractive and offsetting returns to gold in that environment within a multicurrency portfolio.

Implications for Gold Investment

Our study further strengthens an earlier finding that gold has an important diversification role in multicurrency portfolios. For the larger sample period, gold continued to be independent of, and uncorrelated with, prices of stocks, bonds, and money markets for each of the six countries. Extracting from the data we find that result held in each country independent of whether inflation was accelerating or decelerating.

Our study again confirms gold's superior returns compared to other financial assets over the past 16 years across six countries. During accelerating inflation, gold was markedly superior everywhere. While some loss of purchasing power occurred during decelerating inflation, for the combined 1977–83 period, gold generally outperformed all other financial assets. While it is uncertain whether these patterns will hold over subsequent inflation cycles, investors can benefit from being aware of the differentials described here and from close attention to unfolding patterns during the next round of accelerating inflation.

The study further points out that, to take maximum advantage of gold's superiority during accelerating inflation, a multicurrency approach is needed. We found substantial differences in both nominal and real rates of return between gold and other financial assets across the six countries. Returns can be maximized by selectively focusing on those countries that promise to yield the highest returns for the gold portion of the portfolio. The differentials outlined in our study can be helpful in this regard. Additional inflation cycles will be needed to more carefully predict which countries promise the best returns to gold in the future, and at what stage of the cycle gold is preferable to other financial assets in each currency.

Investors holding gold as a long-term inflation hedge can also benefit from awareness of gold's differential rates of return across the various countries. Even when gold lost purchasing power, it did so at markedly different rates across the six countries. For the long-term investor, careful attention to the patterns outlined in our study and to emerging new patterns of gold's relative performance will maximize returns of the gold portion of the portfolio.

Summary: Total Return and Correlation (R^2) of Each Asset Vs. Gold Across Six Countries

Table 6–1
Gold, Stocks, Bonds, Money Markets, C.P.I. (Percent per Annum, Compounded for Periods Ending December 31, 1983).

	United States				Japan				United Kingdom			
	Return		R^2		Return		R^2		Return		R^2	
	B/H	PA	B/H	PA	B/H	PA	B/H	PA	B/H	PA	B/H	PA
GOLD												
5 years	11.04	11.34			14.99	16.36			18.82	18.14		
10 years	13.01	18.39			10.88	15.39			18.47	21.06		
Total Period	16.06	21.89			12.90	17.85			19.78	24.52		
STOCKS												
5 years	17.31	16.62	16.26	22.07	14.49	14.66	0.10	5.45	22.67	22.86	1.88	7.60
10 years	10.62	12.27	2.51	8.53	11.94	12.64	0.20	2.96	18.32	23.22	0.31	4.62
Total Period	7.87	7.44	1.09	4.44	15.53	14.85	0.20	1.97	13.80	13.44	0.32	2.87
BONDS												
5 years	6.62	8.15	0.68	5.17	7.24	7.74	0.36	6.04	14.80	15.74	0.06	4.68
10 years	6.32	5.84	0.30	2.99	10.41	9.79	0.21	2.76	14.08	13.71	1.17	4.80
Total Period	5.84	5.54	0.12	2.54	7.89	8.92	0.05	2.38	11.59	12.48	1.27	4.49
MONEY MARKETS												
5 years	11.20	11.52	8.58	14.21	7.71	7.90	2.89	6.42	13.36	13.58	0.02	3.54
10 years	8.75	8.83	1.07	7.80	6.00	5.98	0.27	5.37	12.79	12.78	1.49	4.37
Total Period	8.60	8.59	1.65	7.23	5.82	5.81	0.54	4.62	12.81	12.85	0.70	4.11
CONSUM. PRICES	Rate of Increase				Rate of Increase				Rate of Increase			
5 years	8.44	8.50			4.62	4.70			10.95	11.01		
10 years	8.20	8.52			7.11	7.11			13.34	13.47		
Total Period	7.10	7.53			7.34	7.34			11.16	12.39		

B/H = Buy/Hold
PA = Period Average
Note: Total Period = For gold, stocks, and consumer prices, total period is 1968–1983.
For bonds and money markets, total period is 1973–1983.

Germany				Canada				Switzerland			
Return		R²		Return		R²		Return		R²	
B/H	PA	B/H	PA	B/H	PA	B/H	PA	B/H	PA	B/H	PA
20.38	19.90			11.99	12.29			17.80	17.75		
13.11	16.83			15.43	21.43			8.59	12.90		
13.32	16.74			17.04	23.26			11.24	14.09		
11.67	11.67	2.09	5.33	18.87	16.11	23.54	24.25	9.31	7.83	1.74	5.79
11.75	9.65	0.07	3.02	11.94	15.35	8.05	12.23	5.28	5.96	0.63	3.38
7.32	6.07	0.25	1.83	11.84	11.41	3.64	6.16	5.59	3.89	1.31	3.12
6.42	6.98	0.01	3.40	10.26	11.18	0.08	2.83	4.05	4.24	3.65	1.97
8.81	8.28	0.22	1.88	8.12	7.32	0.13	2.43	6.75	6.62	2.37	6.43
8.23	8.26	0.82	2.56	7.56	6.96	0.00	2.56	6.12	6.45	9.72	5.64
8.25	8.67	1.89	6.24	13.28	13.79	2.27	7.34	5.17	5.59	8.03	11.09
6.66	6.53	0.26	5.53	10.84	10.99	1.05	5.14	4.42	4.05	0.26	6.46
6.58	6.47	0.00	4.82	10.47	10.62	2.19	5.19	4.49	4.18	0.18	5.62
Rate of Increase				Rate of Increase				Rate of Increase			
4.87	5.02			9.11	9.57			4.74	4.96		
4.55	4.51			9.14	9.30			3.74	3.57		
4.58	4.83			7.52	8.03			4.53	4.73		

United States Summary

Table 6–2
Total Return and Correlation (R^2) of Each Asset Versus Gold—Gold, Stocks, Bonds, Money Markets, C.P.I. (Percent per Annum, Compounded for Periods Ending December 31, 1983).

	Return		R^2	
	B/H	PA	B/H	PA
GOLD				
5 years	11.04	11.34		
10 years	13.01	18.39		
Total Period	16.06	21.89		
STOCKS				
5 years	17.31	16.62	16.26	22.07
10 years	10.62	12.27	2.51	8.53
Total Period	7.87	7.44	1.09	4.44
BONDS				
5 years	6.62	8.15	0.68	5.17
10 years	6.32	5.84	0.30	2.99
Total Period	5.84	5.54	0.12	2.54
MONEY MARKETS				
5 years	11.20	11.52	8.58	14.21
10 years	8.75	8.83	1.07	7.80
Total Period	8.60	8.59	1.65	7.23

	Rate of Increase	
CONSUM. PRICES		
5 years	8.44	8.50
10 years	8.20	8.52
Total Period	7.10	7.53

B/H = Buy/Hold
PA = Period Average
Note: Total Period = For gold, stocks, and consumer prices, total period is 1968–1983.
For bonds and money markets, total period is 1973–1983.

Table 6-3
Gold Price: U.S. Dollars per Ounce.*

	Jan.	Feb.	March	April	May	June	July	Aug.	Sept.	Oct.	Nov.	Dec.
1959	35.000	35.000	35.000	35.000	35.000	35.000	35.000	35.000	35.000	35.000	35.000	35.000
1960	35.000	35.000	35.000	35.000	35.000	35.000	35.000	35.000	35.000	35.000	35.000	35.000
1961	35.000	35.000	35.000	35.000	35.000	35.000	35.000	35.000	35.000	35.000	35.000	35.000
1962	35.160	35.125	35.087	35.075	35.080	35.100	35.122	35.122	35.130	35.140	35.092	35.075
1963	35.060	35.080	35.101	35.096	35.076	35.076	35.075	35.097	35.081	35.079	35.081	35.079
1964	35.079	35.077	35.079	35.079	35.077	35.099	35.075	35.077	35.089	35.110	35.101	35.126
1965	35.126	35.141	35.156	35.141	35.104	35.099	35.122	35.149	35.136	35.112	35.114	35.131
1966	35.145	35.165	35.149	35.130	35.124	35.154	35.176	35.182	35.185	35.157	35.161	35.177
1967	35.184	35.171	35.157	35.174	35.180	35.186	35.187	35.187	35.187	35.192	35.197	35.194
1968	35.196	35.199	35.199	39.100	41.950	40.900	38.850	39.800	39.600	39.000	39.850	41.900
1969	42.440	42.700	42.900	43.600	43.075	41.200	41.390	40.950	40.675	39.750	35.600	35.200
1970	34.990	35.020	35.300	35.850	35.450	35.490	35.300	35.800	36.400	37.250	37.540	37.375
1971	38.050	38.800	38.875	39.700	40.840	40.100	42.400	40.650	42.600	42.340	43.600	43.625
1972	47.150	48.200	48.380	49.600	59.450	64.650	68.300	66.875	64.200	64.390	63.600	64.900
1973	66.000	85.000	90.000	90.725	114.750	123.250	115.600	103.500	100.000	98.000	101.000	112.250
1974	132.500	162.500	173.000	169.250	156.750	144.250	156.000	156.000	151.250	167.000	184.000	186.500
1975	175.800	181.750	177.250	167.000	167.000	166.250	166.700	159.800	141.250	142.900	138.150	140.250
1976	128.150	132.300	129.600	128.400	125.500	123.800	112.500	104.000	116.000	123.150	130.250	134.500
1977	132.300	142.750	148.900	147.250	142.950	143.000	144.100	146.000	154.050	161.500	160.050	164.950
1978	175.750	182.250	181.600	170.850	184.150	183.050	200.250	208.700	217.100	242.600	193.400	226.000
1979	233.700	251.300	240.100	245.300	274.600	277.500	296.450	315.100	397.250	382.090	415.650	524.000
1980	653.000	637.000	494.500	518.000	535.500	653.500	614.250	631.250	666.750	629.000	619.500	589.500
1981	506.500	489.000	513.750	482.750	479.250	426.000	406.000	425.000	428.750	427.000	414.500	400.000
1982	387.000	362.000	320.000	361.250	325.250	317.500	342.900	411.500	397.000	423.250	436.000	456.900
1983	499.750	408.500	414.750	429.250	437.500	416.000	422.000	414.250	405.000	382.000	405.000	381.500

*London afternoon fixings, last day of month.

Table 6-4
U.S. Dollar Gold Performance (Cumulative Rate of Return, Percent Per Year).

	1968	1969	1970	1971	1972	1973	1974	1975	1976	1977	1978	1979	1980	1981	1982	1983
1968	19.06															
1969	0.02	-15.98														
1970	2.03	-5.54	6.18													
1971	5.53	1.36	11.33	16.73												
1972	13.03	11.57	22.63	31.78	48.77											
1973	21.33	21.79	33.63	44.28	60.40	72.95										
1974	26.91	28.26	39.58	49.46	62.30	69.52	66.15									
1975	18.87	18.84	25.91	30.28	33.90	29.28	11.78	-24.80								
1976	16.07	15.70	21.11	23.79	25.25	19.98	6.21	-15.08	-4.11							
1977	16.71	16.45	21.29	23.62	24.81	20.50	10.09	-4.02	8.44	22.63						
1978	18.42	18.36	22.95	25.22	26.48	23.11	15.02	4.91	17.23	29.62	37.01					
1979	25.24	25.82	31.00	34.09	36.44	34.76	29.27	22.94	39.02	57.35	78.24	131.87				
1980	24.21	24.65	29.20	31.76	33.55	31.76	26.73	21.14	33.26	44.69	52.89	61.51	12.51			
1981	18.96	18.95	22.45	24.05	24.80	22.39	17.21	11.51	19.08	24.35	24.79	20.96	-12.63	-32.15		
1982	18.64	18.61	21.80	23.20	23.80	21.55	16.88	11.85	18.38	22.60	22.60	19.24	-4.47	-11.97	14.22	
1983	16.06	15.87	18.56	19.56	19.80	17.47	13.01	8.27	13.32	16.06	15.00	11.04	-7.63	-13.50	-2.34	-16.50

Table 6-5
U.S. Dollar Stock Performance (Cumulative Rate of Return, Percent Per Year).

	1968	1969	1970	1971	1972	1973	1974	1975	1976	1977	1978	1979	1980	1981	1982	1983
1968	10.98															
1969	0.83	-8.40														
1970	1.87	-2.40	4.00													
1971	4.84	2.87	9.02	14.29												
1972	7.52	6.67	12.23	16.59	18.94											
1973	3.44	1.99	4.77	5.03	0.68	-14.77										
1974	-1.47	-3.40	-2.37	-3.90	-9.30	-20.79	-26.39									
1975	2.69	1.56	3.32	3.18	0.58	-4.89	0.48	37.15								
1976	4.83	4.09	6.01	6.35	4.83	1.57	7.68	30.24	23.68							
1977	3.56	2.77	4.25	4.29	2.71	-0.26	3.74	16.31	7.11	-7.24						
1978	3.84	3.15	4.52	4.58	3.27	0.86	4.32	13.82	6.96	-0.53	6.66					
1979	4.99	4.46	5.85	6.05	5.07	3.22	6.57	14.75	9.75	5.47	12.46	18.57				
1980	6.88	6.55	8.02	8.43	7.80	6.48	9.92	17.52	13.95	11.64	18.75	25.30	32.40			
1981	6.00	5.62	6.88	7.15	6.46	5.16	7.96	14.03	10.57	8.12	12.35	14.31	12.24	-4.85		
1982	6.97	6.69	7.95	8.28	7.75	6.69	9.39	14.94	12.08	10.25	14.13	16.07	15.25	7.53	21.53	
1983	7.87	7.67	8.92	9.31	8.90	8.03	10.62	15.75	13.32	11.91	15.47	17.31	17.00	12.28	21.96	22.41

Table 6-6
U.S. Stocks: Proportion of Return Explained by Gold (R^2).

	1968	1969	1970	1971	1972	1973	1974	1975	1976	1977	1978	1979	1980	1981	1982	1983
1968	20.05															
1969	16.40	6.09														
1970	7.76	2.96	0.16													
1971	2.66	0.18	3.31	16.49												
1972	1.37	0.15	0.75	3.83	3.08											
1973	0.10	0.73	2.42	4.69	3.61	2.76										
1974	0.16	0.02	0.02	0.00	0.33	1.24	10.60									
1975	0.00	0.09	0.35	0.46	0.19	0.20	0.18	1.15								
1976	0.10	0.36	0.81	1.04	0.76	0.86	0.07	1.15	6.69							
1977	0.13	0.40	0.83	1.04	0.76	0.89	0.17	3.90	7.74	2.27						
1978	0.50	0.92	1.49	1.81	1.54	1.71	1.05	6.25	8.69	7.27	10.52					
1979	0.24	0.48	0.87	1.06	0.84	0.85	0.39	2.80	2.77	1.13	2.54	0.12				
1980	0.08	0.02	0.00	0.00	0.00	0.01	0.31	0.06	0.31	1.44	1.31	8.25	29.67			
1981	0.20	0.10	0.03	0.03	0.08	0.10	0.64	0.45	0.97	2.48	2.93	10.93	23.93	3.18		
1982	1.17	0.96	0.76	0.83	1.09	1.20	2.71	3.12	4.61	7.43	8.43	18.92	33.89	37.74	56.73	
1983	1.09	0.90	0.72	0.78	1.01	1.10	2.51	2.99	4.20	6.47	7.49	16.26	28.00	26.30	33.44	3.72

Table 6–7
U.S. Dollar Bond Performance (Cumulative Rate of Return, Percent Per Year).

	1973	1974	1975	1976	1977	1978	1979	1980	1981	1982	1983
1973	1.13										
1974	-0.98	-3.05									
1975	3.98	5.43	14.66								
1976	7.47	9.66	16.63	18.65							
1977	6.29	7.62	11.43	9.85	1.70						
1978	5.20	6.03	8.43	6.44	0.81	-0.07					
1979	3.80	4.26	5.78	3.67	-0.88	-2.15	-4.19				
1980	2.98	3.24	4.33	2.38	-1.33	-2.32	-3.42	-2.64			
1981	2.53	2.71	3.56	1.81	-1.25	-1.98	-2.61	-1.81	-0.96		
1982	6.06	6.62	7.89	6.96	5.13	5.83	7.36	11.51	19.33	43.79	
1983	5.84	6.32	7.42	6.55	4.92	5.47	6.62	9.50	13.88	22.12	3.71

Table 6–8
U.S. Bonds: Proportion of Return Explained by Gold (R^2).

	1973	1974	1975	1976	1977	1978	1979	1980	1981	1982	1983
1973	1.86										
1974	0.53	5.93									
1975	0.07	1.71	13.19								
1976	0.00	1.09	4.71	0.74							
1977	0.00	0.69	0.58	0.52	1.07						
1978	0.29	0.03	1.40	7.62	12.75	24.64					
1979	0.26	0.09	1.20	2.30	1.12	0.87	0.61				
1980	0.04	0.00	0.17	0.22	0.05	0.02	0.14	0.12			
1981	0.01	0.07	0.00	0.00	0.02	0.03	0.29	0.52	3.59		
1982	0.32	0.64	0.53	0.48	0.61	0.66	1.48	3.77	14.61	29.03	
1983	0.12	0.30	0.20	0.16	0.20	0.23	0.68	1.81	5.37	5.75	9.78

Table 6–9
U.S. Dollar Money Market Performance (Cumulative Rate of Return, Percent Per Year).

	1973	1974	1975	1976	1977	1978	1979	1980	1981	1982	1983
1973	7.21										
1974	7.60	7.99									
1975	7.00	6.90	5.82								
1976	6.51	6.28	5.43	5.04							
1977	6.28	6.05	5.41	5.21	5.38						
1978	6.49	6.34	5.94	5.98	6.45	7.53					
1979	7.02	6.99	6.79	7.03	7.70	8.89	10.26				
1980	7.62	7.68	7.63	8.00	8.75	9.90	11.10	11.95			
1981	8.36	8.50	8.57	9.04	9.86	11.01	12.19	13.17	14.41		
1982	8.58	8.73	8.83	9.27	9.99	10.93	11.80	12.32	12.50	10.62	
1983	8.60	8.75	8.83	9.21	9.82	10.58	11.20	11.44	11.27	9.73	8.84

Table 6–10
U.S. Money Markets: Proportion of Return Explained by Gold (R^2).

	1973	1974	1975	1976	1977	1978	1979	1980	1981	1982	1983
1973	24.75										
1974	9.29	0.94									
1975	0.13	7.48	34.29								
1976	0.98	4.83	16.92	6.44							
1977	0.98	3.57	6.03	0.14	4.27						
1978	1.03	3.38	1.23	2.24	1.27	0.09					
1979	6.32	12.14	15.46	14.43	12.22	9.29	12.17				
1980	0.19	0.78	0.96	0.22	0.14	2.55	11.87	24.93			
1981	1.04	0.56	0.49	1.67	4.54	9.54	19.33	21.87	1.14		
1982	1.74	1.17	1.07.	2.68	6.02	11.12	18.37	22.36	21.61	24.29	
1983	1.65	1.07	0.95	2.22	4.47	6.87	8.58	10.82	8.27	6.03	1.53

Table 6-11
U.S. Dollar Consumer Price Index (Cumulative Rate of Increase, Percent Per Year).

	1968	1969	1970	1971	1972	1973	1974	1975	1976	1977	1978	1979	1980	1981	1982	1983
1968	4.72															
1969	5.41	6.10														
1970	5.43	5.79	5.48													
1971	4.91	4.97	4.42	3.36												
1972	4.61	4.58	4.08	3.39	3.42											
1973	5.29	5.41	5.24	5.15	6.06	8.78										
1974	6.25	6.51	6.59	6.87	8.07	10.47	12.20									
1975	6.35	6.58	6.66	6.90	7.81	9.31	9.58	7.01								
1976	6.18	6.36	6.40	6.55	7.20	8.17	7.97	5.91	4.82							
1977	6.24	6.41	6.44	6.58	7.13	7.89	7.67	6.20	5.79	6.77						
1978	6.50	6.68	6.74	6.90	7.41	8.09	7.96	6.92	6.89	7.94	9.13					
1979	7.04	7.26	7.37	7.58	8.12	8.81	8.82	8.16	8.44	9.68	11.16	13.23				
1980	7.45	7.68	7.83	8.06	8.60	9.27	9.34	8.86	9.24	10.37	11.60	12.86	12.48			
1981	7.55	7.77	7.91	8.13	8.62	9.21	9.27	8.86	9.17	10.06	10.90	11.49	10.63	8.81		
1982	7.32	7.51	7.62	7.80	8.21	8.70	8.69	8.26	8.44	9.06	9.52	9.62	8.45	6.48	4.20	
1983	7.10	7.26	7.35	7.49	7.84	8.25	8.20	7.76	7.86	8.30	8.56	8.44	7.28	5.60	4.03	3.85

Canada Summary

Table 6–12
Total Return and Correlation (R^2) of Each Asset Vs. Gold—Gold, Stocks, Bonds, Money Markets, C.P.I. (Percent per Annum, Compounded for Periods Ending December 31, 1983).

	Return		R^2	
	B/H	PA	B/H	PA
GOLD				
5 years	11.99	12.29		
10 years	15.43	21.43		
Total Period	17.04	23.26		
STOCKS				
5 years	18.87	16.11	23.54	24.25
10 years	11.94	15.35	8.05	12.23
Total Period	11.84	11.41	3.64	6.16
BONDS				
5 years	10.26	11.18	0.08	2.83
10 years	8.12	7.32	0.13	2.43
Total Period	7.56	6.96	0.00	2.56
MONEY MARKETS				
5 years	13.28	13.79	2.27	7.34
10 years	10.84	10.99	1.05	5.14
Total Period	10.47	10.62	2.19	5.19
CONSUM. PRICES	Rate of Increase			
5 years	9.11	9.57		
10 years	9.14	9.30		
Total Period	7.52	8.03		

B/H = Buy/Hold
PA = Period Average
Note: Total Period = For gold, stocks, and consumer prices, total period is 1968–1983.
For bonds and money markets, total period is 1973–1983.

Table 6-13
Gold Price: Canadian Dollars Per Ounce.*

	Jan.	Feb.	March	April	May	June	July	Aug.	Sept.	Oct.	Nov.	Dec.
1960	37.835	37.835	37.835	37.835	37.835	37.835	37.835	37.835	37.835	37.835	37.835	37.835
1961	37.835	37.835	37.835	37.835	37.835	37.835	37.835	37.835	37.835	37.835	37.835	37.835
1962	38.008	37.970	37.929	37.916	37.921	37.943	37.967	37.967	37.976	37.986	37.934	37.916
1963	37.900	37.921	37.944	37.939	37.917	37.920	37.927	37.940	37.923	37.920	37.923	37.920
1964	37.920	37.918	37.920	37.920	37.918	37.917	37.916	37.918	37.931	37.954	37.944	37.971
1965	37.971	37.987	38.004	37.987	37.947	37.942	37.967	37.996	37.982	37.956	37.958	37.977
1966	37.992	38.013	37.996	37.976	37.969	38.001	38.025	38.032	38.035	38.005	38.009	38.026
1967	38.034	38.020	38.005	38.023	38.030	38.036	38.037	38.037	38.037	38.043	38.048	38.045
1968	38.047	38.050	38.050	42.267	45.348	44.213	41.997	43.024	42.808	42.159	43.078	45.294
1969	45.878	46.159	46.375	47.132	45.564	44.537	44.743	44.267	43.970	42.970	38.484	38.051
1970	37.824	37.857	38.159	38.754	38.321	36.644	36.197	36.444	37.052	37.999	38.219	37.764
1971	38.389	39.118	39.179	40.014	41.232	41.019	43.223	41.158	42.992	42.400	43.722	43.621
1972	47.334	48.330	48.177	49.223	58.309	62.834	67.140	65.786	63.154	63.193	63.144	64.556
1973	65.980	84.465	89.955	91.007	114.499	123.054	115.705	104.060	100.490	97.599	100.930	112.240
1974	130.978	158.520	168.279	162.989	150.733	139.995	152.709	153.943	149.081	164.395	181.628	184.626
1975	175.433	181.243	177.676	170.040	171.091	171.112	171.867	165.058	144.710	146.026	139.532	142.498
1976	128.139	130.330	127.514	125.936	122.979	119.815	109.587	102.129	112.776	119.567	134.127	135.846
1977	135.193	149.615	157.193	154.213	150.212	151.807	153.774	157.052	165.340	179.020	177.135	180.514
1978	194.500	203.187	205.550	193.366	206.226	205.362	226.460	240.272	255.218	282.844	226.873	267.783
1979	278.892	300.021	278.486	280.004	318.723	323.807	345.890	367.917	460.956	452.124	486.049	614.742
1980	757.789	729.540	590.863	614.749	621.111	751.052	716.871	729.959	781.277	732.329	734.956	699.601
1981	605.757	587.124	609.035	577.880	575.777	511.173	500.324	510.608	516.012	514.119	487.424	475.131
1982	462.575	444.382	393.934	440.163	404.129	410.444	431.290	510.702	490.451	519.222	541.238	563.129
1983	617.239	501.684	511.558	525.682	538.773	510.637	520.125	511.212	498.938	470.832	501.337	471.507

*London afternoon fixings, last day of month, converted to Canadian dollars at the prevailing exchange rate of that day.

Table 6-14
Canadian Dollar Gold Performance (Cumulative Rate of Return, Percent Per Year).

	1968	1969	1970	1971	1972	1973	1974	1975	1976	1977	1978	1979	1980	1981	1982	1983
1968	19.06															
1969	0.02	-15.98														
1970	-0.24	-8.68	-0.75													
1971	3.48	-1.24	7.06	15.50												
1972	11.15	9.26	19.26	30.73	47.97											
1973	19.76	19.90	31.05	43.77	60.40	73.88										
1974	25.32	26.39	37.14	48.69	61.76	69.12	64.50									
1975	17.95	17.79	24.61	30.41	34.44	30.21	12.67	-22.82								
1976	15.19	14.71	19.93	23.78	25.50	20.44	6.56	-14.23	-4.68							
1977	16.85	16.60	21.48	25.04	26.70	22.83	12.61	-0.75	12.55	32.89						
1978	19.41	19.44	24.20	27.74	29.59	26.75	18.99	9.73	23.40	40.39	48.33					
1979	26.10	26.75	32.07	36.34	39.19	37.98	32.76	27.19	44.12	65.41	84.54	129.60				
1980	25.10	25.62	30.30	33.89	36.11	34.70	29.87	24.86	37.47	50.64	57.07	61.64	13.79			
1981	19.76	19.82	23.41	25.88	26.97	24.83	19.76	14.46	22.23	28.46	27.37	21.07	-12.09	-32.08		
1982	19.68	19.72	23.03	25.25	26.18	24.18	19.63	14.96	21.69	26.74	25.55	20.43	-2.88	-10.28	18.52	
1983	17.04	16.90	19.69	21.43	21.94	19.81	15.43	10.98	16.14	19.46	17.36	11.99	-6.41	-12.32	-0.37	-16.26

Table 6-15
Canadian Stock Performance (Cumulative Rate of Return, Percent Per Year).

	1968	1969	1970	1971	1972	1973	1974	1975	1976	1977	1978	1979	1980	1981	1982	1983
1968	19.15															
1969	10.93	3.28														
1970	10.03	5.74	8.26													
1971	10.75	8.09	10.58	12.94												
1972	14.78	13.72	17.43	22.30	32.43											
1973	11.68	10.25	12.06	13.36	13.57	-2.60										
1974	5.05	2.87	2.79	1.47	-2.09	-15.82	-27.24									
1975	6.61	4.94	5.21	4.62	2.63	-5.73	-7.25	18.23								
1976	6.90	5.46	5.77	5.36	3.91	-2.21	-2.07	13.61	9.17							
1977	6.83	5.54	5.83	5.48	4.29	-0.57	-0.06	11.09	7.69	6.23						
1978	8.79	7.81	8.32	8.33	7.69	40.40	5.42	15.66	14.81	17.74	30.51					
1979	11.77	11.12	11.94	12.36	12.29	9.67	11.86	21.91	22.85	27.77	40.14	50.47				
1980	12.67	12.14	12.99	13.47	13.53	11.37	13.52	22.25	23.08	26.82	34.54	36.60	24.00			
1981	10.82	10.20	10.80	11.04	10.85	8.68	10.18	16.91	16.69	18.25	21.47	18.59	5.28	-10.61		
1982	10.52	9.93	10.46	10.64	10.44	8.45	9.75	15.54	15.16	16.19	18.29	15.42	5.66	-2.47	6.41	
1983	11.84	11.37	11.98	12.27	12.21	10.53	11.94	17.43	17.33	18.55	20.73	18.87	12.06	8.35	19.28	33.70

Table 6-16
Canadian Stocks: Proportion of Return Explained by Gold (R^2).

	1968	1969	1970	1971	1972	1973	1974	1975	1976	1977	1978	1979	1980	1981	1982	1983
1968	8.63															
1969	5.61	0.87														
1970	2.39	0.18	0.22													
1971	0.59	0.10	2.12	7.99												
1972	1.74	0.85	0.29	0.31	4.18											
1973	0.99	2.12	3.99	7.28	9.39	21.45										
1974	0.12	0.03	0.01	0.08	0.57	0.90	34.53									
1975	0.01	0.01	0.03	0.02	0.01	0.06	3.40	0.18								
1976	0.21	0.44	0.62	0.69	0.53	1.30	0.00	8.24	21.94							
1977	0.21	0.43	0.60	0.66	0.50	1.17	0.00	6.32	12.22	0.17						
1978	0.32	0.54	0.75	0.86	0.73	1.28	0.05	3.99	6.46	2.62	6.05					
1979	0.05	0.01	0.00	0.00	0.01	0.00	0.89	0.00	0.00	1.04	0.53	7.41				
1980	1.97	1.85	1.79	1.97	2.31	2.22	6.08	5.01	6.57	13.02	14.41	29.49	48.19			
1981	1.92	1.80	1.77	1.96	2.28	2.14	5.44	4.68	6.06	11.23	12.70	22.28	26.11	1.88		
1982	3.61	3.52	3.56	3.88	4.33	4.24	8.37	8.06	9.94	15.59	17.15	26.24	30.86	17.52	44.49	
1983	3.64	3.54	3.56	3.86	4.27	4.16	8.05	7.97	9.57	14.48	15.98	23.54	26.87	15.14	27.49	16.23

Table 6–17
Canadian Bond Performance (Cumulative Rate of Return, Percent Per Year).

	1973	1974	1975	1976	1977	1978	1979	1980	1981	1982	1983
1973	2.15										
1974	4.72	7.35									
1975	3.95	4.86	2.43								
1976	6.44	7.91	8.20	14.28							
1977	6.26	7.32	7.31	9.83	5.56						
1978	5.37	6.02	5.70	6.81	3.26	1.01					
1979	4.71	5.15	4.71	5.29	2.45	0.94	0.87				
1980	4.43	4.76	4.34	4.72	2.46	1.45	1.67	2.48			
1981	4.33	4.60	4.21	4.51	2.66	1.95	2.27	2.97	3.47		
1982	7.25	7.84	7.90	8.70	7.80	8.25	10.14	13.42	19.32	37.60	
1983	7.56	8.12	8.21	8.95	8.21	8.66	10.26	12.74	16.38	23.43	10.71

Table 6–18
Canadian Bonds: Proportion of Return Explained by Gold (R^2).

	1973	1974	1975	1976	1977	1978	1979	1980	1981	1982	1983
1973	32.60										
1974	0.08	12.59									
1975	1.04	13.73	19.32								
1976	0.57	8.75	8.11	1.63							
1977	0.47	7.14	4.08	0.01	2.42						
1978	0.38	4.26	1.27	0.07	0.11	1.20					
1979	0.01	1.03	0.00	1.43	0.76	0.28	1.84				
1980	0.04	0.66	0.03	0.09	0.01	0.00	0.02	0.21			
1981	0.04	0.06	0.12	0.47	0.45	0.44	0.68	0.46	10.06		
1982	0.03	0.37	0.06	0.00	0.00	0.00	0.00	0.59	2.05	9.51	
1983	0.00	0.13	0.00	0.09	0.11	0.09	0.08	0.12	0.35	2.81	13.66

Table 6–19
Canadian Money Market Performance (Cumulative Rate of Return, Percent Per Year).

	1973	1974	1975	1976	1977	1978	1979	1980	1981	1982	1983
1973	6.87										
1974	8.15	9.45									
1975	7.96	8.50	7.57								
1976	8.25	8.72	8.36	9.15							
1977	8.09	8.39	8.05	8.28	7.42						
1978	8.19	8.45	8.21	8.42	8.05	8.69					
1979	8.72	9.03	8.94	9.29	9.34	10.31	11.95				
1980	9.25	9.59	9.62	10.03	10.26	11.22	12.50	13.06			
1981	10.19	10.61	10.78	11.32	11.76	12.88	14.31	15.51	18.00		
1982	10.58	11.01	11.20	11.73	12.17	13.14	14.28	15.07	16.09	14.21	
1983	10.47	10.84	11.00	11.43	11.76	12.50	13.28	13.62	13.81	11.76	9.37

Table 6–20
Canadian Money Markets: Proportion of Return Explained by Gold (R^2).

	1973	1974	1975	1976	1977	1978	1979	1980	1981	1982	1983
1973	16.54										
1974	11.52	61.68									
1975	5.53	0.25	5.91								
1976	7.13	0.08	0.11	9.19							
1977	6.44	0.51	2.32	8.18	3.14						
1978	4.31	0.35	0.30	2.21	0.01	0.76					
1979	0.32	4.35	8.22	5.40	7.48	4.49	6.07				
1980	0.06	0.41	1.21	0.13	0.01	0.38	2.54	6.45			
1981	2.86	1.58	1.00	3.10	4.93	7.66	11.94	7.62	6.78		
1982	2.89	1.67	1.06	3.19	5.07	7.62	11.05	8.55	9.25	7.19	
1983	2.19	1.05	0.57	1.76	2.56	2.93	2.27	1.61	0.95	0.64	27.23

Table 6-21
Canadian Consumer Price Index (Cumulative Rate of Increase, Percent Per Year).

	1968	1969	1970	1971	1972	1973	1974	1975	1976	1977	1978	1979	1980	1981	1982	1983
1968	4.11															
1969	4.31	4.50														
1970	3.39	3.03	1.59													
1971	3.79	3.68	3.27	4.97												
1972	4.03	4.01	3.85	5.00	5.03											
1973	4.87	5.03	5.16	6.37	7.08	9.17										
1974	5.94	6.24	6.60	7.89	8.88	10.85	12.55									
1975	6.37	6.70	7.07	8.20	9.03	10.39	11.01	9.48								
1976	6.32	6.60	6.90	7.81	8.39	9.24	9.26	7.65	5.86							
1977	6.63	6.91	7.21	8.04	8.56	9.28	9.31	8.25	7.64	9.44						
1978	6.80	7.08	7.37	8.11	8.57	9.17	9.17	8.33	7.96	9.02	8.60					
1979	7.03	7.30	7.59	8.28	8.70	9.23	9.24	8.59	8.37	9.21	9.10	9.61				
1980	7.35	7.62	7.91	8.57	8.97	9.48	9.52	9.02	8.93	9.71	9.80	10.41	11.23			
1981	7.68	7.96	8.25	8.88	9.28	9.76	9.84	9.45	9.45	10.18	10.37	10.96	11.64	12.06		
1982	7.79	8.05	8.33	8.91	9.28	9.71	9.77	9.43	9.42	10.03	10.15	10.54	10.85	10.66	9.27	
1983	7.52	7.75	7.99	8.49	8.79	9.14	9.14	8.77	8.68	9.08	9.03	9.11	8.99	8.25	6.39	3.59

United Kingdom Summary

Table 6–22
Total Return and Correlation (R^2) of Each Asset Vs. Gold—Gold, Stocks, Bonds, Money Markets, C.P.I. (Percent per Annum, Compounded for Periods Ending December 31, 1983).

	Return		R^2	
	B/H	PA	B/H	PA
GOLD				
5 years	18.82	18.14		
10 years	18.47	21.06		
Total Period	19.78	24.52		
STOCKS				
5 years	22.67	22.86	1.88	7.60
10 years	18.32	23.22	0.31	4.62
Total Period	13.80	13.44	0.32	2.87
BONDS				
5 years	14.80	15.74	0.06	4.68
10 years	14.08	13.71	1.17	4.80
Total Period	11.59	12.48	1.27	4.49
MONEY MARKETS				
5 years	13.36	13.58	0.02	3.54
10 years	12.79	12.78	1.49	4.37
Total Period	12.81	12.85	0.70	4.11

	Rate of Increase	
CONSUM. PRICES		
5 years	10.95	11.01
10 years	13.34	13.47
Total Period	11.16	12.39

B/H = Buy/Hold
PA = Period Average
Note: Total Period = For gold, stocks, and consumer prices, total period is 1968–1983.
For bonds and money markets, total period is 1973–1983.

Table 6-23
Gold Price: British Pounds Per Ounce.*

	Jan.	Feb.	March	April	May	June	July	Aug.	Sept.	Oct.	Nov.	Dec.
1959	12.509	12.509	12.509	12.509	12.509	12.509	12.509	12.509	12.509	12.509	12.509	12.509
1960	12.509	12.509	12.509	12.509	12.509	12.509	12.509	12.509	12.509	12.509	12.509	12.509
1961	12.509	12.509	12.509	12.509	12.509	12.509	12.509	12.509	12.509	12.509	12.509	12.509
1962	12.566	12.554	12.540	12.536	12.538	12.545	12.553	12.553	12.556	12.559	12.542	12.536
1963	12.531	12.538	12.545	12.544	12.537	12.538	12.540	12.544	12.538	12.538	12.538	12.538
1964	12.538	12.537	12.538	12.538	12.537	12.537	12.536	12.537	12.541	12.549	12.545	12.554
1965	12.554	12.560	12.565	12.560	12.547	12.545	12.553	12.563	12.558	12.549	12.550	12.556
1966	12.561	12.568	12.563	12.556	12.554	12.564	12.572	12.574	12.575	12.565	12.567	12.573
1967	12.575	12.571	12.566	12.572	12.574	12.576	12.576	12.576	12.576	12.578	14.677	14.676
1968	14.677	14.678	14.678	16.305	17.493	17.055	16.200	16.597	16.513	16.263	16.617	17.472
1969	17.697	17.806	17.889	18.181	17.962	17.180	17.260	17.076	16.961	16.576	14.845	14.678
1970	14.591	14.603	14.720	14.949	14.783	14.799	14.720	14.929	15.179	15.533	15.654	15.585
1971	15.867	16.180	16.211	16.555	17.030	16.722	17.681	16.516	17.163	16.991	17.496	17.109
1972	18.185	18.508	18.509	19.015	22.732	26.364	27.900	27.338	26.527	27.637	27.062	27.687
1973	27.760	34.279	36.359	36.498	44.807	47.818	46.366	42.182	41.470	40.307	43.067	48.359
1974	58.580	70.544	72.176	69.714	65.521	60.643	65.708	67.377	64.878	71.617	79.258	79.461
1975	73.981	74.972	73.647	71.009	72.291	76.160	77.617	75.736	69.197	68.983	68.542	69.360
1976	63.158	65.283	67.690	69.719	71.358	69.494	63.106	58.649	69.719	77.024	78.984	79.069
1977	77.253	83.554	86.631	85.702	83.271	83.185	82.975	83.836	88.288	88.242	88.192	86.728
1978	90.119	94.273	97.952	93.437	100.987	98.368	103.664	107.663	110.142	115.633	99.266	111.136
1979	117.121	124.282	116.172	119.302	133.056	128.103	129.997	140.037	180.680	183.988	189.464	235.079
1980	288.115	279.589	228.029	228.602	229.840	276.759	262.104	264.115	279.169	258.201	262.485	246.823
1981	212.275	221.236	228.783	226.910	231.606	219.036	218.261	230.346	237.356	232.198	211.506	210.632
1982	205.505	198.848	179.652	200.782	181.718	182.341	197.096	239.975	234.525	252.719	270.167	283.118
1983	327.833	269.288	279.873	275.180	272.958	271.398	277.299	277.875	271.116	255.972	276.188	263.304

*London afternoon fixings, last day of month, converted to pounds
at the prevailing exchange rate on that day.

Table 6-24
British Pound Gold Performance (Cumulative Rate of Return, Percent Per Year).

	1968	1969	1970	1971	1972	1973	1974	1975	1976	1977	1978	1979	1980	1981	1982	1983
1968	19.06															
1969	0.02	-15.98														
1970	2.03	-5.54	6.18													
1971	3.92	-0.69	7.97	9.78												
1972	13.55	12.21	23.57	33.30	61.86											
1973	22.00	22.60	34.74	45.87	68.15	74.68										
1974	27.30	28.73	40.20	50.28	60.87	69.43	64.34									
1975	21.44	21.78	29.55	34.81	41.91	35.82	19.77	-12.71								
1976	20.59	20.78	27.21	31.10	35.83	30.01	17.81	-0.25	14.00							
1977	19.45	19.49	24.87	27.80	31.08	25.66	15.73	2.96	11.83	9.69						
1978	20.22	20.33	25.23	27.84	30.66	26.07	18.11	8.75	17.02	18.56	28.15					
1979	26.01	26.66	31.97	35.20	38.76	35.75	30.16	24.23	35.69	43.80	64.64	111.52				
1980	24.26	24.70	29.26	31.82	34.53	31.46	26.22	20.79	28.90	32.92	41.71	49.02	4.99			
1981	20.97	21.11	24.86	26.71	28.54	25.29	20.20	14.94	20.34	21.64	24.84	23.75	-5.35	-14.66		
1982	21.82	22.02	25.57	27.34	29.07	26.18	21.70	17.21	22.26	23.69	26.70	26.33	6.39	7.10	34.42	
1983	19.78	19.83	22.91	24.30	25.59	22.72	18.47	14.24	18.14	18.75	20.33	18.82	2.87	2.17	11.80	-7.01

Table 6-25
United Kingdom Stock Performance (Cumulative Rate of Return, Percent Per Year).

	1968	1969	1970	1971	1972	1973	1974	1975	1976	1977	1978	1979	1980	1981	1982	1983
1968	51.42															
1969	15.07	-12.54														
1970	7.68	-9.19	-5.72													
1971	14.82	4.70	14.56	39.21												
1972	14.46	6.73	14.05	25.44	13.03											
1973	6.64	-0.59	2.65	5.60	-8.02	-25.16										
1974	-4.54	-11.61	-11.42	-12.79	-25.38	-39.37	-50.88									
1975	7.66	2.54	5.29	7.64	0.94	-2.80	10.78	149.82								
1976	7.24	2.72	5.11	7.03	1.55	-1.14	8.47	61.19	4.01							
1977	10.25	6.43	9.08	11.37	7.31	6.20	15.90	54.30	21.27	41.40						
1978	9.98	6.52	8.88	10.85	7.30	6.38	14.13	40.90	16.42	23.17	7.29					
1979	10.11	6.96	9.14	10.93	7.82	7.10	13.69	34.47	15.18	19.16	9.39	11.54				
1980	11.64	8.84	11.03	12.86	10.25	9.91	16.12	34.02	18.32	22.20	16.40	21.24	31.78			
1981	11.70	9.12	11.15	12.83	10.48	10.20	15.66	30.71	17.34	20.20	15.42	18.26	21.77	12.52		
1982	12.76	10.41	12.40	14.06	12.01	11.91	17.03	30.44	18.88	21.56	17.94	20.76	24.00	20.28	28.58	
1983	13.80	11.65	13.62	15.26	13.46	13.50	18.32	30.47	20.29	22.82	19.96	22.67	25.63	23.64	29.61	30.64

Table 6-26
United Kingdom Stocks: Proportion of Return Explained by Gold (R^2).

	1968	1969	1970	1971	1972	1973	1974	1975	1976	1977	1978	1979	1980	1981	1982	1983
1968	0.96															
1969	0.67	9.42														
1970	0.22	3.59	0.91													
1971	1.11	0.16	2.51	7.62												
1972	0.08	0.00	0.00	0.33	1.36											
1973	0.35	0.54	0.70	1.33	0.76	0.19										
1974	0.01	0.00	0.02	0.07	0.95	3.03	9.20									
1975	1.88	2.15	2.51	2.89	3.12	3.61	4.83	25.68								
1976	2.48	2.79	3.16	3.51	3.79	4.32	5.29	13.08	10.31							
1977	2.31	2.60	2.98	3.32	3.65	4.08	4.63	10.41	5.34	1.99						
1978	2.11	2.36	2.68	2.97	3.24	3.57	3.87	7.89	3.43	0.03	0.18					
1979	1.81	1.94	2.23	2.50	2.66	2.82	2.95	5.75	2.32	0.69	0.47	1.01				
1980	0.37	0.40	0.48	0.57	0.61	0.59	0.42	0.79	0.43	3.65	5.31	7.88	54.41			
1981	0.50	0.55	0.63	0.72	0.78	0.77	0.57	0.88	0.05	1.22	1.49	2.15	10.61	7.46		
1982	0.45	0.49	0.57	0.65	0.71	0.69	0.50	0.78	0.03	0.88	1.06	1.46	5.97	1.39	0.16	
1983	0.32	0.36	0.42	0.47	0.52	0.49	0.31	0.44	0.14	1.22	1.38	1.88	6.43	0.02	1.83	11.39

Table 6–27
United Kingdom Bond Performance (Cumulative Rate of Return, Percent Per Year).

	1973	1974	1975	1976	1977	1978	1979	1980	1981	1982	1983
1973	-10.56										
1974	-3.51	4.09									
1975	6.82	16.74	30.93								
1976	6.67	13.12	17.93	6.23							
1977	11.91	18.36	23.53	19.99	35.54						
1978	8.98	13.37	15.82	11.18	13.74	-4.56					
1979	8.27	11.78	13.38	9.38	10.45	-0.30	4.15				
1980	9.31	12.49	13.96	10.84	12.02	5.13	10.33	16.88			
1981	8.36	10.99	12.02	9.14	9.74	4.09	7.15	8.68	1.05		
1982	11.37	14.12	15.44	13.38	14.62	10.84	15.06	18.95	20.00	42.49	
1983	11.59	14.08	15.25	13.43	14.49	11.32	14.80	17.63	17.87	27.31	13.74

Table 6–28
United Kingdom Bonds: Proportion of Return Explained by Gold (R^2).

	1973	1974	1975	1976	1977	1978	1979	1980	1981	1982	1983
1973	0.58										
1974	0.81	4.50									
1975	5.14	8.37	12.86								
1976	9.41	14.24	22.01	39.80							
1977	5.59	7.04	7.17	5.39	17.76						
1978	3.75	4.49	4.07	1.85	3.91	21.47					
1979	2.75	3.25	2.86	1.28	0.07	0.41	0.23				
1980	1.13	1.12	0.65	0.06	0.89	1.32	0.42	13.52			
1981	1.21	1.17	0.74	0.15	0.46	0.38	0.08	2.13	17.12		
1982	0.81	0.71	0.35	0.03	0.46	0.34	0.12	2.12	0.11	0.04	
1983	1.27	1.17	0.76	0.31	0.03	0.00	0.06	0.14	0.95	0.89	32.31

Table 6–29
United Kingdom Money Market Performance (Cumulative Rate of Return, Percent Per Year).

	1973	1974	1975	1976	1977	1978	1979	1980	1981	1982	1983
1973	12.96										
1974	14.69	16.45									
1975	13.63	13.96	11.53								
1976	13.61	13.83	12.55	13.57							
1977	12.67	12.60	11.34	11.25	8.98						
1978	12.35	12.23	11.20	11.09	9.86	10.75					
1979	12.58	12.52	11.75	11.81	11.23	12.37	14.00				
1980	13.10	13.12	12.57	12.78	12.59	13.81	15.38	16.76			
1981	13.20	13.23	12.78	12.99	12.88	13.87	14.93	15.40	14.05		
1982	13.09	13.10	12.69	12.85	12.73	13.50	14.20	14.26	13.03	12.02	
1983	12.81	12.79	12.39	12.50	12.35	12.92	13.36	13.20	12.04	11.04	10.07

Table 6–30
United Kingdom Money Markets: Proportion of Return Explained by Gold (R^2).

	1973	1974	1975	1976	1977	1978	1979	1980	1981	1982	1983
1973	10.95										
1974	0.32	12.58									
1975	1.45	18.52	15.42								
1976	4.08	18.82	14.56	19.37							
1977	4.18	11.57	4.95	8.44	0.49						
1978	2.38	6.01	1.01	2.13	0.38	6.31					
1979	3.69	7.48	5.71	6.68	7.06	4.00	8.22				
1980	1.48	3.29	1.71	1.46	0.45	0.04	0.58	0.01			
1981	1.01	2.43	0.92	0.73	0.06	0.09	0.02	0.52	0.16		
1982	0.40	1.14	0.20	0.11	0.07	0.80	0.73	2.91	14.81	19.82	
1983	0.70	1.49	0.40	0.35	0.01	0.03	0.02	0.53	3.09	1.52	0.12

Table 6-31
United Kingdom Consumer Price Index (Cumulative Rate of Increase, Percent Per Year).

	1968	1969	1970	1971	1972	1973	1974	1975	1976	1977	1978	1979	1980	1981	1982	1983
1968	5.77	5.31	6.15	6.84	7.01	7.60	9.17	11.03	11.47	11.54	11.25	11.74	11.99	12.00	11.54	11.16
1969		4.85	6.34	7.19	7.32	7.97	9.75	11.80	12.20	12.20	11.81	12.29	12.53	12.49	11.97	11.52
1970			7.85	8.38	8.15	8.77	10.76	13.00	13.29	13.16	12.61	13.07	13.25	13.15	12.54	12.02
1971				8.92	8.30	9.08	11.50	14.06	14.23	13.93	13.22	13.66	13.81	13.65	12.94	12.34
1972					7.69	9.16	12.37	15.38	15.32	14.79	13.85	14.27	14.37	14.13	13.31	12.63
1973						10.64	14.79	18.07	17.31	16.27	14.91	15.24	15.23	14.87	13.88	13.09
1974							19.09	21.96	19.62	17.72	15.78	16.02	15.90	15.41	14.25	13.34
1975								24.91	19.89	17.27	14.97	15.42	15.38	14.89	13.66	12.72
1976									15.06	13.62	11.84	13.16	13.56	13.30	12.14	11.28
1977										12.20	10.26	12.54	13.19	12.95	11.66	10.75
1978											8.36	12.71	13.52	13.14	11.55	10.52
1979												17.23	16.19	14.78	12.36	10.95
1980													15.16	13.57	10.78	9.44
1981														12.01	8.66	7.59
1982															5.41	5.45
1983																5.49

Germany Summary

Table 6-32
Total Return and Correlation (R^2) of Each Asset Vs. Gold—Gold, Stocks, Bonds, Money Markets, C.P.I. (Percent per Annum, Compounded for Periods Ending December 31, 1983).

	Return		R^2	
	B/H	PA	B/H	PA
GOLD				
5 years	20.38	19.90		
10 years	13.11	16.83		
Total Period	13.32	16.74		
STOCKS				
5 years	11.67	11.67	2.09	5.33
10 years	11.75	9.65	0.07	3.02
Total Period	7.32	6.07	0.25	1.83
BONDS				
5 years	6.42	6.98	0.71	3.40
10 years	8.81	8.28	0.22	1.88
Total Period	8.23	8.26	0.82	2.56
MONEY MARKETS				
5 years	8.25	8.67	1.89	6.24
10 years	6.66	6.53	0.26	5.53
Total Period	6.58	6.47	0.00	4.82
CONSUM. PRICES	Rate of Increase			
5 years	4.87	5.02		
10 years	4.55	4.51		
Total Period	4.58	4.83		

B/H = Buy/Hold
PA = Period Average
Note: Total Period = For gold, stocks, and consumer prices, total period is 1968–1983.
For bonds and money markets, total period is 1973–1983.

Table 6-33
Gold Price: German Marks Per Ounce.*

	Jan.	Feb.	March	April	May	June	July	Aug.	Sept.	Oct.	Nov.	Dec.
1959	146.994	146.995	146.995	146.996	146.995	146.994	146.995	146.994	146.994	146.994	146.994	146.994
1960	146.996	146.994	146.995	146.995	146.995	146.994	146.995	146.995	146.994	146.995	146.995	146.995
1961	146.995	146.995	140.000	140.001	140.000	140.001	140.000	140.001	140.001	140.000	140.001	140.000
1962	140.640	140.500	140.349	140.301	140.321	140.400	140.489	140.489	140.520	140.561	140.368	140.301
1963	140.240	140.321	140.404	140.384	140.305	140.317	140.341	140.389	140.324	140.316	140.325	140.316
1964	140.316	140.309	140.317	140.317	140.309	140.304	140.301	140.308	140.357	140.441	140.405	140.504
1965	140.504	140.565	140.625	140.565	140.416	140.396	140.488	140.596	140.544	140.448	140.456	140.525
1966	140.581	140.661	140.597	140.520	140.497	140.615	140.705	140.728	140.741	140.628	140.645	140.708
1967	140.737	140.685	140.628	140.697	140.720	140.744	140.749	140.748	140.748	140.768	140.788	140.776
1968	140.785	140.796	140.796	156.400	167.801	163.601	155.400	159.200	158.401	156.001	159.400	167.601
1969	169.761	170.801	171.600	174.401	172.300	164.801	165.561	163.800	162.701	145.485	130.296	128.832
1970	128.063	128.173	129.198	131.211	129.747	129.893	129.198	131.028	133.224	136.335	137.396	136.792
1971	139.263	142.008	142.282	145.302	145.152	140.241	146.723	138.028	141.294	141.268	144.252	142.746
1972	151.282	153.590	153.463	157.654	188.458	203.844	216.787	213.299	205.569	206.307	203.206	207.778
1973	208.344	241.743	255.241	257.389	313.268	298.577	271.895	254.870	241.502	239.463	264.453	303.415
1974	366.473	433.634	435.960	414.160	395.203	368.925	403.651	415.660	401.118	430.862	455.646	449.004
1975	411.641	415.440	415.354	397.295	391.913	391.648	429.258	412.925	376.083	365.043	363.339	367.810
1976	332.872	339.219	328.701	325.625	325.426	318.912	286.599	262.552	283.334	296.241	313.190	317.557
1977	320.228	342.099	355.643	347.329	336.716	334.117	329.624	338.937	356.312	363.977	356.279	347.390
1978	370.388	370.964	367.099	353.229	386.159	379.823	408.705	415.307	420.734	419.083	372.001	411.316
1979	435.028	464.898	448.383	466.431	523.794	512.677	544.851	575.682	692.204	690.074	719.691	902.317
1980	1135.228	1129.065	961.788	932.903	956.126	1148.182	1096.424	1130.866	1207.794	1200.421	1192.519	1161.014
1981	1070.981	1041.556	1079.894	1069.519	1112.916	1017.915	999.353	1040.382	997.681	960.938	914.989	898.178
1982	894.524	862.916	771.981	840.968	763.341	777.982	841.929	1028.815	1003.750	1084.517	1081.426	1088.479
1983	1227.799	994.419	1005.901	1055.236	1103.947	1055.527	1115.279	1120.271	1066.505	1005.547	1091.001	1039.722

*London afternoon fixings, last day of month, converted to marks
at the prevailing exchange rate on that day.

Table 6–34
German Mark Gold Performance (Cumulative Rate of Return, Percent Per Year).

	1968	1969	1970	1971	1972	1973	1974	1975	1976	1977	1978	1979	1980	1981	1982	1983
1968	19.06															
1969	-4.33	-23.12														
1970	-0.94	-9.65	6.18													
1971	0.36	-5.20	5.26	4.35												
1972	8.11	5.53	17.28	23.25	45.57											
1973	13.66	12.61	23.89	30.42	45.80	46.03										
1974	18.03	17.86	28.37	34.61	46.53	47.00	47.99									
1975	12.76	11.89	19.11	21.88	26.70	20.97	10.10	-18.09								
1976	9.47	8.32	13.76	15.07	17.35	11.19	1.53	-15.90	-13.66							
1977	9.46	8.44	13.20	14.24	15.98	10.83	3.44	-8.19	-2.81	9.40						
1978	10.24	9.40	13.77	14.76	16.33	12.06	6.28	-2.16	3.81	13.82	18.42					
1979	16.75	16.54	21.50	23.33	25.93	23.35	19.93	14.99	25.16	41.65	61.19	119.40				
1980	17.63	17.51	22.13	23.85	26.23	24.00	21.14	17.16	25.86	38.29	49.52	68.02	28.67			
1981	14.16	13.79	17.57	18.67	20.20	17.67	14.54	10.42	16.05	23.13	26.82	29.75	-0.22	-22.63		
1982	14.62	14.30	17.85	18.87	20.29	18.02	15.26	11.71	16.77	22.80	25.67	27.55	6.46	-3.17	21.19	
1983	13.32	12.94	16.09	16.89	18.00	15.77	13.11	9.78	13.88	18.47	20.05	20.38	3.61	-3.61	7.58	-4.49

Table 6-35
German Stock Performance (Cumulative Rate of Return, Percent Per Year).

	1968	1969	1970	1971	1972	1973	1974	1975	1976	1977	1978	1979	1980	1981	1982	1983
1968	13.56															
1969	13.26	12.97														
1970	-0.74	-7.19	-23.76													
1971	2.18	-1.35	-7.81	11.46												
1972	4.81	2.73	-0.48	13.71	16.00											
1973	0.34	-2.11	-5.55	1.43	-3.24	-19.29										
1974	0.92	-1.05	-3.63	2.18	-0.74	-8.19	4.44									
1975	5.27	4.14	2.74	9.05	8.45	6.05	21.56	41.49								
1976	4.21	3.10	1.76	6.78	5.86	3.47	12.40	16.61	-3.89							
1977	4.98	4.07	3.01	7.53	6.89	5.15	12.34	15.11	3.83	12.16						
1978	5.41	4.63	3.74	7.81	7.30	5.91	11.82	13.75	5.77	10.96	9.77					
1979	4.28	3.48	2.57	6.01	5.35	3.91	8.37	9.18	2.33	4.49	0.85	-7.35				
1980	4.26	3.52	2.70	5.81	5.20	3.92	7.74	8.30	2.67	4.37	1.90	-1.82	4.04			
1981	4.30	3.62	2.88	5.72	5.16	4.02	7.38	7.80	3.03	4.47	2.63	0.35	4.44	4.84		
1982	5.24	4.67	4.06	6.79	6.38	5.46	8.64	9.18	5.21	6.81	5.77	4.79	9.18	11.84	19.31	
1983	7.32	6.92	6.50	9.28	9.10	8.49	11.75	12.59	9.42	11.46	11.35	11.67	17.00	21.67	31.07	43.99

Table 6–36
German Stocks: Proportion of Return Explained by Gold (R^2).

	1968	1969	1970	1971	1972	1973	1974	1975	1976	1977	1978	1979	1980	1981	1982	1983
1968	0.36															
1969	1.85	4.73														
1970	1.37	6.56	5.37													
1971	0.01	0.09	5.84	7.83												
1972	0.70	0.98	6.08	4.84	6.28											
1973	0.99	1.12	0.33	1.11	2.80	12.17										
1974	0.16	0.15	0.01	0.08	0.27	1.55	4.13									
1975	0.19	0.19	0.03	0.19	0.58	1.85	0.61	4.78								
1976	0.08	0.09	0.00	0.04	0.20	0.94	1.02	1.34	0.32							
1977	0.09	0.09	0.01	0.04	0.20	0.89	0.80	0.69	0.46	0.10						
1978	0.00	0.00	0.04	0.01	0.01	0.25	1.70	1.85	4.25	7.56	32.38					
1979	0.03	0.03	0.00	0.01	0.08	0.38	0.32	0.04	0.49	0.16	1.53	0.78				
1980	0.03	0.04	0.17	0.08	0.04	0.00	1.14	0.80	2.63	2.95	5.82	4.75	15.40			
1981	0.01	0.01	0.09	0.04	0.01	0.03	0.75	0.46	1.13	1.06	1.67	0.57	2.76	3.97		
1982	0.01	0.00	0.01	0.00	0.02	0.14	0.24	0.07	0.20	0.07	0.14	0.03	0.13	3.27	10.04	
1983	0.25	0.25	0.17	0.27	0.46	0.82	0.07	0.28	0.40	0.87	0.95	2.09	1.33	7.14	12.73	15.01

Table 6–37
German Bond Performance (Cumulative Rate of Return, Percent Per Year).

	1973	1974	1975	1976	1977	1978	1979	1980	1981	1982	1983
1973	2.58										
1974	6.19	9.93									
1975	9.38	12.94	16.04								
1976	10.40	13.14	14.78	13.54							
1977	11.55	13.92	15.28	14.90	16.28						
1978	9.76	11.25	11.59	10.14	8.48	1.21					
1979	8.41	9.42	9.32	7.70	5.82	0.94	0.68				
1980	7.56	8.29	8.02	6.48	4.79	1.21	1.22	1.76			
1981	7.24	7.84	7.55	6.19	4.78	2.09	2.39	3.25	4.76		
1982	8.49	9.16	9.07	8.11	7.23	5.50	6.60	8.66	12.28	20.33	
1983	8.23	8.81	8.68	7.80	7.00	5.53	6.42	7.90	10.03	12.76	5.66

Table 6–38
German Bonds: Proportion of Return Explained by Gold (R^2).

	1973	1974	1975	1976	1977	1978	1979	1980	1981	1982	1983
1973	16.41										
1974	9.48	4.47									
1975	12.56	7.85	11.15								
1976	8.06	2.70	0.11	6.86							
1977	7.03	2.02	0.00	4.40	0.26						
1978	4.79	1.28	0.22	0.64	0.17	1.33					
1979	4.51	2.16	1.67	0.24	0.26	0.45	0.32				
1980	0.97	0.15	0.01	0.26	0.48	1.52	1.58	2.90			
1981	0.97	0.24	0.09	0.02	0.02	0.11	0.05	0.17	5.94		
1982	0.40	0.02	0.01	0.21	0.22	0.33	0.25	1.02	0.72	5.94	
1983	0.82	0.22	0.09	0.00	0.00	0.00	0.01	0.04	0.30	0.12	31.68

Table 6–39
German Money Market Performance (Cumulative Rate of Return, Percent Per Year).

	1973	1974	1975	1976	1977	1978	1979	1980	1981	1982	1983
1973	5.75										
1974	7.56	9.40									
1975	6.54	6.94	4.53								
1976	5.93	6.00	4.33	4.14							
1977	5.56	5.51	4.24	4.10	4.06						
1978	5.20	5.09	4.04	3.88	3.75	3.43					
1979	5.39	5.33	4.54	4.54	4.68	4.98	6.56				
1980	5.85	5.86	5.29	5.44	5.76	6.34	7.82	9.10			
1981	6.51	6.60	6.21	6.49	6.96	7.70	9.16	10.49	11.90		
1982	6.69	6.79	6.47	6.75	7.19	7.83	8.96	9.77	10.11	8.34	
1983	6.58	6.66	6.36	6.59	6.94	7.43	8.25	8.68	8.54	6.89	5.46

Table 6–40
German Money Markets: Proportion of Return Explained by Gold (R^2).

	1973	1974	1975	1976	1977	1978	1979	1980	1981	1982	1983
1973	5.54										
1974	1.08	10.63									
1975	0.18	12.13	7.60								
1976	1.16	12.10	0.35	9.34							
1977	1.29	9.70	0.05	9.25	15.57						
1978	0.77	5.09	1.86	0.05	0.07	20.12					
1979	2.40	8.54	11.94	18.31	18.65	15.62	7.90				
1980	1.43	4.62	3.93	3.94	2.08	0.61	1.29	21.85			
1981	0.00	0.31	0.00	0.05	0.84	2.32	9.44	5.91	19.25		
1982	0.00	0.19	0.00	0.08	0.89	2.27	7.65	5.83	5.56	4.00	
1983	0.00	0.26	0.01	0.02	0.40	0.94	1.89	0.92	1.16	0.15	0.72

Table 6-41
German Consumer Price Index (Cumulative Rate of Increase, Percent Per Year).

	1968	1969	1970	1971	1972	1973	1974	1975	1976	1977	1978	1979	1980	1981	1982	1983
1968	2.16															
1969	2.13	2.10														
1970	2.74	3.04	3.99													
1971	3.44	3.87	4.78	5.57												
1972	4.01	4.47	5.27	5.92	6.28											
1973	4.63	5.13	5.90	6.55	7.04	7.81										
1974	4.81	5.26	5.91	6.39	6.67	6.87	5.93									
1975	4.88	5.28	5.82	6.19	6.34	6.36	5.65	5.36								
1976	4.78	5.11	5.55	5.81	5.86	5.75	5.07	4.65	3.93							
1977	4.65	4.93	5.29	5.48	5.46	5.30	4.68	4.26	3.72	3.50						
1978	4.45	4.68	4.97	5.09	5.03	4.82	4.23	3.81	3.30	2.98	2.46					
1979	4.51	4.72	4.99	5.10	5.04	4.87	4.39	4.08	3.76	3.70	3.81	5.17				
1980	4.58	4.78	5.03	5.13	5.08	4.94	4.53	4.30	4.09	4.13	4.34	5.29	5.42			
1981	4.69	4.88	5.12	5.22	5.19	5.07	4.73	4.56	4.43	4.52	4.78	5.57	5.77	6.12		
1982	4.69	4.87	5.09	5.18	5.15	5.04	4.73	4.58	4.47	4.56	4.78	5.37	5.43	5.44	4.76	
1983	4.58	4.74	4.93	5.01	4.96	4.84	4.55	4.40	4.28	4.32	4.46	4.87	4.79	4.59	3.83	2.90

Switzerland Summary

Table 6–42
Total Return and Correlation (R^2) of Each Asset Vs. Gold—Gold, Stocks, Bonds, Money Markets, C.P.I. (Percent per Annum, Compounded for Periods Ending December 31, 1983).

	Return		R^2	
	B/H	PA	B/H	PA
GOLD				
5years	17.80	17.75		
10 years	8.59	12.90		
Total Period	11.24	14.09		
STOCKS				
5years	9.31	7.83	1.74	5.79
10 years	5.28	5.96	0.63	3.38
Total Period	5.59	3.89	1.31	3.12
BONDS				
5years	4.05	4.24	3.65	1.97
10 years	6.75	6.62	2.37	6.43
Total Period	6.12	6.45	9.72	5.64
MONEY MARKETS				
5years	5.17	5.59	8.03	11.09
10 years	4.42	4.05	0.26	6.46
Total Period	4.49	4.18	0.18	5.62

CONSUM. PRICES	Rate of Increase	
5years	4.74	4.96
10 years	3.74	3.57
Total Period	4.53	4.73

B/H = Buy/Hold
PA = Period Average
Note: Total Period = For gold, stocks, and consumer prices, total period is 1968–1983.
For bonds and money markets, total period is 1973–1983.

Table 6-43
Gold Price: Swiss Francs Per Ounce.*

	Jan.	Feb.	March	April	May	June	July	Aug.	Sept.	Oct.	Nov.	Dec.
1959	151.410	151.410	151.410	151.410	151.410	151.410	151.410	151.410	151.410	151.410	151.410	151.410
1960	151.410	151.410	151.410	151.410	151.410	151.410	151.410	151.410	151.410	151.410	151.410	151.410
1961	151.410	151.410	151.410	151.410	151.410	151.410	151.410	151.410	151.410	151.410	151.410	151.410
1962	152.102	151.951	151.786	151.734	151.756	151.843	151.938	151.938	151.972	152.016	151.808	151.734
1963	151.669	151.756	151.847	151.825	151.739	151.752	151.778	151.830	151.760	151.752	151.760	151.752
1964	151.752	151.743	151.752	151.752	151.743	151.739	151.734	151.743	151.795	151.886	151.847	151.955
1965	151.955	152.020	152.085	152.020	151.860	151.838	151.938	152.055	151.998	151.894	151.903	151.977
1966	152.037	152.124	152.055	151.972	151.946	152.076	152.171	152.197	152.210	152.089	152.106	152.176
1967	152.206	152.150	152.089	152.163	152.189	152.215	152.219	152.219	152.219	152.241	152.262	152.249
1968	152.258	152.271	152.271	169.147	181.476	176.933	168.065	172.175	171.310	168.714	172.391	181.259
1969	183.595	184.720	185.585	188.614	186.342	178.231	179.053	177.150	175.960	171.958	154.006	152.275
1970	151.367	151.496	152.708	155.087	153.357	153.530	152.708	154.871	157.466	161.143	162.398	161.684
1971	164.604	167.849	168.173	171.742	166.938	163.914	173.315	161.930	168.616	169.026	172.526	171.118
1972	182.773	186.772	185.677	191.749	228.698	242.328	257.924	252.910	244.239	244.738	240.335	245.052
1973	239.542	268.626	293.614	296.000	358.700	364.293	333.301	315.957	304.505	305.453	325.738	367.388
1974	439.510	511.480	524.842	497.104	469.629	435.804	467.382	472.799	448.502	482.643	502.165	477.057
1975	442.605	439.465	452.770	430.118	421.713	419.485	455.366	432.498	391.110	377.402	373.064	370.402
1976	335.737	341.612	331.084	324.950	309.015	308.260	280.404	259.428	286.452	302.371	320.428	331.865
1977	335.365	367.313	381.304	374.222	360.489	354.459	348.659	352.078	362.728	363.150	348.915	332.952
1978	349.480	342.219	341.821	333.372	351.811	342.432	351.766	345.750	338.566	361.473	335.935	369.291
1979	397.403	421.889	406.472	425.529	477.464	464.899	496.259	525.828	620.308	640.736	672.905	841.711
1980	1068.657	1084.176	918.327	871.469	897.397	1065.200	1023.805	1049.273	1108.288	1087.982	1084.961	1050.817
1981	978.109	967.710	990.045	983.531	998.370	870.702	871.120	915.956	855.803	792.114	738.240	724.502
1982	718.687	690.049	623.263	709.426	654.946	668.754	720.008	882.287	867.191	942.005	935.254	918.191
1983	1009.845	847.464	869.615	890.507	922.825	878.940	903.727	914.658	865.872	824.009	880.553	837.528

*London afternoon fixings, last day of month, converted to Swiss francs at the prevailing exchange rate on that day.

Table 6-44
Swiss Franc Gold Performance (Cumulative Rate of Return, Percent Per Year).

	1968	1969	1970	1971	1972	1973	1974	1975	1976	1977	1978	1979	1980	1981	1982	1983
1968	19.06															
1969	0.02	-15.98														
1970	2.03	-5.54	6.18													
1971	2.97	-1.90	6.01	5.83												
1972	9.99	7.83	17.18	23.10	43.20											
1973	15.82	15.18	24.63	31.46	46.52	49.92										
1974	17.72	17.50	25.65	31.05	40.73	39.51	29.83									
1975	11.76	10.75	15.96	18.03	21.29	14.76	0.40	-22.35								
1976	9.05	7.85	11.77	12.73	14.16	7.88	-3.33	-16.59	-10.39							
1977	8.14	6.99	10.27	10.87	11.73	6.32	-2.43	-11.30	-5.19	0.32						
1978	8.39	7.37	10.34	10.87	11.61	7.07	0.10	-6.20	-0.10	5.48	10.90					
1979	15.31	14.98	18.64	20.11	22.03	19.27	14.81	12.03	22.78	36.37	58.99	127.94				
1980	16.02	15.77	19.19	20.58	22.34	19.96	16.19	14.07	23.19	33.39	46.68	68.68	24.83			
1981	11.79	11.25	13.88	14.61	15.52	12.80	8.86	6.15	11.83	16.90	21.45	25.19	-7.22	-31.05		
1982	12.73	12.29	14.82	15.57	16.50	14.12	10.71	8.53	13.85	18.48	22.49	25.57	2.94	-6.52	26.74	
1983	11.24	10.74	12.95	13.48	14.15	11.82	8.59	6.45	10.74	14.14	16.62	17.80	-0.13	-7.28	-7.52	-8.79

Table 6-45
Swiss Stock Performance (Cumulative Rate of Return, Percent Per Year).

	1968	1969	1970	1971	1972	1973	1974	1975	1976	1977	1978	1979	1980	1981	1982	1983
1968	30.99															
1969	17.31	5.05														
1970	6.12	-4.49	-13.16													
1971	8.40	1.77	0.17	15.55												
1972	11.32	6.88	7.50	19.61	23.82											
1973	6.10	1.72	0.90	6.08	1.64	-16.56										
1974	-0.32	-4.76	-6.61	-4.90	-10.87	-24.38	-31.47									
1975	4.52	1.20	0.58	3.57	0.78	-5.90	-0.07	45.71								
1976	4.38	1.46	0.95	3.52	1.27	-3.69	1.02	22.65	3.25							
1977	4.48	1.88	1.49	3.78	1.94	-1.95	2.09	16.60	4.30	5.37						
1978	3.94	1.56	1.18	3.13	1.47	-1.84	1.40	11.83	2.39	1.97	-1.32					
1979	4.45	2.33	2.06	3.91	2.54	-0.19	2.84	11.53	4.32	4.68	4.34	10.34				
1980	4.33	2.37	2.13	3.80	2.57	0.19	2.84	10.04	4.03	4.22	3.85	6.53	2.86			
1981	3.40	1.53	1.24	2.67	1.46	-0.76	1.41	7.25	1.91	1.65	0.74	1.44	-2.74	-8.03		
1982	4.12	2.42	2.22	3.62	2.60	0.69	2.82	8.17	3.66	3.73	3.40	4.62	2.78	2.74	14.77	
1983	5.59	4.08	4.01	5.46	4.66	3.08	5.28	10.42	6.66	7.16	7.46	9.31	9.05	11.20	22.27	30.27

217

Table 6-46
Swiss Stocks: Proportion of Return Explained by Gold (R^2).

	1968	1969	1970	1971	1972	1973	1974	1975	1976	1977	1978	1979	1980	1981	1982	1983
1968	11.72															
1969	14.20	15.63														
1970	7.78	3.46	9.02													
1971	7.52	5.40	2.09	6.66												
1972	8.97	8.24	7.51	9.08	12.65											
1973	3.83	3.23	2.79	2.95	3.96	1.92										
1974	4.67	4.38	4.79	5.38	7.70	7.60	14.37									
1975	1.62	1.24	0.90	0.95	0.85	0.08	0.04	1.06								
1976	1.25	0.90	0.60	0.67	0.54	0.01	0.00	1.33	1.07							
1977	1.31	0.95	0.66	0.74	0.60	0.03	0.03	0.85	0.00	5.84						
1978	1.42	1.07	0.79	0.88	0.76	0.10	0.11	0.38	0.56	5.37	6.18					
1979	1.17	0.95	0.73	0.75	0.69	0.19	0.17	0.27	0.59	1.74	1.55	0.07				
1980	1.83	1.63	1.45	1.51	1.53	0.91	1.05	0.25	4.29	7.38	8.10	7.97	27.48			
1981	1.68	1.45	1.28	1.37	1.36	0.75	0.88	0.27	3.00	4.87	5.11	5.03	8.02	6.37		
1982	1.82	1.62	1.47	1.55	1.56	0.99	1.17	0.57	3.56	5.16	5.27	5.14	8.48	2.15	5.99	
1983	1.31	1.13	0.96	1.02	0.98	0.53	0.63	0.21	1.60	2.22	2.06	1.74	3.11	0.16	0.02	5.08

Table 6–47
Swiss Bond Performance (Cumulative Rate of Return, Percent Per Year).

	1973	1974	1975	1976	1977	1978	1979	1980	1981	1982	1983
1973	0.04										
1974	1.32	2.62									
1975	5.48	8.32	14.34								
1976	8.03	10.84	15.19	16.05							
1977	8.55	10.79	13.65	13.31	10.64						
1978	7.88	9.52	11.32	10.34	7.58	4.62					
1979	6.75	7.91	9.00	7.71	5.06	2.38	0.19				
1980	6.02	6.91	7.64	6.35	4.05	1.95	0.64	1.09			
1981	5.42	6.11	6.62	5.39	3.37	1.63	0.66	0.90	0.70		
1982	6.21	6.92	7.47	6.52	5.01	3.92	3.75	4.96	6.95	13.59	
1983	6.12	6.75	7.22	6.37	5.05	4.15	4.05	5.04	6.39	9.36	5.28

Table 6–48
Swiss Bonds: Proportion of Return Explained by Gold (R^2).

	1973	1974	1975	1976	1977	1978	1979	1980	1981	1982	1983
1973	2.82										
1974	5.18	8.12									
1975	0.04	0.10	20.19								
1976	0.35	0.30	14.72	13.28							
1977	0.39	0.33	11.35	7.83	0.77						
1978	0.37	0.38	10.21	6.44	0.66	0.00					
1979	0.36	0.55	6.72	3.53	0.08	1.39	8.25				
1980	1.69	2.27	8.10	6.01	3.55	2.72	2.59	9.78			
1981	2.86	3.62	9.22	7.61	6.17	6.07	6.49	15.53	52.23		
1982	2.54	3.10	7.30	6.00	4.80	4.73	5.07	8.35	6.37	1.81	
1983	1.97	2.37	5.68	4.50	3.48	3.43	3.65	5.68	2.87	0.18	16.93

Table 6–49
Swiss Money Market Performance (Cumulative Rate of Return, Percent Per Year).

	1973	1974	1975	1976	1977	1978	1979	1980	1981	1982	1983
1973	5.15										
1974	7.40	9.71									
1975	6.20	6.74	3.85								
1976	5.05	5.01	2.74	1.65							
1977	4.55	4.40	2.69	2.11	2.57						
1978	3.92	3.67	2.22	1.68	1.70	0.83					
1979	3.64	3.39	2.17	1.76	1.80	1.41	2.00				
1980	3.92	3.74	2.78	2.57	2.80	2.88	3.92	5.88			
1981	4.51	4.43	3.69	3.67	4.07	4.45	5.69	7.59	9.31		
1982	4.53	4.46	3.82	3.82	4.19	4.51	5.46	6.63	7.01	4.76	
1983	4.49	4.42	3.85	3.85	4.17	4.44	5.17	5.98	6.01	4.40	4.04

Table 6–50
Swiss Money Markets: Proportion of Return Explained by Gold (R^2).

	1973	1974	1975	1976	1977	1978	1979	1980	1981	1982	1983
1973	0.19										
1974	0.39	0.48									
1975	2.09	10.22	0.64								
1976	4.19	7.59	0.75	54.47							
1977	3.89	5.62	0.16	7.81	1.42						
1978	2.49	2.63	0.77	0.29	2.65	2.78					
1979	1.09	1.02	0.63	9.62	7.29	28.27	30.81				
1980	0.64	0.61	0.33	1.36	0.24	0.20	1.25	27.34			
1981	0.17	0.26	1.88	2.05	4.73	6.43	14.82	15.06	4.42		
1982	0.26	0.36	1.74	1.93	4.33	5.85	12.38	12.68	16.53	5.69	
1983	0.18	0.26	1.48	1.65	3.51	4.50	8.03	5.71	6.97	0.55	4.12

Table 6–51
Swiss Consumer Price Index (Cumulative Rate of Increase, Per Cent Per Year).

	1968	1969	1970	1971	1972	1973	1974	1975	1976	1977	1978	1979	1980	1981	1982	1983
1968	2.33															
1969	2.30	2.28														
1970	3.35	3.86	5.46													
1971	4.15	4.76	6.03	6.59												
1972	4.68	5.28	6.30	6.72	6.84											
1973	5.86	6.58	7.69	8.44	9.37	11.97										
1974	6.09	6.73	7.64	8.20	8.74	9.70	7.47									
1975	5.76	6.26	6.94	7.24	7.40	7.58	5.46	3.48								
1976	5.25	5.63	6.11	6.22	6.15	5.98	4.05	2.38	1.29							
1977	4.84	5.12	5.48	5.49	5.30	5.00	3.32	1.98	1.23	1.17						
1978	4.43	4.65	4.91	4.85	4.60	4.23	2.75	1.60	0.98	0.83	0.48					
1979	4.51	4.71	4.96	4.91	4.70	4.39	3.18	2.35	2.07	2.32	2.90	5.39				
1980	4.51	4.69	4.92	4.86	4.67	4.40	3.37	2.70	2.54	2.85	3.42	4.92	4.46			
1981	4.69	4.88	5.09	5.06	4.91	4.70	3.82	3.31	3.28	3.69	4.32	5.64	5.76	7.07		
1982	4.71	4.88	5.08	5.05	4.91	4.72	3.95	3.52	3.52	3.90	4.45	5.47	5.49	6.01	4.96	
1983	4.53	4.68	4.85	4.81	4.66	4.46	3.74	3.34	3.32	3.61	4.02	4.74	4.58	4.62	3.42	1.90

Japan Summary

Table 6–52
Total Return and Correlation (R^2) of Each Asset Vs. Gold—Gold, Stocks, Bonds, Money Markets, C.P.I. (Percent per Annum, Compounded for Periods Ending December 31, 1983).

	Return		R^2	
	B/H	PA	B/H	PA
GOLD				
5 years	14.99	16.36		
10 years	10.88	15.39		
Total Period	12.90	17.85		
STOCKS				
5 years	14.49	14.66	0.10	5.45
10 years	11.94	12.64	0.20	2.96
Total Period	15.53	14.85	0.20	1.97
BONDS				
5 years	7.24	7.74	0.36	6.04
10 years	10.41	9.79	0.21	2.76
Total Period	7.89	8.92	0.05	2.38
MONEY MARKETS				
5 years	7.71	7.90	2.89	6.42
10 years	6.00	5.98	0.27	5.37
Total Period	5.82	5.81	0.54	4.62

CONSUM. PRICES	Rate of Increase			
5 years	4.62	4.70		
10 years	7.11	7.11		
Total Period	7.34	7.34		

B/H = Buy/Hold
PA = Period Average
Note: Total Period = For gold, stocks, and consumer prices, total period is 1968–1983.
For bonds and money markets, owing to limitations of available data, total period is 1973–1983.

Table 6-53
Gold Price: Japanese Yen per Ounce*.

	Jan.	Feb.	March	April	May	June	July	Aug.	Sept.	Oct.	Nov.	Dec.
1959	12600	12600	12600	12600	12600	12600	12600	12600	12600	12600	12600	12600
1960	12600	12600	12600	12600	12600	12600	12600	12600	12600	12600	12600	12600
1961	12600	12600	12600	12600	12600	12600	12600	12600	12600	12600	12600	12600
1962	12657	12645	12631	12626	12628	12635	12643	12643	12646	12650	12633	12626
1963	12621	12628	12636	12634	12627	12628	12630	12634	12629	12628	12629	12628
1964	12628	12627	12628	12628	12627	12627	12626	12627	12632	12639	12636	12645
1965	12645	12650	12656	12650	12637	12635	12643	12653	12648	12640	12641	12647
1966	12652	12659	12653	12646	12644	12655	12663	12665	12666	12656	12657	12663
1967	12666	12661	12656	12662	12664	12666	12667	12667	12667	12669	12670	12669
1968	12670	12671	12671	14075	15101	14723	13985	14327	14255	14040	14345	15083
1969	15278	15371	15443	15695	15506	14831	14900	14741	14642	14310	12815	12671
1970	12596	12607	12707	12905	12761	12776	12707	12887	13103	13310	13514	13455
1971	13697	13967	13995	14291	14702	14435	15263	13658	14233	13908	14268	13728
1972	14571	14631	14650	15081	18091	19431	20528	20098	19296	19345	19052	19535
1973	19838	22346	23849	24043	30347	32552	30376	27416	26516	25981	28239	31384
1974	39560	46651	47506	47254	44061	40908	46479	47192	44856	50028	55111	55999
1975	52313	52041	51770	48735	48568	49272	49480	47551	42730	43022	41799	42708
1976	38863	39923	38752	38362	37580	36685	32960	29986	33273	36169	38550	39335
1977	38100	40304	41267	40766	39590	38061	38311	38973	40526	40296	39143	39526
1978	42382	43467	40402	38172	40868	37407	37992	39637	41027	42781	38190	43871
1979	46906	50752	50288	54329	60325	60339	64281	69332	88697	90804	103514	125291
1980	155876	159212	123447	123494	120020	142421	139572	138045	140316	132999	133929	119791
1981	104062	101981	108373	103593	107076	96199	96994	97501	99495	99281	88769	87790
1982	88221	85594	79114	84659	79080	80524	87821	106829	106315	117148	109706	107117
1983	119409	96871	98767	101692	104358	99271	101777	102079	95271	89211	93794	88180

*London afternoon fixings, last day of month, converted to yen at the prevailing exchange rate on that day.

Table 6-54
Japanese Yen Gold Performance (Cumulative Rate of Return, Percent Per Year).

	1968	1969	1970	1971	1972	1973	1974	1975	1976	1977	1978	1979	1980	1981	1982	1983
1968	19.06															
1969	0.02	-15.98														
1970	2.03	-5.54	6.18													
1971	2.03	-3.08	4.09	2.03												
1972	9.05	6.69	15.52	20.50	42.31											
1973	16.33	15.79	25.46	32.63	51.21	60.68										
1974	23.66	24.44	34.61	42.83	59.78	69.30	78.40									
1975	16.41	16.03	22.45	25.99	32.81	29.78	16.64	-23.74								
1976	13.42	12.73	17.57	19.58	23.43	19.12	7.81	-16.19	-7.90							
1977	12.05	11.30	15.28	16.64	19.27	15.13	5.93	-10.97	-3.80	0.47						
1978	11.96	11.27	14.80	15.92	18.05	14.44	6.93	-5.92	0.90	5.61	11.02					
1979	21.04	21.23	25.75	28.14	31.84	30.41	25.95	17.48	30.88	47.14	78.07	185.61				
1980	18.87	18.85	22.66	24.44	27.22	25.45	21.09	13.52	22.92	32.11	44.74	65.26	-4.37			
1981	14.83	14.51	17.51	18.59	20.39	18.18	13.72	6.64	12.77	17.43	22.09	26.03	-16.29	-26.71		
1982	15.30	15.03	17.85	18.88	20.54	18.55	14.62	8.45	14.04	18.18	22.08	25.01	-5.08	-5.44	22.02	
1983	12.90	12.50	14.87	15.56	16.77	14.69	10.88	5.18	9.49	12.23	14.32	14.99	-8.40	-9.71	0.22	-17.68

Table 6-55
Japanese Stock Performance (Cumulative Rate of Return, Percent Per Year).

	1968	1969	1970	1971	1972	1973	1974	1975	1976	1977	1978	1979	1980	1981	1982	1983
1968	25.58															
1969	30.02	34.60														
1970	14.45	9.26	-11.32													
1971	19.35	17.34	9.56	35.34												
1972	34.47	36.79	37.53	71.27	116.74											
1973	21.79	21.04	17.87	29.59	26.81	-25.81										
1974	16.75	15.34	11.83	18.50	13.37	-18.01	-9.40									
1975	17.34	16.21	13.40	19.12	15.37	-6.50	4.97	21.61								
1976	17.71	16.77	14.42	19.38	16.42	-0.33	9.98	21.16	20.72							
1977	15.22	14.12	11.79	15.55	12.54	-1.28	6.02	11.72	7.09	-5.01						
1978	16.01	15.09	13.11	16.60	14.14	2.58	9.44	14.73	12.53	8.64	24.25					
1979	15.37	14.48	12.65	15.68	13.43	3.41	9.29	13.47	11.52	8.62	16.15	8.57				
1980	15.00	14.16	12.47	15.17	13.12	4.29	9.49	13.00	11.36	9.13	14.30	9.62	10.68			
1981	15.70	14.97	13.47	16.04	14.27	6.42	11.33	14.66	13.54	12.15	16.91	14.55	17.67	25.10		
1982	15.04	14.33	12.90	15.19	13.52	6.41	10.76	13.58	12.47	11.15	14.70	12.43	13.75	15.31	6.29	
1983	15.53	14.89	13.60	15.78	14.29	7.83	11.94	14.60	13.75	12.79	16.06	14.49	16.02	17.86	14.39	23.11

Table 6-56
Japanese Stocks: Proportion of Return Explained by Gold (R^2).

	1968	1969	1970	1971	1972	1973	1974	1975	1976	1977	1978	1979	1980	1981	1982	1983
1968	1.25															
1969	0.32	0.90														
1970	0.65	1.98	3.06													
1971	1.70	4.75	11.42	22.92												
1972	4.06	7.48	9.28	10.64	0.36											
1973	0.23	0.43	0.71	0.36	0.10	0.09										
1974	0.17	0.30	0.61	0.35	0.06	1.45	3.35									
1975	0.34	0.50	0.75	0.63	0.19	0.07	0.78	15.33								
1976	0.17	0.26	0.39	0.33	0.04	0.05	0.08	0.56	1.11							
1977	0.32	0.44	0.63	0.61	0.21	0.00	0.33	0.72	0.01	17.58						
1978	0.31	0.42	0.57	0.56	0.20	0.00	0.34	0.73	0.08	3.47	0.41					
1979	0.32	0.43	0.63	0.55	0.29	0.22	0.71	0.80	0.65	5.92	1.56	28.47				
1980	0.53	0.67	0.89	0.84	0.57	0.48	1.24	1.66	1.88	7.54	6.41	16.43	18.87			
1981	0.29	0.37	0.49	0.47	0.24	0.08	0.42	0.52	0.32	1.20	0.47	0.60	0.37	2.66		
1982	0.36	0.44	0.57	0.55	0.33	0.17	0.56	0.67	0.53	1.40	0.79	0.98	0.56	0.11	2.69	
1983	0.20	0.25	0.33	0.32	0.14	0.02	0.20	0.23	0.10	0.37	0.11	0.10	0.01	0.94	0.21	8.73

Table 6-57
Japanese Bond Performance (Cumulative Rate of Return, Percent Per Year).

	1973	1974	1975	1976	1977	1978	1979	1980	1981	1982	1983
1973	14.41										
1974	-0.96	14.61									
1975	4.98	16.26	17.93								
1976	6.40	14.41	14.31	10.79							
1977	9.00	15.79	16.18	15.32	20.02						
1978	8.43	13.68	13.45	11.99	12.60	5.63					
1979	6.98	11.03	10.33	8.50	7.75	2.09	-1.33				
1980	6.88	10.33	9.63	8.04	7.36	3.45	2.37	6.22			
1981	7.38	10.47	9.89	8.61	8.18	5.40	5.33	8.82	11.49		
1982	7.54	10.30	9.77	8.66	8.30	6.10	6.22	8.86	10.21	8.94	
1983	7.89	10.41	9.96	9.00	8.75	6.97	7.24	9.50	10.61	10.18	11.43

Table 6-58
Japanese Bonds: Proportion of Return Explained by Gold (R^2).

	1973	1974	1975	1976	1977	1978	1979	1980	1981	1982	1983
1973	1.55										
1974	0.43	6.58									
1975	0.17	1.96	1.02								
1976	0.51	0.82	0.55	10.28							
1977	0.85	0.40	0.59	4.85	5.40						
1978	0.69	0.26	0.85	3.10	1.34	0.10					
1979	0.91	0.19	3.29	5.03	3.56	0.05	7.12				
1980	0.01	0.77	0.08	0.47	1.49	5.61	7.99	20.69			
1981	0.04	0.30	0.01	0.01	0.19	0.92	1.07	6.89	18.13		
1982	0.07	0.16	0.05	0.01	0.04	0.39	0.42	2.93	6.77	1.69	
1983	0.05	0.21	0.01	0.00	0.08	0.34	0.36	3.02	2.09	0.03	11.38

Table 6–59
Japanese Money Market Performance (Cumulative Rate of Return, Percent Per Year).

	1973	1974	1975	1976	1977	1978	1979	1980	1981	1982	1983
1973	4.03										
1974	4.70	5.37									
1975	4.92	5.37	5.37								
1976	4.82	5.09	4.95	4.53							
1977	4.63	4.78	4.59	4.20	3.87						
1978	4.27	4.31	4.05	3.61	3.16	2.46					
1979	4.55	4.64	4.49	4.28	4.19	4.35	6.28				
1980	5.38	5.57	5.61	5.66	5.94	6.64	8.79	11.36			
1981	5.62	5.82	5.88	5.97	6.26	6.86	8.37	9.43	7.54		
1982	5.75	5.94	6.01	6.10	6.37	6.88	8.01	8.59	7.23	6.93	
1983	5.82	6.00	6.07	6.15	6.39	6.81	7.71	8.07	6.99	6.72	6.51

Table 6–60
Japanese Money Markets: Performance of Return Explained by Gold (R^2).

	1973	1974	1975	1976	1977	1978	1979	1980	1981	1982	1983
1973	0.15										
1974	0.15	0.33									
1975	2.69	0.64	5.17								
1976	1.00	0.53	3.60	100.00							
1977	0.05	0.75	3.27	0.00	1.25						
1978	0.04	0.00	4.94	1.77	1.83	1.96					
1979	3.90	5.77	6.13	12.89	19.03	19.07	5.47				
1980	0.10	0.02	0.01	0.03	0.21	1.30	17.88	17.53			
1981	0.58	0.33	0.27	0.40	0.82	1.89	8.50	1.09	3.28		
1982	0.44	0.22	0.13	0.25	0.58	1.44	5.70	2.03	1.67	18.76	
1983	0.54	0.27	0.17	0.28	0.55	1.12	2.89	0.82	0.22	9.44	1.09

Table 6–61
Japanese Consumer Price Index (Cumulative Rate of Increase, Percent Per Year).

	1968	1969	1970	1971	1972	1973	1974	1975	1976	1977	1978	1979	1980	1981	1982	1983
1968	3.81															
1969	5.07	6.34														
1970	6.08	7.23	8.13													
1971	5.69	6.32	6.31	4.52												
1972	5.61	6.06	5.97	4.90	5.28											
1973	7.73	8.53	9.08	9.40	11.92	18.98										
1974	9.66	10.66	11.55	12.42	15.18	20.47	21.97									
1975	9.42	10.24	10.91	11.47	13.28	16.08	14.65	7.77								
1976	9.53	10.26	10.83	11.29	12.70	14.63	13.21	9.07	10.40							
1977	9.05	9.65	10.07	10.34	11.35	12.60	11.06	7.64	7.58	4.83						
1978	8.60	9.09	9.40	9.56	10.30	11.15	9.65	6.77	6.44	4.51	4.20					
1979	8.30	8.72	8.96	9.05	9.63	10.26	8.87	6.43	6.09	4.70	4.63	5.07				
1980	8.20	8.58	8.78	8.85	9.34	9.86	8.61	6.53	6.29	5.28	5.44	6.06	7.06			
1981	8.02	8.36	8.53	8.56	8.97	9.39	8.25	6.42	6.20	5.37	5.51	5.95	6.40	5.74		
1982	7.60	7.87	7.99	7.98	8.30	8.61	7.51	5.83	5.55	4.77	4.75	4.89	4.83	3.74	1.77	
1983	7.34	7.58	7.67	7.63	7.89	8.13	7.11	5.57	5.30	4.59	4.55	4.62	4.51	3.67	2.65	3.54

Summaries for All Six Countries

Table 6–62
Rates of Return of Financial Assets Across Six Countries: 1977–80;
1980–83; 1977–83 (Cumulative Rate of Return, Percent Per Year).

Country	Gold	C.P.I.	Stocks	Bonds	Money Markets
			Accelerating Inflation, 1977–1980		
U.S.	44.7	10.4	11.6	–1.3	8.8
Canada	50.6	9.7	26.8	2.5	10.3
U.K.	32.9	13.2	22.2	12.0	12.6
Germany	38.3	4.1	4.4	4.8	5.8
Switzerland	33.4	2.9	4.3	4.1	2.8
Japan	32.1	5.3	9.1	7.4	5.9
Mean	38.7	7.6	13.1	4.9	7.7
			Decelerating Inflation, 1980–1983		
U.S.	–7.6	7.3	17.0	9.0	11.4
Canada	–6.4	9.0	26.9	12.7	13.6
U.K.	2.9	9.5	25.6	17.6	13.2
Germany	3.6	4.8	17.0	7.9	8.7
Switzerland	–0.1	4.6	9.1	5.0	6.0
Japan	–8.4	4.5	16.0	9.5	8.1
Mean	–4.8	6.6	18.6	10.3	10.7
			Total Period, 1977–1983		
U.S.	16.1	8.3	11.9	4.9	9.8
Canada	19.5	9.1	18.6	8.2	11.8
U.K.	18.8	10.8	22.8	14.5	12.4
Germany	18.5	4.3	11.5	7.0	6.9
Switzerland	14.1	3.6	7.2	5.1	4.2
Japan	12.2	4.6	12.8	8.8	6.4
Mean	16.5	6.8	14.1	8.1	8.6

Table 6–63
Differential Rates of Return of Financial Assets Across Six Countries: 1977–80; 1980–83; 1977–83 (Cumulative Rate of Return, Percent Per Year).

Country	Gold less C.P.I.	Gold less Stocks	Gold less Bonds	Gold less Money Markets	Stocks less C.P.I.	Bonds less C.P.I.	Money Markets less C.P.I.
Accelerating Inflation, 1977–1980							
United States	34.3	33.1	46.0	35.9	1.2	-11.7	-1.6
Canada	40.9	23.8	48.1	40.3	17.1	-7.2	0.6
U.K.	19.7	10.7	20.9	20.3	9.0	-1.2	-0.6
Germany	34.2	33.9	33.5	32.5	0.3	0.7	1.7
Switzerland	30.5	29.9	29.3	30.6	1.4	1.2	-0.1
Japan	26.8	23.0	24.7	26.2	3.8	2.1	0.6
Mean	31.1	25.7	33.8	31.0	5.5	-2.7	0.1
Decelerating Inflation, 1980–1983							
United States	-14.9	-24.6	-16.6	-19.0	9.7	1.7	4.1
Canada	-15.4	-33.3	-19.1	-20.0	17.9	3.7	4.6
U.K.	-6.6	-28.5	-14.7	-10.3	16.1	8.1	3.7
Germany	-1.2	-20.6	-4.3	-5.1	12.2	3.1	3.9
Switzerland	-4.6	-9.2	-5.1	-6.1	4.5	0.4	1.4
Japan	-12.9	-24.4	-17.9	-16.5	11.5	5.0	3.6
Mean	-9.3	-23.4	-13.0	-12.8	12.0	3.7	3.6
Total Period, 1977–1983							
United States	7.8	4.2	11.2	6.3	3.6	-3.4	1.5
Canada	10.4	0.9	11.3	7.7	9.5	-0.9	2.7
U.K.	8.0	-4.0	4.3	6.4	12.0	3.7	1.6
Germany	14.2	7.0	11.5	11.6	7.2	2.7	2.6
Switzerland	10.5	6.9	9.0	9.9	3.6	1.5	0.6
Japan	7.6	-0.6	3.4	5.8	8.2	4.2	1.8
Mean	9.7	2.4	8.4	7.9	7.3	1.3	1.8

Definitions and Sources of Data[1]

Cumulative Rates of Return, Percent per Year. This is the total rate of return, with income reinvested where appropriate, percent per annum, compounded, based on monthly data.

Proportion of Return of Domestic Asset Explained by Gold (R^2). Correlation coefficient: R^2 = the proportion of return of each domestic asset that is explained by movement in the price of gold.

Buy/Hold. Results shown based on end-of-period pricing. It is assumed that assets were bought and held for the duration of the simulation period.

Period Average. The cumulative rate of return from the start of each year to the end of every subsequent year averaged for the entire period. This measure diminishes the significance of the particular starting and ending dates. For this reason it is typically more valid than buy/hold measures.

Gold Price Index in Local Currency Terms. London afternoon gold fix at month-end, converted from U.S. dollars to local currency at month-end exchange rate.

Stock Data. The national equity indices utilized are those prepared by Capital International Perspective, Geneva. These indices are widely used performance benchmarks. In the United States the S&P 500 is used. Each of the indices has been adjusted by InterSec to include dividend payments.

Bond Data. The national bond indices utilized are based on proprietary intermediate-term indices calculated by InterSec Research Corp. The indices measure the combined effects of price movement, interest income, and reinvestment of interest income. Bonds included in the indices are government

[1]The same definitions were used in our earlier studies.

issues of common maturity, normally seven to ten years. Calculations are based on monthly prices. The U.S. dollar domestic index is Salomon Brothers High Grade Corporate Bond Index.

Money Market Data. The national deposit indices utilized are based on proprietary indices calculated by InterSec Research Corp. The indices are calculated from three-month deposit rates in local currencies.

Consumer Price Index Data. The consumer price index data utilized is prepared by the Federal Reserve Bank of St. Louis, based on data published in the International Monetary Fund's *International Financial Statistics.*

V

Gold in the International Monetary System

No analysis of gold is complete without a study of its role in the international monetary system. The first article in this part, written by Mr. Eugene J. Sherman, reviews the evolution from the classic gold standard of the 19th century to adoption of flexible exchange rates and the subsequent multicurrency reserve system. This chronological study reveals the recent re-emergence of the monetary role of gold despite attempts to demonetize it.

The second article, written by Dr. Richard A. Stuckey, focuses on the current and future official role of gold with particular emphasis on developments that took place after publication of the first article. Merits and demerits of floating exchange rates and a controversial gold standard proposal as an alternative to the present system are discussed.

Finally, in order to bring the whole study up-to-date, a review of recent developments written by Mr. Itsuo Toshima appears at the end.

7
Gold in the Monetary System
—A Re-Examination

The financial system is dynamic. Its structure seems constantly in evolution. Moreover, the pace of change has picked up in recent years. The role of gold in that system is once again emerging in importance. If gold in the financial system is viewed in terms of a short historical perspective, the emergence of gold may seem like something new. However, when viewed historically, it can readily be seen that gold has very long-term standing as a monetary asset. In that sense, the efforts in the mid-1970s to demonetize gold can be seen as the aberration. The evidence of the re-emergence of gold is substantial.

1. A growing number of central banks are valuing their gold based on some formula linked to current market prices.
2. Gold is being used more widely as collateral for loans in the international lending market.

3. The European Monetary System requires gold as an important portion of its pooled assets or resources.

4. A growing number of central banks have been accumulating substantial amounts of gold, while fewer central banks are selling gold.

The purpose of this article is to show the monetary role of gold in historical perspective and to call attention to its re-emergence since the failure at efforts to demonetize it. The renewed acknowledgement by central banks, although perhaps at this stage only tacit, is still another reason for private investors to examine the investment merits of gold as an appropriate vehicle for achieving long-term objectives.

The format here is chronological. Thus, if readers choose to concentrate on one or two particular time periods, as against the entire history, they may do so. However, a broader historical view is worthwhile. Thus the attempt is made here to provide a survey of the subject in one place.

A broad array of sources was drawn upon, especially various Federal Reserve publications, data published by the International Monetary Fund, the Chamber of Mines of South Africa, and a cross-section of other reliable sources.

EUGENE J. SHERMAN
Vice President, Economist
May, 1981

Summary and Conclusions

Gold has served as a store of value and a medium of exchange for more than six thousand years owing to its unique properties and universal acceptance. At various times in history, when a confluence of favorable factors made it possible, gold was at the very center of domestic and international money systems. Such instances were the classic gold standard era of the 19th century in which pound sterling was the key currency and Great Britain the dominant force in international trade, finance, and economics, and the Bretton Woods system subsequent to the second World War in which the U.S. dollar and the United States served the same functions.

However, international economic stability, low and consonant inflation rates, and peace and prosperity—especially in combination—are not the normal circumstances of economic history. As a result, alternatives had to evolve, such as the multicurrency floating exchange rate system that has come into being in recent years. At the same time, recognizing the absence, at least in the near term, of a universally accepted monetary system or numeraire, a growing number of participants in the international monetary system and especially central banks have once again begun to look upon gold as a monetary asset that serves the most important function of store of value.

In the prevailing circumstance of economic uncertainty and instability, gold is once again emerging as an internationally acceptable financial asset. At this stage, central banks are preferring to make international settlements in currency, such as dollars, and are, in most cases, holding onto their gold as the major portion of their reserve assets. This is precisely in accord with what would be expected under Gresham's law—the less valuable money is spent while the more valuable money is retained.

As private investors become aware of this evolution and the re-emergence of gold in the monetary system, they too are likely to look upon gold as having an appropriate place in some proportion in their portfolios.

The Use of Gold as Money in History

Gold has unique qualities that make it particularly useful as a medium of exchange.

First, as an element, it has a very high atomic weight and specific gravity and is very stable. It is also malleable and yet doesn't lose its properties despite fabrications. Therefore, it is resistant to corrosion and loss owing to evaporation, breakdown, or change of chemistry when combined with other elements. Since its history as a metal dates to prerecorded times and its qualities have been recognized throughout, it has had a longstanding record as a useful, scarce, and attractive metal.

Secondly, gold contains all the basic requisites of money: it is scarce; it is indestructable; it cannot be manufactured; it is recognizable; it is measurable to minute fineness; it can be easily divided into finite amounts; and it is portable. Its dual role as a means of adornment as well as money has contributed further to its desirability. After all, even if people were to reject gold as a form of money, it would still be widely used in jewelry and for decorative purposes.

Thus, for all of these reasons, gold has served as a store of value. In more recent times, it has been found to have numerous uses in electronics, dentistry, heat shields, and other things.

The history of gold as money dates back more than 6,000 years, to Ancient Egypt and the civilizations of Mesopotamia. Most of the great civilizations of history since then have used gold as a medium of exchange and as a store of value. These include the Chinese, Minoa of Crete, Mycenae, and the city-states of Ancient Greece, the Persians, the Romans, the Byzantines, the Islamic and Ottoman empires, India, and the African kingdoms. The Aztecs and Incas used gold reverentially, and it played an important role in their cultures; yet they did not have the concepts of medium of exchange or store of value. Nevertheless, it is particularly noteworthy that, prior to the discoveries of Columbus, the eastern hemisphere and the western hemisphere did not know of each other's existence. Yet gold was highly regarded on both sides of the ocean. Clearly, the unique properties of gold make it ideal as a basis of value.

The history of gold coins is almost as long. Lydia, in 560 B.C., was the first known kingdom to strike a gold coin. This became the forerunner of more than 20,000 types of gold coins struck over the centuries by over 1,200 different cities and governments. In fact, the issuance of gold coins came to be recognized as a reflection of the stability of a government and the prosperity of a state. The debasement of these coins almost always was a reflection of the deterioration of that society. People's recognition that coins were being debased led to a behavior pattern which later became known as Gresham's law, which states simply that bad money drives good money out of circulation. If there are two or more qualities of money available, people will spend the less valuable money first and hold on to the more highly valued money. Gold and gold coins throughout history have been the more valued money that has been held from circulation in times of political unrest, inflation, and money debasement. In modern times, central banks and governments are the holders of the substantial reserves of gold and rarely, if ever, in current times make payments with it. At most, they use it for collateral against loans. Thus, in the broadest sense, gold retains its identity as a money and store of value, and Gresham's law is still at work.

The International Gold Standard

The gold standard had its heyday in the three or four decades before the first World War. It was pioneered by Britain, the world's leading industrial power for most of the 19th century, and was adopted by an increasing number of countries with economic ties with the British. By 1870 all the world's leading trading nations were linked to gold. Prior to the evolution to a gold standard, there was no formal, widely accepted international financial system, but rather a plethora of settlement arrangements which, among other things, included silver as a means of payment.

The gold standard was based on two rules: (1) Gold had to be convertible into the currency of a country on the standard, either bullion or freely circulating coin; and (2) participating countries were obligated to allow the free import and export of gold. Ideally, if these rules were observed, the gold standard worked with splendid precision and served as an equilibrating force in economic adjustments. Under the gold standard, a currency's value was stated in terms of a fixed amount of gold and was convertible from paper into gold by anyone on demand. It was a rigid system that presupposed approximate balance among countries in international payments, assumed that there would be accommodating adjustments for periods of imbalance, and required final settlements in gold.

As the currency of a country on the standard was defined in terms of a fixed content of gold, this meant that the exchange rate between currencies was also fixed. Thus, before 1914 the pound sterling was equal to 4.866 U.S. dollars, a rate derived by relating the gold content of the British pound (113 grams) to that of the American dollar (23.22 grams).

As an example, let us suppose that because of especially heavy British imports from the U.S. there was a shortage of American currency available to British merchants. As a result, the rate of the dollar against sterling would appreciate until it reached what was called the *gold export point*, that is, $4.827 to the pound. At that level it was economic to export gold from London to New York, allowing for transport and insurance charges. This differential was necessary as gold transfers were required for the purchase of dollars or their equivalent with which British importers could pay American exporters. In the reverse case, there would be a shortage of sterling bills of exchange available for purchase by American merchants, so that sterling would appreciate against the dollar. In that case, the gold import point would be $4.890 to the pound, and gold would be shipped from New York to London.

One-way gold flows could not continue indefinitely, because corrective mechanisms reversed the process.

In the short run, a *deficit country* could expect its interest rates to rise because of reduced domestic liquidity as a result of less gold in the country. The higher interest rates would encourage an inflow of foreign funds. As a supplementary measure the central bank could raise the discount rate if the liquidity shortage was not by itself sufficient to attract overseas short-term capital. Over the long run, adjustments would take place through a combination of reduced investment and consumption in the deficit country because of higher interest rates, and lower prices resulting from reduced liquidity. All of this would make for a stronger balance of trade by curbing imports and encouraging exports.

By the same token, *surplus countries*, which by definition would be receiving gold, would find their positions eroded by rising prices and greater domestic investment and consumption resulting from lower interest rates. Also, the residents of a country in balance-of-payments surplus would tend to spend more than those of a deficit country, some of which consumption would be devoted to imports, so that there would be a natural tendency for equilibrium to be restored.

The gold standard also regulated the amount of notes on issue. The Bank Charter Act of 1844 in the United Kingdom regulated the issue of bank notes in two ways: First, it decreed that:

1. Existing banks, except the Bank of England, could not increase the quantity of notes they had in use (at that stage about 180 British banks were handing out paper promises to pay legal tender—gold coins at Bank of England rates of exchange—on demand).
2. No new banks could issue notes.
3. If any bank failed, changed its character, or amalgamated, its right of issue lapsed into the hands of the Bank of England.

Second, the act regulated the Bank of England monopoly. The Bank of England was allowed to issue notes up to 14 million pounds on the security of its loan to the State; it could also put out notes equal to two-thirds of the issues of other banks, thus bringing its issue to 20 million pounds. Beyond that point every note had to be backed in full with gold and every increase in issue had to be accompanied by an addition to the gold reserve. If the gold reserve declined, the notes issued would be reduced accordingly.

Other central banks tended to follow the British example with small modifications. The German Reichsbank, established in 1875, had the monopoly of note issue. It was allowed some fiduciary notes, but required gold backing for other note issues. To cope with emergencies, however, the Reichsbank was allowed to put out uncovered notes, provided it paid a tax of 5 percent on these and did not let its gold reserves fall below 30 percent of the total issue.

A number of countries followed Britain onto the gold standard, among them France, Belgium, Switzerland, Italy, Greece, Norway, Sweden, and, somewhat later, Austria-Hungary, Russia, and Japan. By the outbreak of World War I, virtually all major countries were on the system.

In the United States the Redemption Act required that paper money issued by the Treasury be made redeemable in coin on demand. Since the Treasury complied with this Act by redeeming in gold coin, the country effectively adopted the gold standard with the return to convertibility in 1879. In 1900 the Gold Standard Act formally recognized the defacto gold standard.

There were strong forces making for the unity of theory and practice. The free movement of gold was essential for equilibrating balance-of-payments distortions between different countries, for otherwise the international character of the standard would have been destroyed. In practice, this was made possible because the pre-1914 gold standard was in effect a sterling standard. Most countries kept their currencies stable in terms of sterling; the alternative would have been a failure to attract British investment and difficulties in financing their trade with London. Sterling was the key currency, particularly for international transactions on both current and capital account. Britain had deficits with Europe and the United States and surpluses with the new countries. Britain was a long-term investor in new countries, which made possible their payments for British goods.

But the gold standard did not work entirely according to classical theory. The movements of exports and imports between deficit and surplus countries on the gold standard were supposed to diverge, but in fact there was a high degree of parallelism in the movements of these trade flows. Also, export prices in a number of countries moved together over time, although more frequent divergencies would have been expected in terms of the classical theory. Furthermore, while adjustment was supposed to have been facilitated for deficit countries by price flexibility downwards, in practice prices did not decline in response to payments disequilibria as readily as the theoretical model suggested. In fact, substantial price changes were largely in response to variations in the flow of new gold to monetary stocks.

The exhaustion of old mines, the discovery of new

ones, and breakthroughs in mining and refining technologies produced significant changes in the cost of producing gold during the 19th century. Since the monetary price of gold was fixed, the resulting changes in the rate of gold production generated similar fluctuations in the growth of money supplies of countries on the gold standard.

The world's monetary gold stock increased only 1.4 percent a year from 1816 to 1848. The annual growth of monetary gold stocks then jumped to 6.2 percent from 1849 to 1873, fell back to 1.4 percent from 1874 to 1892, and recovered to 3.6 percent from 1893 to 1913.

These fluctuations in the growth of monetary gold stocks were reflected in the behavior of U.S. and foreign prices. For example, in the period of gold shortage from 1872 to 1896, wholesale prices fell 50 percent in the United States, 39 percent in the United Kingdom, 36 percent in Germany, and 43 percent in France. But from 1896 to 1913, when gold production had recovered, prices rose 49 percent in the United States, 32 percent in the United Kingdom, 41 percent in Germany, and 41 percent in France. Similarly, during bimetallism—that is, a dual silver and gold system—from 1814 to 1849, an overall shortage of gold and silver had prompted an average price decline of 46 percent in these countries.

The use of both paper currency and demand deposits increased markedly during those years. Paper money and demand deposits probably accounted for less than a third of the U.S. money supply in the first part of the 19th century, but possibly for as much as nine-tenths by 1913. And the monetary gold stock— gold coins and gold reserves of the Treasury—declined sharply relative to the nation's money supply over the corresponding period.

If, as under a true gold standard, gold was to be the sole regulator of the rate of monetary expansion, monetary gold should have maintained a constant ratio to the money supply. But if this had happened during the 19th century, prices in the United States and other countries would have fallen severely, instead of remaining relatively stable.

The discipline of gold was consistent with relatively stable prices only because it was not fully operative during a period of gold shortage. The monetary price of gold was too low to call forth production of monetary gold in proportion to the growth in economic activity. If demand deposits and paper money had not been substituted for gold, there would have been a severe deflation.

The price swings indicate that a gold standard does not necessarily bring about price stability. The reasons can be broadly summarized as follows:

1. Monetary stability in the issue of bank notes does not necessarily mean price stability because the velocity of circulation of money can change.
2. Central banks did not always stick to the "rules of the game" particularly in times of economic emergency.
3. The amount of newly mined gold produced in the world was of prime importance in determining international liquidity.

In spite of deviations from theory, the pre-1914 gold standard functioned relatively smoothly and the external adjustment mechanism worked with a high degree of efficiency. Exchange rate adjustments, at least among the major economic powers, were infrequent, trade and capital movements met few obstacles, and quantitative restrictions on trade were largely absent. The main reason for this apparently ideal situation was probably due to a fact mentioned before, that the gold standard was actually a sterling standard. Britain was the leading trading country throughout the 19th century and was the most important source of investable funds. In spite of a persistent trade deficit, it maintained a continuous surplus on current account be- cause of its large "invisible" earnings from shipping and foreign investments. Britain's gold reserves tended, however, to be fairly low during the 19th cen- tury because the current account surplus was substan- tially offset by capital outflows. Sterling as an interna- tional currency nonetheless had the complete confidence of its holders during this period. Sterling balances tended to be neither too large nor too small. Britain's demand for imports was inelastic but the de- mand for its exports was elastic, so that during a time of depression, Britain would have a current account deficit. This would be balanced by a decline in capital exports. During a time of boom, the situation was re- versed.

In addition to the mutually beneficial nature of the pre-1914 gold standard, other factors contributed to its success. First and perhaps most important, the world economy was growing rapidly. Changes in demand, reflected in price changes, did not therefore lead auto- matically to widespread unemployment and lower profits. Because of the international economy's dyna- mism and flexibility, necessary adjustments could readily be made by alterations in industrial structures that did not give rise to deflationary tendencies. Sec- ond, the rules of the game were not as invariably ob- served as the common view of the gold standard would have it. In principle, central banks had little dis- cretion in implementing their discount policies: if there was a deficit, interest rates were raised; if there was a surplus, they were lowered. It followed that the do- mestic situation would depend entirely on the state of the balance of payments. In practice, central banks, in- cluding the Bank of England, were aware of the need to achieve external balance without excessive restric- tions on domestic activity. Interest rates were there- fore often allowed to decline so as to counteract the deflationary effects of gold out-flows. A third reason for the system working smoothly was the growth of a multilateral settlements network. This provided for a variety of ways of offsetting payments between countries and thus considerably reduced the need for gold in international transactions.

To sum up, the smooth working of the international gold standard before 1914 is not a myth, but its success was very closely bound up with historically transient factors, particularly the predominance of Britain in the international economy and rapid economic growth and international expansion. Sterling was increasingly used as a supplement to gold in settling global economic transactions. It is indeed difficult to see how the international monetary system could have functioned smoothly had this not been so, as it would otherwise have been heavily dependent on such accidental factors as the discovery of gold and its rate of production.

The Gold Exchange Standard

The international gold standard broke down under the strains of World War I. Belligerent countries generally sought to get gold coins out of circulation and into official hands and to prevent the exportation of gold abroad. Neutral governments frequently suspended the free coinage of gold and ceased to buy gold freely at the official price so as to avoid importing inflation.

Partly because of the severe inflation experienced in many countries during the war, popular sentiment favored restoration of the international gold standard. The United States was the first to return to the gold standard in 1919, with the removal of its embargo on gold exports. And by 1927 the number of countries on a gold standard was larger than ever before. But the restored international gold standard bore only a superficial resemblance to the previous one.

Once again, central banks bought and sold gold at fixed prices, and gold was allowed to move freely internationally. But with the exception of the United

States, most countries operated on a gold bullion standard, rather than a gold coin standard. These countries redeemed their money in gold bars of large denomination only, and some—like Great Britain and the Netherlands—restricted gold sales to people wanting it for export or industrial uses only. By reducing the amount of gold used in domestic circulation, these measures made more gold available for international payments. Without such measures, gold would have tended to be in short supply.

Of even more significance was the widespread adoption of gold exchange standard for international reserves. To economize further on gold, central banks began to hold a significant proportion of their reserves in the form of financial investments in London and, to a lesser extent, in New York and Paris. Because these reserves could be withdrawn anytime, and especially because the gold reserves of Great Britain were not large, this system contained the seeds of its own destruction.

Another problem with the restored gold standard was that the new gold parities did not adequately reflect the different degrees of inflation after 1914. Of particular significance, because of its role as a reserve currency, was the overvaluation of the British pound sterling. To reassert its financial leadership and to attempt to restore prices to prewar levels, Britain returned to gold in 1925 at the prewar parity for the pound sterling. But because many other countries had devalued their currencies from prewar parities, Britain's trade balance became depressed, and the pound sterling was at or near the gold export point most of the time. However, the losses of gold, and consequent monetary deflation in the British economy, did not reduce wages and prices enough.

Finally, in 1931, a series of continental bank failures led to heavy withdrawals from the London money market, forcing the Bank of England to announce that its gold reserves had fallen to the point where it could no longer maintain the gold standard. The pound sterling was allowed to float downward, creating losses for the central banks that held their reserves in London. Pressure then shifted to other countries, forcing most of them off the gold standard also.

The Depression brought an important modification to the gold standard of the United States. In 1933, apparently as a temporary measure for alleviating the banking panic of that year, the Roosevelt Administration prohibited private holdings of gold coin, gold bullion, and gold certificates. But in 1934, the Gold Reserve Act gave the government permanent title to all monetary gold and allowed gold certificates to be held only by Federal Reserve banks. This put the United States on a limited gold bullion standard, under which redemption in gold was restricted to dollars held by foreign central banks and licensed private users.

Also under this act, President Roosevelt devalued the dollar by increasing the monetary price of gold from $20.67, as established in 1834, to $35 an ounce. The devaluation of the dollar was not undertaken for the purpose of defending the country's balance of payments but, rather, in the belief that it would raise the dollar price of exports and, hence, help stimulate prosperity. This assumed that demand and market share would not be affected by the higher prices.

One effect, however, was to overvalue the currencies of the few countries that were still on gold—notably France. These countries had earlier repudiated the gold exchange standard and decided to depend on gold as the only reliable international reserve. But the deflationary effects stemming from its overvalued exchange rate prompted France to devalue the franc 26 percent in 1936 and to float it in 1937. When the French franc was once again pegged in 1938, it was to the pound sterling rather than gold.

The limited gold bullion standard could have been the basis for complete regulation of the money supplied by gold if that had been desired. In this system, when the U.S. Treasury bought gold, the cash balances to pay for it were created by issuing gold certificates to Federal Reserve banks. The total amount of credit that Reserve banks could create was, in turn, limited by law to a multiple of their holding of gold certificates. Each dollar of Federal Reserve credit generated several dollars of money in circulation. So, if the Federal Reserve had varied its credit creation in proportion to gold flows, the effect would have been to make the money supply vary in proportion to the monetary gold stock of the Treasury.

In practice, such gold backing requirements did not significantly limit the operations of most central banks during the interwar period. For instance, in the 1920s, the amount of gold certificates held by Reserve banks was nearly twice the amount legally required, giving the Federal Reserve System considerable leeway in its money-creating powers.

Some central banks were constrained, however, by the effects of their operations on the balance of payments—and, hence, on their limited gold stocks. For example, because of a precarious balance-of-payments position, the Bank of England did not allow money and credit to expand as much as would otherwise have been desirable for the domestic economy. But balance-of-payments constraints were asymmetrical. The United States and France both experienced large gold inflows in the 1920s, which, under the rules of the gold standard, should have led to expanded money supplies. But rather than allow such expansions to inflate their economies, these countries neutralized the monetary effects of gold inflows.

The attempted restoration of the gold standard in the 1920s did not meet the test of consistency. Exchange rates were pegged on an ad hoc basis following the upheavals of the war, but hoped-for price adjustments in countries with payments deficits were too slow in coming. And the looser ties between money and gold allowed countries to follow more independent monetary policies than before. Also, international reserves varied in a haphazard manner as central banks substituted more or less reserve currencies for gold.

Though the worldwide Depression subjected it to abnormal stress, the system was basically fragile. Gold parities were adopted without a complete enough acceptance of the other rules of the gold standard game and, therefore, could not have been permanently viable.

The Bretton Woods System

Growing out of discussions among the major powers during World War II was a new international monetary organization, formally created at a 1944 conference at Bretton Woods, New Hampshire, and called the International Monetary Fund. The purpose of the Fund was to re-establish a fixed exchange rate system, with gold as the primary reserve asset. At the same time, rigidities and inconsistencies of the previous gold exchange standard were to be avoided.

Member countries were obligated to declare fixed parities for their currencies in terms of gold or, alternatively, the gold content of the U.S. dollar in 1944. Thus, these parities were unequivocally expressed in gold. But other countries were not required to join the United States in making their currencies convertible to gold for foreign central banks. The requirement of maintaining a fixed parity for a currency could also be fulfilled by stabilizing its dollar value within plus or minus 1 percent of parity through central bank intervention in the foreign exchange market.

The U.S. Treasury continued to buy and sell gold at $35 an ounce in transactions with foreign central banks and licensed users. But foreign countries that had been on the gold standard before World War II did not return to it. Even though their citizens could, in many cases, freely hold gold, no currency other than the U.S. dollar was again made convertible to gold.

Thus the Bretton Woods system restored a gold exchange standard, with the United States assuming Britain's earlier role as the main reserve currency country. Because of vast inflows of gold during the 1930s, the United States was in a better position to assume this role than Britain had been before.

An important implication of the use of dollars as a reserve currency was that the total supply of international reserves varied with the payments position of the United States. When the United States ran a payments deficit, other countries were obligated to purchase the excess supply of dollars in the foreign exchange market to maintain the exchange values of their currencies at parity.

If these dollars were converted to gold, the total amount of international reserves did not change, but the process increased foreign reserves at the expense of U.S. reserves. However, to the extent that foreign countries were satisfied with holding inflows of reserves in dollars, there was an increase in reserves abroad but no decrease in the gold reserves of the United States. Similarly, as long as no gold changed hands, a payments surplus for the United States produced a decline in total international reserves.

There had been a problem with the gold exchange standard of the 1920s. Exchange rates were fixed in terms of gold parities, but monetary policies of central banks were not harmonized sufficiently to ensure that fixed rates could be easily maintained. So, under the Bretton Woods system, member countries were allowed to change the par values of their currencies in case of a fundamental disequilibrium.

Although this term was not defined in the "Articles of Agreement," it seemed to mean that internal economic stability should not be unduly sacrificed to achieve a balance in international payments. Nevertheless, it was widely believed that national monetary policies could be harmonized enough so that the need for changes in par values would be infrequent. In actual practice, this basic assumption was the flaw that led to the system's demise. Lacking a mandatory and automatic adjustment mechanism, the system took on an inflationary bias that became more pronounced over time. Moreover, since the process was "sanctioned" by international agreement, it became immutable.

To facilitate the financing of temporary and reversible swings in a country's payments position, a new credit facility was established. Each member country paid into the IMF an amount of gold plus its own currency equal to a quota that was roughly proportionate to its economic size. Countries with temporary payments deficits could obtain foreign exchange from the IMF's pool of funds by purchasing it with their own currencies. Later, they would sell an equivalent amount of foreign exchange back to the Fund. Interest on credits extended in this manner was normally paid in gold. Countries could automatically purchase foreign exchange in an amount equal to the gold they had deposited with the Fund. Further drawings were conditional on the Fund being satisfied that the countries' economic policies were consistent with an improved balance in their international payments.

Although quotas have been increased from time to time, credits extended by the IMF have, in fact, constituted only a small proportion of total international reserves. Gold and the U.S. dollar—and, to a much lesser extent, the British pound sterling—have been far more important.

By allowing a degree of flexibility in exchange rates, the Bretton Woods system was supposed to discourage exchange controls. But maladjustments inherited from the war were so great that most currencies did not become freely exchangeable for one another at near their official parities until 1958. Although reappearance of the prewar dollar shortage had been expected, this did not materialize. Marshall Plan aid and very substantial devaluations of foreign currencies against the dollar in 1949 had helped restore the competitive positions of war-torn countries relatively quickly.

The Search for an Alternative

Dollar liabilities of the United States to foreign official institutions exceeded U.S. gold holdings for the first time in 1964. A run on the U.S. gold stock then became conceivable but was not likely so long as U.S. payments deficits could be corrected. The Fund agreement did not require that the gold value of the dollar remain fixed. But the special position of the dollar as a reserve currency made it difficult for U.S. officials to contemplate a dollar devaluation in terms of gold. Also, the economic importance of the United States made it difficult for them to devalue the dollar without triggering sympathetic devaluations by other countries, leading to uncertain results.

Actually, it was not clear that U.S. payments deficits ought to be eliminated before something was done about the shortage of monetary gold. The Bretton Woods system needed the international reserves being created by U.S. deficits because world production of gold barely exceeded private demand. But if the United States continued to run payments deficits, its position as the world's banker would deteriorate. Further deficits would increase its dollar liabilities and reduce its holdings of gold, leading to weakened confidence in its ability to maintain convertibility of the dollar to gold.

On the other hand, if the United States restored confidence in the dollar by taking steps to curb its payments deficits, an important source of international reserves would be cut off. If this happened, the expansion of international reserves would tend to lag behind the growth of international trade and payments, making it more likely that countries would resort to tariffs, exchange controls, or deflationary policies for balancing their international payments.

A devaluation of all currencies by the same amount would have maintained exchange rates exactly as before, but would also have increased the value of gold reserves. The difficulty with this idea was that a large increase in the price of gold might generate such large increases in gold production and reserves as to encourage inflationary monetary policies. But only a small increase could generate expectations of further increases, which might swell private hoarding of gold and decrease its availability to central banks. In addition, a higher gold price would have penalized the countries that had, in good faith, held most of their reserves in dollar or pound sterling balances.

In 1967 the members of the IMF agreed to the creation of a new international reserve asset—called Special Drawing Rights (SDRs)—to supplement dollars and gold. These bookkeeping entries in the accounts of the Fund were allocated to participating members in proportion to their membership quotas and have been used to settle payments imbalances between members.

Special Drawing Rights were to be similar to gold in that they would be generally acceptable as a reserve asset without being a legal debt. They were called "paper gold." Initially, their value was defined in terms of gold, and they had a gold-value guarantee. However, their establishment did not prevent a breakdown of the Bretton Woods system as a result of overly rigid exchange rates.

Steps were taken to insulate the gold stocks of central banks from the effects of the gold shortage. To keep the market price of gold from being bid up above the official price of $35 an ounce, the major central banks stood ready to feed gold into the London market, that is, the "Gold Pool" arrangement. But by 1968, speculative buying of gold had so depleted the stocks of central banks that this practice was abandoned. Instead, the free-market price of gold was allowed to find its own level.

Also in that year, an act of Congress eliminated the requirement that the Federal Reserve hold gold certificates equal to at least 25 percent of the value of Federal Reserve notes, thereby freeing all Treasury gold for international use. A similar reserve requirement against other Federal Reserve liabilities had been dropped in 1965.

By the time of the first allocation of SDRs in 1970, the U.S. payments position had worsened, rather than improved. The U.S. trade balance, which had been in surplus by over $6 billion in 1964, registered surpluses of less than $1 billion in 1968 and 1969 and fell into deficit by over $2 billion in 1971. The deterioration was due partly to rising inflation in the United States and partly to more rapid productivity increases abroad.

Countries with payments surpluses might have revalued their currencies upward in the light of the fundamental disequilibrium that had occurred. But surplus countries were reluctant to revalue because of the resulting impact on employment in their export industries. Moreover, they did not seem willing to accept a devaluation of the U.S. dollar without countering with some devaluations of their own, at least partially nullifying its effects.

A basic weakness of the Bretton Woods system was that the responsibility for adjustment was unclear. A multilateral agreement on a new structure of exchange rates that was acceptable to all countries was needed. To private holders of dollars, however, a depreciation of the dollar, one way or another, was inevitable. And the resulting massive outflow of dollars in the summer of 1971 induced the United States to suspend convertibility, as Britain had done 40 years before.

In December 1971, parties at an international conference at the Smithsonian Institution agreed to a new structure of exchange rates. But the attempted return to a fixed parity system was unsuccessful. The reserves of central banks amounted to less than half of the short-term funds that could be switched from one currency to another.

Moreover, even when reserves of central banks could be used to defend fixed parities, the cost in terms of economic stability had become too high. Central banks of countries with payments surpluses, by buying foreign exchange to maintain their currencies at parity, injected new money into their economies. And the resulting inflation was not easily offset by other means. In early 1973, after another bout of massive speculative flows of money into surplus countries, the major central banks decided to allow their currencies to float, rather than try to defend the Smithsonian parities or negotiate a new structure of rates.

Meanwhile, as monetary officials struggled to regain control over the monetary system, they began to look upon the role of gold in the system as an encumbrance. Accordingly, from 1968 onwards, a determined attempt was made to demonetize gold. In March of that year the two-tier system for gold transactions mentioned above was established. In 1971 the United States ended the gold convertibility of its currency, and in March 1973 the link was severed altogether. When floating exchange rates became widespread, the IMF made a determined attempt to reduce the role of gold by changing the provisions relating to it in the Fund's Article of Agreement.

The new provisions were ratified in April 1978. Gold ceased to be the common denominator of par values of member countries. Obligatory gold payments to the IMF were abolished. One-sixth of its gold reserves were restituted to members. The IMF sold a further one-sixth of its official gold reserves in the private market through regular auctions with the proceeds used to help its poorer members finance their large payments deficits. In sum, the IMF reduced its holdings by 1,555 metric tons in the four-year period ending May 1980. In addition, final settlement among central banks in gold ended. At the same time, the U.S. Treasury conducted a series of gold auctions from May 1978 to November 1979, during which it sold 491 metric tons.

In the spring of 1978, the managing director of the IMF proposed the creation of a "substitution account." This was intended to allow official dollar holders to hold, or substitute, SDRs for dollars. The purpose was to reduce the temptation to sell dollars on foreign exchange markets at a time when the dollar was already weakening. The problem was that the SDR still maintained a high weighting of dollars and no one was willing to accept the exchange risk for the differential between dollars and substituted SDRs. Thus, if a central bank held dollars and the dollars went down relative to other currencies, it lost value in its own currency terms. Alternatively, if it exchanged dollars for the SDRs and the dollar declined, so too would the SDR, based on the dollar's weighting. Although the central bank might lose less in the SDRs, it would lose anyway. Meanwhile, it would earn less on its holdings of SDRs, owing to the interest rate formula, than it would if it held dollars and invested in interest yielding dollar denominated money market instruments.

From the U.S. point of view, one country's balance of payments deficit was another country's surplus and both had an obligation to move their balance to zero, so that the adjustment process and burden should have been mutually shared. Therefore, the U.S. was not willing to assume the full foreign exchange risk. The problem of making the "substitution account" sufficiently attractive to provide a substitute asset of international liquidity to the dollar and other hard currencies is still "being considered" within the IMF, but progress, if any, in this direction is expected to be slow.

In summary, like the gold exchange standard of the 1920s, the Bretton Woods system suffered from basic inconsistencies. Because exchange rate adjustment was made only in cases of fundamental disequilibrium, private speculation could anticipate coming devaluations or revaluations, setting the stage for an international monetary crisis. The Fund agreement did not establish a procedure for making timely and frequent adjustments of exchange rates. Instead, it assumed that exchange adjustments would be rare because of a hoped-for harmonization of national monetary policies. Yet there was no mechanism to coordinate national monetary policies, as had automatically occurred under the 19th-century gold standard.

There was a similar lack of consistency in the rules regarding gold. Gold was to be the primary international reserve asset, and its price was fixed because of the uncertainties and inequities involved in changing it. But there was no assurance that there would be enough gold production at a fixed price. When a gold shortage arose, the dollar and SDRs had to be substituted for gold in international reserves. The price of gold was not permitted to rise because this would imply a devaluation of the dollar.

Moreover, since the dollar was convertible to gold for foreign central banks, the United States could not continue feeding it into the private market to keep its price there at the official level of $35 an ounce. Instead, there had to be a separation of the private market price from the official price. But central banks then became unwilling to trade gold at the official price when the market was telling them it was really worth much more. The resulting immobilization of gold suggested that a rethinking of its role in the international monetary system was badly needed.

A Multicurrency Reserve System

In the absence of a single alternative financial unit that could be acceptable worldwide as a numeraire such as gold, the international financial system has evolved a multicurrency reserve system. This is necessary since an interdependent world economy requires an acceptable medium of exchange and a store of value.

The dollar is still the most widely held and widely used currency. The share of dollars as a proportion of all currencies in central bank foreign exchange holdings in recent years has been in excess of 70 percent. However, excluding the major industrial countries and the largest oil-producing nations, the proportion of dollars held by other nations is much lower, perhaps 50-60 percent. Among the industrialized countries and large OPEC members a part—and probably a large part—of the explanation for so large a proportion of dollar holdings is the absence of viable alternatives of substantial size. The large dollar holdings of those countries are also the result of accumulation arising out of persistent U.S. balance-of-payments deficits and some of those countries' dollar support operations. Among the countries with the smaller proportion in dollars, diversification of currency holdings is probably more feasible, primarily because the amounts involved are not nearly so large.

The main impulse toward a multicurrency reserve system comes from the fact that, in a world of floating exchange rates, diversification of currency holdings reduces risk. For a central bank, ownership of a diversified portfolio of foreign exchange means less risk than ownership of a dollar portfolio. The measure of risk is variability. The variability of a diversified portfolio, with respect to any floating currency, is bound to be less than the variability of any one floating currency including the dollar. The principle is the same as the diversification of an investment portfolio of common stocks. The risk of even the most promising single stock is higher than that of a diversified portfolio. So is the risk of even the strongest single currency, making allowance for total return in that currency, compared with other currencies, rather than expectations of appreciation alone.

Of course, this does not mean that all central bankers would tend to prefer the same kind of diversification among currencies. The precise composition of a diversified portfolio will differ for different central banks. This in turn would often depend on the country's trade relations, and on the currencies in which its foreign debt, if any, is denominated.

The most serious liability of a multicurrency reserve system is switches amongst currencies constituting the system. Shifts between sterling and gold, sterling and dollars, and dollars and gold in the past have plagued the international monetary community even when the amounts that could or did move were relatively moderate and fixed exchange rates limited some of the consequences of such shifts. Today, with large international reserves lodged in floating currencies, the potentially destabilizing effects of switching could be even greater.

In an effort to further expand world liquidity and achieve greater use of its form of international reserves, the IMF has ambitious plans for the SDR. In the meetings held in September 1980, the Fund approved a plan to allow countries to borrow up to 600 percent of their quota over three years, virtually tripling the existing credit range. Prior to this, countries were permitted to borrow 200 percent over two years. And in those cases, the IMF exacted stringent commitments of sound fiscal, monetary, and international financial policies. The new extended borrowings will be with much less severe strictures. As a result, instead of serving as a barrier to inflation as was the case prior to this step, the IMF seems now ready to become part of the inflationary process. In short, these borrowings will be used to finance balance-of-payments and national deficits with strong potential inflationary consequences. Clearly, the SDRs will proliferate. The IMF plans to borrow in international markets to raise the funds to meet member countries' borrowing requirements. This development is likely to

provide central banks with renewed incentive to diversify reserves.

8

Gold in the International Monetary System: Current and Prospective Official Roles

This chapter picks up where the last chapter left off. The U.S. Gold Commission report raised other questions with special emphasis on the debts of developing countries. The strength of the dollar has also been a major international financial issue. Both of these have raised questions regarding the structure and stability of the international financial system, and prospects for further evolution of it. The purpose of this chapter is to review these matters and try to put the entire subject into perspective with a view to the future. Chapter 8 should therefore be seen as an extension of the last chapter on the subject.

Eugene J. Sherman
Vice President, Economist
September, 1983

Introduction

What role can we expect gold to play in the international financial system in the next decade? From an official monetary standpoint, a role little changed from the current one, no matter how the exchange rate structure evolves in the coming years. Yet even though gold's prospects as numeraire for the world monetary system atrophy, several factors act to further legitimize gold as a financial asset in the 1980s: increasing central bank swapping, leasing and trading activities, and the development worldwide of new markets for gold futures and options instruments, along with the creation of various gold-backed assets. And, officially, neither central banks nor the International Monetary Fund (IMF) in general plan to reduce the size or importance of their gold reserves.

For the present time, pressures to seek price stability through the discipline of the gold standard have been relieved by successes that most industrialized nations have achieved in reducing inflation rates. But lingering frustrations arising from erratic money supply growth, as well as perceptions that exchange rate movements are both excessively volatile and fundamentally out of line, continue to breathe life into gold monetization proposals. So it should not really be very surprising to find a turnaround towards a reconsideration of the gold-money link. Domestically their aim is to bring needed discipline to monetary and fiscal profligates, and, if it is established internationally, the hope is to provide an anchor for a stable, fixed exchange rate environment.

Until recently, discussions pertaining to the gold standard were relegated strictly to theses on economic history. It has been widely assumed that the gold standard lacks the flexibility required to operate in today's vast, liquid, international money markets. Moreover, there is the question of the political palatability of reduced domestic economic control. The view expressed here holds these conundrums to still be effective barriers to a return to a fixed monetary system. We can expect neither a unilateral return to any form of the gold standard by the U.S. nor an international resurrection of a gold-centered fixed exchange rate system. The benefits of long-run price stability under the gold standard are not enough to outweigh the recurrent short-run dislocations endemic to the system, even in the unlikely case where practical problems associated with returning to gold are surmountable.

It is perplexing to many to find that, although gold is no longer a numeraire for worldwide currency values, we find ourselves returning to it in times of uncertainty. One can never "count gold out." Hence it would be remiss to ignore the gold proposals altogether. However, it is a fact that gold's importance from an official monetary perspective has declined for 70 years, from the heyday of the pure gold coin standard before World War I, to its reduced role with the advent of the floating exchange rate system in the early 1970s, which coincided with a wave of gold demonitization sentiment not seen before in U.S. history. Furthermore, proposing a gold solution for domestic and international problems ignores the severe, protracted deflations forced on economies by the pure gold standard, and the frequent heavy depletions of foreign exchange reserves under the Bretton Woods system. The rather simple conclusion reached here, and expressed by others as well, is that the stability of prices and confidence in a domestic currency can be restored only by other more fundamental means. The road to credibility has no shortcuts, though gold is frequently thought to be one.

This topic is considered during a period of dissatisfaction with the current floating rate system. The May 1983 Williamsburg summit was held in an environment of heightened international discontent with the strong value of the dollar widely attributed primarily to high U.S. interest rates. Additionally, protectionism has been increasing, partly in response to the two-year decline in world trade and little world economic growth since the late 1970s. Quick and preferably easy solutions are sought. None surface. Therefore, any serious reconsideration of moving towards a less flexible exchange rate system is important not only for assessing the future official monetary role of gold but also for portfolio managers following international diversification strategies. Hence, the inclusion of the following discussion of alternative trends in the structure of the foreign exchange markets.

U.S. Gold Commission Findings

The U.S. is the only major economic power to have recently given serious consideration to any gold standard proposal. It therefore seems appropriate to begin with those conclusions reached by the U.S. Gold Commission, regarding gold's proper role in domestic and international monetary systems. This approach not only provides the reader with an overview of a high-level position of the U.S. in terms of implementing gold rules associated with the operation of monetary policy, but it is an appropriate starting point for discussing gold's current and future official role. Simply put, in March 1982 the Commission rejected the notion of returning to a monetary system based on gold in any form. The major conclusion can be stated that "under present circumstances, restoring a gold standard does not appear to be a fruitful method for dealing with the continuing problem of inflation."

In terms of domestic monetary policy arrangements, the gold standard was rejected for two practical reasons, though many Commission members had sound theoretical misgivings as well. First, there is no sound guide by which one can determine the appropriate fixed dollar price of gold. Second, it is not feasible to consider gold-dollar convertibility given the large volume of dollar obligations held worldwide.

Internationally, two recommendations were forthcoming. They favored no shift from the current floating exchange rate system to a less flexible system. And they opposed any action by the U.S. to seek restitution of IMF gold to member countries, figuring that if the U.S. needs the security of gold to weather crises then so does an institution such as the IMF.

Actually, it is somewhat presumptuous that a body composed solely of U.S. members would consider gold's international role. Therefore, the domestic recommendations realistically carry more weight. The Commission's domestic determinations were comprehensive. They reviewed a wide range of domestic proposals for basing the nation's money supply, from a pure gold standard where gold coins would circulate interchangeably with other forms of money, to the inconvertible paper standard. Other issues studied included gold transfers between central banks, and gold intervention operations designed to dampen foreign exchange market swings. To summarize, the Commission's view was that currently existing monetary policy tools would not be easily improved upon, and certainly not with gold.

Gold's Current Role— Official International Institutions

The purpose of this section is to summarize gold's changing role among official or governmental international institutions, in particular central banks, the European Monetary System (EMS), the Bank for International Settlements (BIS), and the International Monetary Fund (IMF). Gold remains an important reserve asset in many instances, and in others is even advancing in terms of its uses as collateral for loans and as an income-producing instrument. The gradual reduction in gold's importance from an official monetary viewpoint has been halted by political and economic realities. The mood to demonitize gold in the

1970s has disappeared as the "markets" have deemed gold to be a highly desirable asset.

Even so, gold no longer stands as the official benchmark for currency valuation, the convertibility of currencies to gold was long ago eliminated, and gold is not used in the settlement of imbalances between central banks. The creation of the Special Drawing Right (SDR) or "paper gold" further indicates the concerted efforts mounted in the past to reduce gold's importance. Looked at positively, gold remains an integral part of the international financial system as the ultimate reserve asset. Looked at negatively, it is a stockpiled asset to be used only infrequently, under duress, without possessing any real liquidity.

Central Banks

GOLD COVER. Gold currently plays no major role in effectively limiting the creation of money, however measured, in any modern economy. A few countries require gold or foreign exchange cover, but without specifying the proportions of each. Realistically, any time gold has been a constraining factor, monetary authorities have found a way around it. The Kuwait gold cover requirement was abandoned in the 1970s after repeated gold borrowings were required. As it turns out, the perspicacious policy would have been to buy rather than borrow.

The well-known Swiss case, which requires a specific percentage of gold to back its currency note issues, is considered a solvable inconvenience. The 40-percent gold cover for notes in circulation is currently nonbinding even given the policy of valuing gold reserves at far below current market prices. Although a constraint may arise sometime after 1985, the Swiss central bank will not permit it to become a deterrent to economic growth. The legal requirement will either be eliminated (though attempts to abolish it in the past have failed), or Swiss gold reserves will be valued at a higher official price.

Central banks value gold reserves in many different ways. The lack of uniform valuation is partly due to an inability to determine whether gold reserves could be mobilized at a known price. Table 8–1 presents the various valuation methods. The important point to consider is that 34 central banks (about 30 percent of the 111 countries reporting gold holdings to the IMF) value gold reserves at market or market-related prices. This policy tends to improve the financial standing of gold as an international asset.

OFFICIAL RESERVES. Gold finds its greatest support among central banks as the ultimate reserve asset. But even within the central banking community, attitudes regarding the necessity of holding gold reserves differ according to the relative size of gold stocks already owned and the perceived need. Since most of the world's official gold reserves are held by major industrialized nations, their gold reserve policies can be expected to differ from those of developing countries.

Current central bank policies of large gold holders can be stated as "don't sell" unless the country faces bankruptcy and is unable to borrow needed funds, yet "don't buy" either, or if you do buy, do so slowly and discreetly. A major change in this policy is unlikely. For one thing, world uncertainty argues for retention of gold by central banks in the event of a system breakdown. The sale of gold in France would undoubtedly create major political repercussions, and any European central bank would probably be severely criticized if steps were undertaken to significantly reduce gold holdings. And gold aids Switzerland in maintaining the policy of political neutrality. Of course, one can expect sophisticated central bankers to approach the management of international reserves in ways similar to other portfolio managers. They will attempt to enhance returns and reduce risk through diversification

Table 8–1
Summary of National Valuation Procedures For Gold.[1]

Industrial Countries	U.S. $42.22/ Ounce	SDR35/ Ounce	National Currency Alternatives	Cost of Acquisition	Market Related Price
	United States	Japan	Switzerland [2]	Germany [3]	France
	Belgium	Canada			Italy
	Luxembourg	Sweden			Austria
		Greece			Netherlands
		Norway			United Kingdom
		Ireland			Spain [4]
		Iceland			Australia
		New Zealand			Denmark
					Finland
OPEC	Venezuela	Algeria	Iraq	United Arab	Indonesia
	Ecuador	Saudi Arabia	Kuwait [5]	Emirates	Gabon
		Iran	Libya		
		Qatar	Nigeria		

272

Other Developing Countries

1. Africa		Zambia 6 Ivory Coast Senegal Togo Benin Niger Upper Volta	Morocco Ethiopia Tunisia Malawi 7 Rwanda	Ghana Kenya Mali	South Africa Zaire Mauritius Cameroon Somalia Burundi Cntrl. Africa Republic Chad Congo, P.R. Mauritania
2. Asia	Nepal Sri Lanka	Malaysia Burma Fiji	India 8	Philippines Korea Papua New Guinea 9	Thailand Pakistan Afghanistan Bangladesh
3. Europe	Turkey Yugoslavia	Romania	Malta		Portugal
4. Middle East	Lebanon Egypt Yemen, P.D.R.	Israel Yemen Arab Republic	Syria Bahrain	Cyprus Oman	Jordan

	U.S. $42.22/Ounce	SDR35/Ounce	National Currency Alternatives	Cost of Acquisition	Market Related Price
5. Western Hemisphere	Argentina Colombia[10] Bolivia Netherlands Antilles Guatemala El Salvador Suriname Paraguay Nicaragua Honduras	Peru[11] Bahamas			Uruguay Brazil Mexico Chile Dom. Republic Costa Rica Haiti
International Institutions		IMF[12]			EMCF

1/ Within the various country groupings, countries are ranked from highest to lowest, according to the size of their reported gold reserves in fine troy ounces as of February 1982.

2/ One Swiss franc is defined by law as 0.12759 grams of gold, which translates to 142.93 Swiss francs per fine troy ounce.

3/ Gold reserves are valued at the lower of cost of acquisition and current market value.

4/ As of December 31, 1981, Spain made a one-time revaluation of their gold reserves to U.S. $200/ounce. Prior to this, their reserves were valued at U.S. $42.22/ounce.

5/ According to the 1978 edition of the Central Bank of Kuwait's Economic Report, gold reserves are valued at KD 12.500 per fine troy ounce.

6/ According to the December 1979 edition of the Bank of Zambia's Report on Statement of Accounts, gold reserves are valued at the cost of acquisition, prior to this, they were valued at SDR 35/oz.

7/ According to the December 1979 edition of the Reserve Bank of Malawi's Financial and Economic Review, any gold purchased from the IMF is valued at cost.

8/ According to the 1979 edition of the Reserve Bank of India's Report on Currency and Finance, gold reserves are valued at 84.39 rupees per 10 grams.

9/ Gold reserves are valued at the lower of cost of acquisition and current market value.

10/ New gold acquired after April 1978 valued on basis of average daily closing quotations on London and Zurich markets during week prior to purchase; older gold valued at US $42.22/oz.

11/ Gold acquired before June 1979 is based on a valuation of SDR 35/oz., gold acquired after June 1979 is based on cost of acquisition.

12/ To avoid appearance of supporting a certain official price of gold, the IMF publishes statistics on its gold holdings valued at SDR 35/oz. and at a market-related price.

Source: The World Gold Market in the 1980's, Economic Consulting Services, May 1982.

274

while still maintaining liquidity. This is part of the explanation for Canada's gold sales, because Canada has an overwhelming percentage of reserves in gold when it is valued at current market prices.

Conversely the developing countries will attempt to buy gold when they can, and sell when they must. Other factors play a major role however. Gold-producing developing countries such as Brazil, Zaire, Ghana, Chile, Colombia, and the Philippines are examples of countries that will take local gold output into reserves. This partly explains the increase in official gold reserves from 1980 through 1982. In addition, oil-producing countries, as a result of large balance of payments surpluses, have been reported to be buyers of gold, though reported IMF figures for the Mid-East are unreliable. Middle Eastern countries have other reasons to purchase gold as well. Gold has been obtained in the wake of events including the freeze of Iranian assets by the U.S., wars, and other political upheavals. Future gold purchases by these countries will be depressed by reduced oil revenues. However, some Middle Eastern central banks are reported to still be buyers.

Recent less developed country (LDC) loan defaults provide additional clues about gold sales policies. The inability to meet debt payments on schedule has brought out gold into the open market, but not in what would be termed overwhelming amounts. Brazil is widely reported to have sold some gold outright, although most of that country's gold has been in swaps (see next section). Debtor countries in somewhat less shaky financial shape, such as Chile and Venezuela, are even more likely to engage in gold swaps rather than sales of gold. In this case gold enhances a country's ability to borrow, using the gold as collateral.

How important is the liquidity provided by gold reserves? At around $400 an ounce, gold figures to be approximately 55 percent of international reserves. Free world gold reserves total 36,044 tons or

1,158,814,600 ounces, giving a dollar value of $463 billion. This compares to a value of nongold reserves of $373 billion at the end of 1982. Table 8–2 presents official gold reserves in descending order held by major industrialized countries. The net official purchases and sales worldwide are shown in Table 8–3. The figures show a reversal of the trend to sell gold in the latter half of the 1970s that was associated with U.S. and IMF gold demonitization efforts. Note that, even though central bankers have been net puchasers for the period 1981–83, the totals are not large. The major buyers, besides the gold-producing countries, were the oil producers such as Indonesia, Qatar, and the United Arab Emirates.

Whether one can consider large gold reserves as

Table 8–2
Official Gold Stocks (Year-End 1982).

	Million Troy Ounces	Metric Tons	Percent of Total
U.S.	264.03	8,212.4	21.4
West Germany	95.18	2,960.5	7.7
Switzerland	83.28	2,590.4	6.8
France	81.85	2,545.9	6.7
Italy	66.67	2,073.7	5.4
Netherlands	43.94	1,366.7	3.6
Belgium	34.18	1,063.1	2.8
Japan	24.23	753.7	2.0
Austria	21.12	656.9	1.7
Canada	20.26	630.2	1.6
U.K.	19.01	591.3	1.5
Total Eleven Major Industrialized Countries	753.75	23,444.8	61.2
Other Countries*	281.36	8,751.3	22.8
IMF	103.4	3,216.2	8.4
BIS	7.3	227.1	0.6
EMCF	85.7	2,665.6	7.0
Total	1,231.51	38,305.0	100

*Includes estimates for Soviet and Chinese reserves
Note: One metric ton equals 32,150 ounces of gold.
Source: International Financial Statistics, IMF;
    International Gold Corporation Ltd.

Table 8–3
Official Gold Net Sales, Purchases.

	1972	1973	1974	1975	1976	1977	1978	1979	1980	1981	1982
Metric Tons	151	(6)	(20)	(9)	(58)	(269)	(362)	(544)	230	276	98
Million Troy Ounces	4.85	(.19)	(.64)	(.29)	(1.86)	(8.65)	(11.64)	(17.49)	7.39	8.87	3.15

Sales in Parentheses
Source: Gold 1983, Consolidated Gold Fields Plc.

truly liquid is questionable, since the dollar value is not proportional to the transactional use. If one defines liquidity as the ability to buy and sell large quantities of an asset without significantly altering the price, gold reserves are considerably less liquid. Morever, the development and expansion of highly efficient world money markets reduces the practical significance of official gold reserve levels. Today it is much easier to borrow funds; note the case of France. And, the size of short-term capital flows can swamp intervention efforts, in whatever form taken, much more quickly than in the past.

OTHER CENTRAL BANK ACTIVITIES. Activities such as swapping and leasing, rather than outright purchases or sales, have become much more popular as a means of practically mobilizing previously frozen gold reserves. They represent, along with trading activities, the "new wave" of central bank gold operations. Swaps enable countries to overcome short-term balance-of-payments difficulties without having to give up gold reserves. Several central banks have arranged swaps with leading international banks. Portugal has borrowed from the BIS using gold collateral (a portion of which was eventually sold to meet loan payments), and the Brazilians, Chileans and Venezuelans have used gold reserves as collateral to borrow to alleviate debt payment difficulties. The South Africans and Soviets also conduct swap activities.

The formal swap is simple and similar to a repurchase agreement in the government securities market, which is used by dealers to finance bond inventories. Bullion dealers will accept gold from a central bank at a discount from the market price. The borrower must maintain gold balances at prescribed levels. Thus a fall in price obliges the borrower to put up more collateral. The central bank later buys the gold back, paying interest in the interim at a margin over the London Interbank Offered Rate (LIBOR). Countries that borrow regularly in the international money markets will, however, attempt to use their gold as the basis for attracting credit rather than formally pledging it.

Central banks and other holders of gold also lease gold to the market for a small rate of interest. These leasing activities attempt to earn interest on a reserve asset that would otherwise produce no income. The rate of interest is usually very low and can vary with the need from bullion dealers and industrial users and supply from central banks. The demand for leased gold comes partly from jewelry manufacturers, who utilize the lease as a financing tool to acquire gold bullion for inventory in fabricating jewelry products. Demand also arises from various activities connected with bullion dealer operations.

European Monetary System

The European Monetary System (EMS) is an interesting study of a fixed rate exchange system within the larger structure of the international floating rate regime. The EMS is also an example of gold's use in a limited, regional manner, without a fixed price, yet as an integral part of an international reserve asset, the European Currency Unit (ECU). The EMS was created in March 1979 in an effort to integrate the economies of Europe and promote monetary stability and growth. It was also seen as a step towards the creation of a European Union. The EMS is a practical use of economic doctrine that holds that floating exchange rates are not appropriate for regional blocs, such as the European Economic Community (EEC), which are characterized by a high degree of economic cooperation and where trade plays a major role in member country output and income.

At the heart of this system is a semifixed currency relationship—fixed within bands, yet adjustable on an infrequent basis. And each member country is issued ECUs, the numeraire for the EMS, much like SDRs. The ECU was intended to serve as a reserve asset and settlement instrument, of which gold is an ancillary part. Each member central bank initially swapped 20 percent of its gold and dollar holdings for ECUs issued by the European Monetary Cooperation Fund (EMCF). The swaps are for three months duration with dollars valued at the market rate. Gold is valued at the average market price of the previous six months or of the two fixings on the next to last working day, whichever is lower.

The value of the ECU is determined by a basket of 10 European currencies. Each currency has a central rate expressed in terms of the ECU, where the central rates determine a grid with fluctuations of 2.25 percent for most members and 6 percent for the Italian lira. The aim is to make small parity adjustments before crises develop. Intervention with dollars is allowed and is enhanced by mutual credit lines. The ECU also provides a reference point as a divergence indicator, supposed to signal authorities that corrective actions are needed.

Two questions must be answered in the context of this discussion. First, how has the inclusion of gold in the ECU affected the system? Second, how well has the fixed rate system worked in terms of expectations?

The ECU itself, ignoring its current makeup, has been used very little because settlements can also be in

U.S. dollars. Member countries have simply been unwilling to give the ECU a larger role. Including gold in the ECU does allow mobilization of gold reserves to a degree, and the concept that a currency should have a strong backing is pervasive. However because of the manner in which the ECU is constructed, the process of ECU creation is determined largely by factors outside the control of the system—namely the exchange rate of the dollar, but more importantly the price of gold. The volume of ECUs will change with the price of gold, enhancing or constricting the liquidity of the system. While a rise in the price of gold and therefore volume of ECUs supposedly aided Belgium in propping the Belgian franc at one time, others consider it to be excess liquidity, which may be only short lived and a detriment to the system. Therefore, some have proposed changing the ECU creation process, but not in a way so as to imply a fixed price of gold.

As to the fixed exchange structure, it has been fairly successful in smoothing day-to-day exchange rate fluctuations. However, any expectations that the EMS would promote greater convergence of economic policies have not nearly been fulfilled. Numerous realignments have been necessary. Some were large, and heavy periods of intervention were needed at times to keep rates aligned. Inflation differentials are still significant, with France on the higher end and Germany on the lower, the result of Germany placing a premium on price stability and France on expansion. Though monetary and fiscal policies are currently undergoing change, the EMS has not been able to subjugate domestic economic policies to regional ones.

Bank for International Settlements

The Bank for International Settlements engages in many activities in the international monetary system that are relatively unknown except to central bankers. The BIS provides short-term liquidity to central banks in times of difficulty. Through its mandate to foster international monetary cooperation, its visibility has been heightened in recent years by its efforts to alleviate the debt payment problems of major LDC borrowers. Furthermore, the BIS performs the functions of agent for the European Monetary Cooperation Fund (EMCF) in connection with EMS central bank intervention and creation and utilization of ECUs.

The BIS is without doubt the most active international institution in the gold market due to its gold-swapping activities. The Portugese swap is just one example. Moreover, the reliance on gold as a convenient denominator is seen on a typical BIS balance sheet. Assets and liabilities are valued in terms of gold francs (equivalent to 0.29032258 grams of fine gold). United States dollar assets and liabilities are converted at $208 per ounce of fine gold.

International Monetary Fund

Present IMF policy towards gold's official role is one of neutrality, neither pushing for a greater role for gold, nor attempting to actively discredit its reserve function. Obviously the IMF would prefer that the SDR assume a greater reserve role. However, its liquidity and acceptability have never been realized as hoped. One cannot accurately predict future IMF gold policy changes. While those policies do change from time to time, they are gradual in nature. The current gold stance is a swing in policy from decided efforts beginning in the late 1960s to remove gold as the numeraire for the exchange system and as a basis for international transactions. In addition to the creation of the SDR, the IMF sold one-sixth of its gold holdings through auctions from June 1976 to May 1980, restituted another one-sixth, and in February 1976 was part of the agreement that the total stock of gold in the hands of the IMF, Switzerland, and G-10 countries would not rise. The U.S. sold almost 500 tons of gold between May 1978 and November 1979.

Future gold policy changes may be related to the seriousness of the international LDC debt situation. Though there are no plans to further liquidate IMF gold reserves, as more debtor countries fall behind in debt payments, the IMF may be pressured to sell a portion of its gold stock. However, such a major new step in IMF gold policy would require approval of 85 percent of the weighted membership, an unlikely proposition. If IMF gold cannot be sold, and IMF quotas are not increased by member countries, the IMF could be forced to borrow in private capital markets. The IMF currently has the authority, requiring only a simple majority of its board of directors. Gold reserves would likely not be used as collateral for any future borrowing since the IMF could borrow on international markets on the credit of its own good name. Part of that standing is based on its gold reserves. Overall, a major shift in policy cannot be foreseen at this time.

The Future Official Role of Gold

No Return to the Gold Standard

There is virtually no prospect that any nation or group of nations will attempt to limit money supply growth with a gold standard. Many commentators consider gold unsuitable as the basis for a monetary system in the current international economic climate. There are indeed those who consider that even serious discussion of returning to a gold standard would play havoc with the gold and capital markets, and a number of European bankers were somewhat surprised at the time of the Gold Commission that the U.S. would even consider such a system.

The technical considerations of fixing the price of gold, both initially and then maintaining that price, are fraught with nearly insurmountable difficulties. The gold price should be set so as to induce growth in gold production at a rate roughly consistent with the growth in currency needed to support economic activity. The probability of meeting this goal is slim when historically the rate of increase in gold production has been too slow to generate sufficient money supply growth. Higher gold prices have not produced sustained increases in production in the last few years, especially since South African mines typically switch to lower-grade ores as gold prices rise. Although 1982 noncommunist mine production exceeded 1,000 metric tons for the first year since 1973, production continues to be lower than a decade ago. Output from other countries has tended to compensate for the reduced production from South Africa.

A unilateral shift to the gold standard has other problems associated with fixing an inappropriate price. Should the gold price be based on a dollar price and fixed higher than supply-demand forces would dictate, the U.S. money supply would have to be increased to purchase gold offered to the Treasury, with resulting inflation. A price of gold set too low would have domestic deflationary effects. However, even if the gold price is set correctly, many Europeans fear a wrenching of capital markets and a soaring demand for the dollar. The widening psychological gap would sharply depreciate foreign currencies, initially raising inflation rates overseas that would require massive deflationary policies to balance the international system. Alternatively, capital markets would have to be closed to external influences. The effects have been compared to another oil shock, with the spectre of rising protectionism, further setbacks for LDCs and a possible disruption of European health and welfare systems.

Shifting political and economic trends towards a dispersal of worldwide strengths among countries also mitigate against a unilateral gold standard system. The U.S. does not dominate the world as it once did, what with the uneven distribution of strategic natural resources and a narrowing of previously disparate military capabilities. A unilateral gold standard could work if a single country and its currency dominated the international economy as the U.S. did in the 1950s and 1960s, or as Britain did in the 19th century. This is not the case today.

Finally, the unilateral gold standard—and an international one for that matter—would be too harsh for governments to accept fully. Its discipline would hamper monetary authorities' ability to deal with short-term domestic economic problems. Policymakers cannot resist tampering to cushion the effects of policies of restraint, fiscal or monetary. Authorities could change the price of gold when gold begins to bite, but that would destroy the intent of the system and negate its stabilizing properties. The option to change like that is available at most once a generation. Too loose a tie to gold means setting it aside as political realities dictate.

The problems associated with an official international shift to gold also include those connected with any international fixed rate exchange system (discussed in the next section). But we should note here that the credibility of any such fixed rate plan depends crucially on a convergence, or at least a coordination, of monetary and fiscal policies world-wide, an unlikely prospect. In a fixed-rate system the need for sterilized intervention is crucial, but it has only very short-term effects. And the size and efficiency of today's Eurocurrency and other capital markets would overwhelm government gold or currency stabilization efforts if the markets realized that underlying economic policies are not synchronized.

The International System— Fixed, Floating, or a Combination?

After more than a decade of floating exchange rates, schemes to re-fix currency values are beginning to appear. Dissatisfaction with floating exchange rates stems from the volatility exchange rates have displayed, and from the perception that speculative forces may push exchange values to areas of fundamental over- or undervaluation for long periods of time with resulting distortions in domestic economies. A serious question policymakers face is whether an alternative to floating rates exists, gold-based or not, and whether it is plausible in today's liquid, efficient capital markets. Assuming the alternative to be a fixed-rate system, is gold a requisite? Or can other fixed-rate structures ensure stability without gold's drawbacks?

There are two essential reasons that the floating foreign exchange system, which was thought to be an essential step towards free markets, is currently under question.

First, exchange rates are considered too erratic and unstable. Even more problematic is the belief that flexible exchange rates allow "hot" capital flows to unduly influence currency values to the point where rates are fundamentally out of line. Whether one measures fundamentally correct exchange rates according to a purchasing power parity doctrine or by other means is unimportant. The important point is that incorrect monetary or fiscal policy may result if indeed speculative forces can cause fundamental changes in currency values.

Second, the theoretical underpinnings and justification for flexible exchange rates, which state that there will be a lessening of the transmission of domestic disturbances worldwide, therefore allowing more autonomous economic policies than under fixed exchange rates, have not been realized. National business cycles have been closely in phase for most industrialized nations, partly due to dramatic oil price changes. Yet a common response to worldwide disturbances is evident. Flexible exchange rates have not performed as expected in terms of protecting smaller economies from the policies of larger ones.

Thus we must ask whether a fixed exchange rate environment is viable in the current economic context. The Bretton Woods system required frequent exchange rate adjustments and was characterized by heavy foreign exchange depletions in its last few years, and it only worked as long as the U.S. acted as the world's banker. The divergence of worldwide macroeconomic policies and inflation preferences precludes the maintenance of exchange rate stability. The need for exchange rate changes is basic unless inflation policies are harmonized and the exchange rate becomes a major policy tool for the domestic economy. Furthermore, intervention in foreign exchange markets to stabilize a currency is credible only to the extent that the market is convinced that imbalances will be followed by appropriate monetary and fiscal policies. Central banks simply will not commit large reserves for intervention purposes when they are not really effective. And take the EMS as an example of the effectiveness of fixed exchange rates. If the EMS has not worked well in such a culturally homogeneous environment, a fixed rate structure has little chance worldwide.

Although the arguments for a flexible structure seem to outweigh the fixed, voices pushing world monetary authorities to create a more stable environment are strong. As to a gold-based system, it suffers from all the deficiencies of any fixed exchange rate system. And it adds the further complexities of linking currencies to gold. Even if currencies were valued according to an international numeraire in the future, it would not likely be gold. The IMF would push the SDR, the Europeans would push the ECU, and developing countries, with little gold reserves, would find little reason to support a gold-based system.

A common ground between the fixed and floating systems is not as unlikely as many realize. Opponents of a floating system usually propose a vague regime of fixed rates with wide exchange bands, fixed or moving, and intervention in between to dampen movements. The idea is to confine rates to some degree, disallowing nonself-correcting speculative waves. The assumption is that, while monetary authorities may not know what the "right" rates should be, they can agree when exchange rates are "wrong." Hence, the desire to push rates back into zones rather than to exact targets. Narrower zones could be set to trigger corrective action. Again, exchange reforms do little good when domestic economic goals and policies are at odds worldwide. Moreover, one could argue that it makes little sense to set limits for exchange rates when inflation and interest rates are not targeted.

Finally, other trends may be followed. Some governments may set limits on short-run capital mobility if speculative forces are deemed excessive. And there may be a drift towards a strengthening of regional currency blocs similar to the EMS. Possibilities include Southeast Asia, Africa, and North America.

Gold's Practical Role

Political, technical, and economic factors preclude reactivating gold as the international monetary standard of value. Yet its active role will not end. Increasing investment demand—along with expanding markets across the world in physical gold, gold futures, and options—further legitimizes gold as an international financial asset. Gold will remain a contingency reserve in uncertain times for central banks and will enhance a country's ability to borrow from external sources, public and private. Furthermore, its contribution to domestic confidence and standing in the world community cannot be overlooked. Finally, countries with large gold holdings may not desire a gold-based system, but would not object to ideas making gold more useful in international settlements, or more mobile. Therefore various schemes will come into practice allowing and even stimulating increasing activity in swapping, leasing, and other active trading strategies from a portfolio perspective.

DR. RICHARD A. STUCKEY
Assistant Vice President Investments

International Monetary System Update

Developments in the international monetary system are reviewed in this update, although nothing drastic in the way of reforms has taken place since the second article went to press.

The Exchange Rate System

Discussions regarding the viability of flexible exchange rates continue without any consensus for an alternative being reached. Some European countries, such as France, strongly advocate the concept of "target zones" for exchange rates. For instance, at the Tokyo meeting of a Group of Ten countries on June 21, 1985, it was argued that convergence of economic performance may not always be sufficient to achieve lasting exchange rate stability and that credible commitments to target zones would contribute to stabilizing market expectations. However, the majority was still opposed to this proposal citing the following reasons:

1. It is difficult to identify equilibrium exchange rates that would serve as an anchor for expectations.
2. The target zones would have to be too wide to serve as an anchor for expectations.
3. Allocation of the burden of policy adjustment among the countries involved would hardly please everybody.
4. Markets would inevitably test the zones, thereby adding to instability.
5. Constraints imposed on domestic policies by target zones might undermine efforts to pursue sound and stable policies in a medium-term framework.

Therefore, the present system is likely to remain in place for the time being. This is so despite the accord of the Group of 5 in September of 1985, which led to more active currency market intervention. Perhaps most important was the shift in United States policy to participate in intervention. This contributed to some currency realignment. Nevertheless, fundamental changes to the international monetary system, if any, are likely to be made within a floating currency framework, with moral suasion and international surveillance being used to promote convergence of economic performance among countries. They, especially the major countries, are called upon to:

1. Pursue sound, noninflationary macroeconomic policies.
2. Place a high priority on the international implications of their domestic policies in setting national policies.
3. Eradicate controls on international capital flows.

International Liquidity

As a result of the recent evolution of international credit markets, financial markets have acquired a crucial role in the provision of liquidity in the world economy. Credit-worthy countries have gained more and more access to international capital markets. Emergence of these new channels has enlarged the concept of international liquidity to include not only the monetary authorities' actual holdings of reserve assets but also countries' credit-worthiness and the availability of external sources of financing. In this context, gold becomes more important for central banks as a means for enhancing countries' ability to borrow from external sources.

Now that market-supplied international liquidity has subjugated official credit arrangements to a supplemental role, only a small share of total liquidity, arising from IMF-related reserve assets and credit provided under bilateral and multilateral official credit arrangements, is amenable to some form of direct control. This reduced scope for influencing the process of liquidity creation requires international institutions to improve the quality of data regarding country risks and to strengthen supervision of banks operating in international markets.

The preponderance of market-supplied international liquidity has also affected the rationale for the SDR. The main purpose of creating the SDR was to make the supply of reserves less dependent on the official settlements balance of the U.S. and to provide an instrument to counteract reserve shortages. However, the expansion of international financial markets has provided a flexible and efficient source of reserves for many countries and reduced their dependence on SDRs.

Index

A

Above-ground gold stocks:
  gold coin and bullion, 11
  risk to dollar gold price, 10–11
  year-end 1984 estimates, 89–96
Aggregate gold demand schedule, 4–5
Aggregate gold supply:
  schedule, 5
  volatile, 1972–83, 21–22
Aggregate industrial gold demand, 8, 40
Aggregate karat jewelry:
  shift in 1978, 7
Alpha, *see* Statistical measures.
Annualized standard deviation:
  definition, 153

B

Bank Charter Act of 1844, the, 243–44
Bank for International Settlements (BIS),
        280–81
  EMCF, 281
  gold francs, 281
  gold swapping, 281

Bank for International Settlements (*cont.*)
  LDC borrowers, 281
  short-term liquidity, 280–81
Bank of England:
  1931 bank failures, 250–51
Belgium, 280
Berman, Dr. Peter I.:
  introduction by, 3–4
  reference to, 1, 173
Beta, *see* Statistical measures.
Bimetallism:
  1814–49, 246
Bonds:
  compared to stocks, 176–77
  sources of data, 232–33
  tables, 149, 180–81, 182, 187, 190, 195,
        198, 203, 206, 211, 214, 219, 222,
        227, 230, 231
Bretton Woods system:
  basic weakness, 258
  breakdown, 257
  to discourage exchange controls, 255
  exchange rate adjustments, 286
  IMF, 253
  internal economic stability, 254

Bretton Woods system (*cont.*)
  macroeconomic policies, 286
  member countries, 253
  new credit facility, 255
  purpose, 253, 255
  reality of, 255–56
  summary, 260–61
  after WWII, 239
Bullion, *see* Gold bullion.
Buy/hold:
  definition, 152, 232
  tables, 180–81, 182, 190, 198, 206, 214,
    222

C

Canada:
  gold sales, 275
  Summary (*tables*), 190–97
Central banks:
  diversified portfolios, 262–63
  gold as reserves, 239
  gold cover, 270–71
  as holders of gold reserves, 89
  leasing of gold, 277–78
    demand, 278
    purpose, 278
  official reserves, 271, 275–77
  policies of larger gold holders, 271
  supply of gold, 277–78
Chamber of Mines of South Africa, the,
    238
Changing role of gold, 269–70
Classic gold standard:
  19th century, 235, 239
Coin, *see* Gold coin.
Communist sector sales:
  instability in gold market, 5
  1972–83, 27–28, 36
  percent of aggregate gold supply, 8–9
  relation to dollar gold price, 22–23
  year-end 1984 estimates, 94–96
Components gold investment activities, 5
Consolidated Gold Fields PLC:
  London, in footnote, 14
  as publisher, 68, 96
  use of annual data, 1, 20, 72
Consumer Price Index (CPI) data:
  source, 233
  tables, 149, 180–81, 182, 189, 190, 197,
    198, 205, 206, 213, 214, 221, 222,
    229, 230, 231

Convertibility of dollar:
  suspended 1971, 258
Correlation (R^2), *see* Statistical measures.
Cost of producing gold:
  19th century, 245–46
Cumulative rates of return:
  definition, 232
  tables, 184, 185, 187, 188, 189, 192, 193,
    195, 196, 197, 200, 201, 203, 204,
    205, 208, 209, 211, 212, 213, 216,
    217, 219, 220, 221, 224, 225, 227,
    228, 229
Currency crisis, 138
Currency values:
  attempts to refix, 284
Current official role of gold, 215

D

Data notes, 68–70
Decorative gold demand:
  1972–83, 98
  see also Fabricated gold demand.
Defacto gold standard, 245
Deficit country, 243
Demand and supply analysis:
  basic technique, 3
  market behavior, 4
  1972–83, 1, 3, 19–20
Demand for nonfabricated gold, 5
Demand/supply-price elasticities, 3
Demonitization of gold:
  to downplay gold, 259–60
  recent failure, 238
Dentistry gold demand, 8, *see also*
    Fabricated gold demand.
Department of Labor:
  administering ERISA, 166–67, 169
  changes, 167
  interpretations, 169
Depression:
  modified U.S. gold standard, 251
  stress to gold standard, 253
Devaluation:
  of all currencies, 257
  of gold
    by U.S. in 1971, 134–35
    second time in 1973, 138
Diversification:
  currency holdings, 262
  see also Portfolio.

Dollar gold price:
  definition, 69
  increases
    causes 1972–83, 6
    demand and supply driven, 6
    1973–74, 1979–80, 11
  relation to supplies of gold, 29
  volatility, 11
Dollar gold price, nominal:
  affected by
    aggregate gold demand schedule, 4–5
    aggregate gold supply schedule, 5
Dollar liabilities:
  of U.S., 256
Dollars:
  as reserve currency, 254
Downward-sloping supply schedules, 8, 9

E

Economic Consulting Services, Inc., 1, 71
Economic role of gold, 267
Elasticity:
  concept
    computation, 18
    definition, 18
  estimates, 6–7
Electronic gold demand, 8
Employee Retirement Income Security Act
    (ERISA):
  requirements, 165–66, 169
Eurocurrency market size:
  gross index, 103
  net, 103
Eurodollar rate:
  1969, 131
  90-day, 104
  real, 104
    revised gold-pricing model, 111–17
European Currency Unit (ECU):
  dollar use preferred, 279–80
  excess liquidity, 280
  how value determined, 279
  as international reserve asset, 278, 279
  restricted use, 280
European Economic Community (EEC),
    279
European Monetary Cooperation Fund
    (EMCF):
  BIS as agent, 281
  issues ECUs, 279

European Monetary System (EMS):
  creation, 278
  fixed exchange rates, 286
  gold as asset, 238
  member banks, 279
    swapping, 279
  overview, 280
  semifixed currency relationship, 279
Excess gold demand conditions, 13–14
Exchange rates, *see* Fixed exchange rates,
    Flexible exchange rates, Floating
    exchange rates, Trade-weighted
    exchange rates.
Exchange rate system, 288–89
  target zones, 288
  Tokyo meeting, 288
External influences:
  affecting gold coin and bullion demand,
    6

F

Fabricating gold demand, 38–63
  demand-price schedules
    gold coin and medals demand, 60–63
    industrial gold demand, 59–60
    karat jewelry demand, 54–59
  1973–74, 1979–80, 6
  overview, 41, 50–52
  sensitivity to dollar gold price change,
    52–54
  summary, 38–41
  tables, 42–43
  upward shifts, 1977–78, 6
Fabricated gold products:
  karat jewelry, 5
Federal Reserve:
  Bank of St. Louis
    CPI data, 233
  creating credit, 252
  currency diversification, 165
  dollar exchange rate series, 101, 102
  gold certificates, 258
  shift in approach, 132
Fixed exchange rates:
  common ground with floating rate,
    286–87
  EMS, 286
  viability, 285–87
Fixed parities:
  of currencies

Fixed parities (*cont.*)
  IMF, 253
  economic stability, 259
Flexible exchange rates:
  disappointing, 285
  viability, 236
Floating currencies:
  1971, 133, 134
  1973, 259
Floating exchange rates:
  common ground with fixed rate, 286–87
  dissatisfaction with, 284–85
  as erratic, 285
  pros and cons, 235
  risk reduction, 262
Foreign exchange crisis:
  in Europe, 133
Foreign exchange markets, 286
France:
  EMS, 280
  overvalued currency, 251
  private stocks of gold coin and bullion,
    83–84
Fundamental disequilibrium:
  exchange rate adjustment, 261
Future role of gold:
  extension of present role, 266
  official role, 235
Futures price index (*figure*), 124

G

Germany:
  EMS, 280
  Reichsbank
    following British example, 244
  Summary (*tables*), 206–213
Gold
  as asset in 1980s, 266
  benefits in portfolio, 148–51
  buying and selling
    developing countries, 275
  as collateral for loans, 237
  compared to
    bonds, 149, 150, 176–77
    money markets, 176–77
    stocks, 148, 150, 176–77
    stocks, bonds, money markets in six
      countries, 173–231
  demand
    compare bullion and gold coin, 6–7

Gold (*cont.*)
  and supply elasticity, 5–6
  tables, 44–45, 46–47, 48–49, 76
  demonitization, 259–60
  as diversifier
    in large, balanced portfolios, 142–43
  as escape from U.S. financial
    environment, 139, 147
  as hedge against inflation, 123, 127, 143
    long-term, 179
  history as money, 240–41
  low volatility, 144
  percentage of international reserves,
    275–76
    dollar value, 276
  production (*table*), 74–75
  as reserves
    in central banks, 239
  as store of money, 240
  as store of value, 238–39
  supply (*tables*), 24–25, 26–27, 30, 31, 76
  swaps, 275
  tables, 149, 180–81, 182, 183, 184, 190,
    191, 192, 198, 199, 200, 206, 207,
    208, 214, 215, 216, 222, 223, 224,
    230, 231
  in times of uncertainty, 266
Gold bullion
  compared to gold coin, 6, 11–12
  dealers, 278
  demand
    compared to gold coin demand, 11–12
    instability, 11–12
    1979, 6
  hoarding and investment, 9, 10–11, 13,
    93
  in Far and Middle East, 93
  1973–74, 1979–80, 6
  private stocks
    compared to gold coin, 79–82
    distribution (*table*), 87
    diversified world demand, 82
    India, 86
    meltdown of coins into bullion, 79–80
    Middle East, 86
    other Asia, 86–87
    other Europe, 85
    rest of world, 87
    U.S., 82–83, (*table*) 83
    Western Europe, 83–85
    since WWII, 72–73, 77–78

Gold bullion (*cont.*)
    year-end 1984 estimates, 94–95
    standard
      compared to gold coin, 250
    state provisions for gold investment
      purchases, 168
Gold coin
    compared to bullion, 6, 11–12
    demand
      compared to bullion demand, 11–12
      stability, 11–12
      unconventional demand schedules,
        40
      see also Fabricated gold demand.
    history, 241
    hoarding and investment, 9, 10–11, 13,
      93
    1973–74, 1979–80, 6
    private stocks
      compared to bullion, 79–82
      India, 86
      meltdown coins into bullion, 79–80,
        (*table*) 81
      Middle East, 86
      other Asia, 86–87
      other Europe, 85
      rest of world, 87
      U.S., 82–83, (*table*) 83
      Western Europe, 83–85
      since WWII, 72–73, 77–78
      year-end 1984 estimates, 94–95
    production
      since WWII, 80
      table, 81
    relation to dollar gold price, 5
Gold coin and medals:
    demand-price schedule, 60–63
Gold convertibility of currency:
    ended in U.S., 259
Gold crisis, 1968, 127
Gold Economics Service:
    background, vii–viii
    studies, ix–x
Gold exchange standard, 1920s
    its demise, 254
Gold export point, 242
Gold import point, 243
Gold investment:
    activities components
      bullion and gold coins, 5
      compared with stocks and bonds, 143

Gold investment (*cont.*)
    purchases
      in individual states in U.S., 168
Gold market:
    as demand driven, 3, 4
    instability, 5
    unconventional demand/supply price, 5
Gold medals demand, 40
    see also Fabricated gold demand.
Gold pool, international:
    allow free market to find level, 126
    arrangement, 257–58
    broken, 127–28
Gold price:
    index
      definition, 232
    projections
      constructing one's own, 119
      three scenarios, 117–119
Gold pricing model:
    to explain gold price, 99–100
    revised, *see* Revised gold pricing model.
Gold production:
    recovered
      1896–1913, 246
Gold Reserve Act (1934), the, 251
Gold reserves:
    as collateral, 277
Gold's appreciation:
    1977–83, 175
    uniform, 176
Gold's changing role, 269–70
Gold's current official role, 235
Gold's diversification role, 171
Gold's economic role, 267
Gold's future role:
    extension of present role, 266
    official role, 235
Gold's long-term standing, 237
Gold's practical role, 287–88
Gold's properties:
    as an element, 240
    as requisites of money, 240
Gold's re-emergence, 239
Gold standard:
    adopted by U.S. 1879, 245
    basis on two rules, 242
    international
      breakdown, 249
      1872–96, 246
      problem, 250

Gold standard (*cont.*)
  restored, 249
  lack of flexibility, 266–67
  no return to it after WWII, 253–54,
    282–84
  possible return to it, 268
  pre-1914, 241–42, 245–49
  regarding price stability, 247
  rejected by U.S., 268
  relation to classical theory, 245–46
  in summary, 249
  unilateral, 284
Gold Standard Act (1900), the, 245
Gold supply-price schedules:
  communist sector sales, 36
  new mine production, 33–36
    in South Africa, 34–35
    outside South Africa, 35–36
  official agency sales, 36–37
Great Britain:
  as dominant force in international
    trade, 239, 245, 247–48
Gresham's law, 239, 241
Gross National Product (GNP):
  1970, 132
  1972, 136
  1973, 137
Ground rules:
  1972–83 study, 19
Group of 5, the, 289

H

Hedge against inflation, 141, *see also* Gold,
  as hedge against inflation.
Hoarding of bullion and gold coin, 9,
  10–11, 13, 94
"Hot" capital flows:
  flexible exchange rates, 285
Hudson Institute:
  Hudson Strategy Group
    gold pricing model, 97, 100
  political tension index (*table*), 108–9
  quasi-money index, 103

I

Industrial gold:
  demand, aggregate:
    1972–83, 8, 40
    see also Fabricated gold demand.
  demand-price schedule, 59–60

Inflation:
  accelerating, 174–79, 258
  and decelerating, 143–44
  decelerating, 174–79
  hedge against, 141, *see also* Gold, as
    hedge against inflation.
  unanticipated
    gold pricing model, 104–5
    revised gold pricing model, 111–17
  in U.S.
    in 1970s, 126
  in U.S. and world
    1968, 127
    1969, 131
    1970, 132
    1971, 133
    1972, 136
    1973, 137
Instability in gold market:
  communist sector sales, 5
  demand for bullion, 5
  official agency activities, 5
Interest rates:
  allowed to decline, 248
  corporate bonds, 131
  Eurodollars, 131
  Treasury bills, 131
Internal economic stability:
  Bretton Woods system, 254
International economic and political
    developments:
  effect on
    bullion and gold coin demand, 11
    gold market, 9–10
International Gold Corporation:
  gold pricing model, 97
  international study, 174
  Ltd., Japan, 96
International liquidity, 289–90
  in revised gold pricing model, 110
International Monetary Fund (IMF):
  Article of Agreement, 259
  creation, 253
  credits extended, 255
  currency diversification, 165
  data, 238
  in footnote, 13
  Fund agreement, 256
  gold demonitization effort, 276
  gold reserves, 266
  International Financial Statistics, 233
  LDC debt situation, 282

International Monetary Fund (*cont.*)
   member countries, 73, 255
   M-1 index, 103
   neutral policy, 281
   new extended borrowings, 265
   new provisions, 259–60
   official agency activities, 68
   pool of funds, 255
   present policy, 281
   purpose, 253
   related reserve assets and credits, 290
   reserve figures, 96
   sales, 22
   SDRs
     IMF's hopes for, 281
     plans for, 263–64
     rate, 102
   "substitution account," 260
   supplying gold 1977–80, 29
   used geometric weighting, 103
   world inflation series, 104–5
International payments:
   balance, 254
Intersec Research Corporation:
   bond data, 232
   money market data, 233
   statistical work, 173
Investment:
   activities
     gold coins, 5, 9
     gold bullion, 5, 9
   risks, 142
Investors' motivation:
   expectations of inflation, 122
Italian lira, 279

J

Japan Summary (*tables*), 222–29

K

Karat jewelry:
   aggregate, 7–8
   compared to bullion and gold coin, 12
   demand
     in developed and less developed
       countries, 39–40
     see also Fabricated gold demand.
   demand-price schedule, 54–59
   industry, 13
   market share, 50–51

Karat jewelry (*cont.*)
   private stocks (*tables*), 88–93
   rebounded, 41
   secondary recovery of gold from scrap,
     89
   strength, 7
   year-end 1984 estimates, 94, 95

L

Less developed countries (LDC):
   loan defaults
     cues to gold policies, 275
     IMF, 282
Link of dollar to gold:
   severed, 134
Liquidity:
   of gold, 110, 277, 289–90
London gold fixings:
   as measure gold price variability, 146
London Interbank Offered Rate (LIBOR),
   278

M

Marshall Plan aid, 256
Mean of the dependent variable (MDV),
     see Revised gold pricing model.
Meltdown of gold coins, 79–80
   other countries, 80
   in U.S., 80
Method of Analysis:
   Consolidated Gold Fields PLC data,
     14–21
Middle Eastern countries:
   buying gold, 275
Mine production, *see* New mine
     production.
Mining production of gold:
   in large quantity, 76
   prehistory–1980, 73, 76
Monetary policy:
   expansionary, 136
Monetary role of gold:
   recent re-emergence, 235, 237–38, 239
Money markets:
   sources of data, 233
   tables, 180–81, 182, 188, 190, 196, 198,
     204, 206, 212, 214, 220, 222, 228,
     230, 231
Morgan Guaranty Trust Company:
   net Eurocurrency market size, 103

Multicurrency:
  floating exchange rate system
    alternative to gold standard, 239
  reserve system
    liability, 263

N

National valuation procedures:
  for gold (*table*), 272–74
New credit facility:
  Bretton Woods system, 255
New mine production:
  compared to fabricated product
    demand, 13
  component of aggregate gold supply, 5
  1973–74, 1979–80, 6
  schedule more inelastic, 8
  shifts after 1978, 8
  in South Africa, 22, 23, 26, 32
  in South Africa and outside South
    Africa, 32–36
  outside South Africa, 10, 22, 23, 27, 32
Noncommunist mine production, 283
Nonfabricated gold demand, 64–68
  demand-price schedule, 67–68
  general, 5
  overview, 66–67
  sensitivity to dollar gold price change,
    67
  summary, 64–66
  table, 42–43

O

Official agency:
  gold activities
    instability in gold market, 5, 22–23, 28
    relationship to dollar gold price, 8
  sales, 36–37
Official convertibility:
  between gold and dollar, 4
Official gold:
  net sales and purchases, 276–77
  table, 277
Official gold reserves:
  major industrial countries, 276
  table, 276
  prior to 1950, 76–77
  after 1950, 77

policies
  of developing countries, 271
  of industrialized nations, 271
  year-end 1984 estimates, 93, 95

P

Patterns:
  of gold supply and demand
    changes since 1950s, 2
Period average:
  definition, 152, 232
  tables, 180–81, 182, 190, 198, 206, 214,
    222
Physical quantity of gold:
  affected by
    aggregate gold demand schedule, 4–5
    aggregate gold supply schedule, 5
Political tension index:
  in gold pricing model, 105–7
  in revised gold pricing model, 111–17
  1971–84 (*table*), 108–9
  seven dimensions of, 106–7
Portfolio:
  diversified
    central banks, 262–63
    five-year, 150–51
  rate of return (*tables*), 152, 162
  Simulation Results (*tables*)
    1974–83, 156–57
    1979–83, 162–63
  ten-year, 149–50
  values, (*tables*), 158, 164
Pound sterling:
  classic gold standard, 239
  exchange rate, 242
  float downward, 251
  key currency, 239, 245, 248
  overvaluation, 250
Practical role of gold, 287–88
Price-fixing of gold:
  difficulties, 282–84
  London, late 1960s, 81
Price of gold:
  acceleration and deceleration, 143
  affected by
    changes in supply or demand, 5–6
    gold investment activities, 5
    international events, 127–28, 130, 131,

Price of gold (*cont.*)
133, 135–36
political and economic forces, 125–38
climbing, 127
fixed
by central banks, 122, 127
1968, 127–29
table, 129
1968–83 (*figure*), 125
1969, 130–31
table, 130
1970, 131–33
table, 132
1971, 133–35
table, 134
1972, 135–36
table, 135
1973, 136–38
table, 137
projections (*tables*), 116, 117
upward trend, 122
U.S. economy, 128–29, 130, 131, 132,
133–35, 136, 137
Price of gold determinants, 122–23
to analyze gold, 122
as a commodity, 122
as a monetary form, 122
variations in investor demand, 122
Private market price:
U.S. official price, 261
Private sector:
supply side, 20
Private stocks of bullion, *see* Gold bullion,
private stocks.
Private stocks of bullion and coin, *see*
Gold bullion, private stocks, or
Gold coin, private stocks.
Private stocks of gold:
bullion compared to gold coin, 79–82
gold jewelry, 78
meltdown coins into bullion, 79–80
prior to 1960s, 78
after 1960s, 78
Production, gold coin, 80
Prudent Man Rule:
Department of Labor, 166
institutional investors, 165
liberalization at federal level, 167, 168
Public sector:
demand side, 20–21

R

Real interest rates:
gold pricing model, 104–5
Real return:
of stocks, bonds, money markets, 177
Redemption Act, the, 244–45
Re-emergence of gold, 235, 237–38, 239
Regression analysis, 14
Relative volatility:
definition, 152
tables, 154, 160
Revaluation of currencies, 258
Revised gold pricing model, 110–17
Cohrane-Orcutt regression, 112–13,
115–17
Durbin-Watson (D-W) statistic, 112–17
MDV, 112–17
multiple regression, 112
political tension index, 111–12
real Eurodollar rate, 111
SEE, 122–17
t statistic, 112, 113
unanticipated inflation, 111–13
U.S. trade-weighted exchange rate,
110–13
world liquidity, 110, 112–17
Reward/variability ratio:
definition, 153
tables, 160, 164
Roosevelt administration:
devalued dollar, 251
prohibited private gold holdings, 251

S

Salomon Brothers index:
of high-grade corporate bonds, 146, 233
table, 148
Scatter diagrams
analysis
intention, 15
interpretation, 16–17
elasticity concept, 18
shifts, 17–18
vs. dollar gold price (*figures*)
communist sector sales, 37
decorative gold demand, 60
dentistry gold demand, 61
developed country karat jewelry

Scatter diagrams (*cont.*)
    demand, 56
    electronic gold demand, 59
    fabricated gold demand, 59
    gold coin demand, 62
    gold coin and medals demand, 64
    gold medals demand, 63
    industrial gold demand, 58
    karat jewelry gold demand, 55
    less developed country karat jewelry
      demand, 57
    new mine production, 33
    new mine production outside South
      Africa, 35
    official agency net sales, 38
    South African new mine production,
      34
Scrap, secondary recovery of gold from:
    changes in pattern of gold use, 88, 89
    from old karat jewelry, 92
Sherman, Eugene J.:
    reference to, 1, 98, 100, 139, 235
    introductions by, vii–viii, 121, 173–74,
      237–38, 265
Shifts:
    between sterling and gold, 263
Sign change analysis, 15, 29–33, 52–54
    purpose, 15
Smithsonian Agreements, 134
South African mine production, *see* New
    mine production in South Africa.
Special Drawing Rights (SDRs):
    affected by international liquidity, 290
    creation in 1967, 257
    definition, 102
    first allocation, 258
    IMF's plans, 263–64
    "paper gold," 257
    purpose, 257, 290
    reduced importance of gold, 270
Speculative forces, 285
Stability of gold market:
    1972–83, 9
Standard & Poor's 500 index (S&P 500):
    in base portfolios, 151
    as measure of price variability, 145, 146,
      147
    stock data source, 232
    table, 148

Standard error of the estimate (SEE), *see*
    Revised gold pricing model.
Statistical measures:
    alpha, 145–48
      long-term interest rates, 147
      S&P 500, 147
      standard error, 146
      table, 148
      timing performance, 145–46
    beta, 144–48
      definition, 152
      long-term interest rates, 147
      measure of volatility of gold, 145
      relation to alpha, 145–46
      S&P 500, 147
      standard error, 146
      table, 148
    correlation (R^2), 112–17, 145, 146, 147,
      152
      tables, 148, 180–81, 182, 186, 187, 188,
        190, 194, 195, 196, 198, 202, 203,
        204, 206, 210, 211, 212, 214, 218,
        219, 220, 222, 226, 227, 228, 230,
        231
    correlation coefficient (R^2)
      definition, 232
    R^2, *see* Statistical measures, correlation,
      and correlation coefficient.
    standard error, 146, 147
Sterling standard:
    pre-1914, 245, 247
Stocks:
    compared to bonds, 176–77
    compared to fabricated gold products
      karat jewelry, 77
    sources of data, 232
    tables, 149, 180–81, 182, 185, 186, 190,
      193, 194, 198, 201, 202, 206, 209,
      210, 214, 217, 218, 222, 225, 226,
      230, 231
Stuckey, Dr. Richard A., x, 235
Summaries for all six countries (*tables*),
    180–81, 230, 231
Supply and demand:
    potential imbalance, 71–72
Surplus countries, 243
Switzerland:
    central banks, 271
    private stocks of gold coin and bullion,

Switzerland (*cont.*)
84–85
Summary (*tables*), 214–21

T

Target zones:
for exchange rate system, 288
Tokyo meeting in 1985, 236
Toshima, Itsuo:
introduction by, ix–x
reference to, 235
update by, 89–96
Total return:
definition, 152
tables, 180–81, 182, 190, 198, 206, 214, 222
Trade-weighted exchange rates:
concept developed, 101
countries included, 102
in revised gold pricing model, 110–17

U

Unanticipated inflation, *see* Inflation, unanticipated.
United Kingdom:
private stocks of gold coin and bullion, 84–85
Summary (*tables*), 198–205
United States (U.S.):
and gold standard
adopted by, 245
limited gold bullion standard, 251
rejected by, 268
return to, 249
and U.S. dollar:
as dominant force, 239
U.S. dollar:
as major alternative currency, 122
holdings by other nations, 262
as influence on gold price, 122
as reserve currency, 254, 256
U.S. Gold Commission, 73, 76, 265, 268–69
U.S. interest rates:
effect on dollar, 267
U.S. payments deficits:
effect of curbing them, 256–57

U.S. payments deficits (*cont.*)
1968, 127–28
U.S. Summary (*tables*), 182–89
U.S. trade-weighted exchange rates, 101–2, 110–11
revised gold pricing model, 110–11
U.S. Treasury:
buying gold, 252
footnote, 13
gold auctions, 260
gold in 1968, 258
Gold Standard Act, the, 245
meltdown of gold coins into bullion, 79–80
monetary gold stock, 246
Redemption Act, the, 244
sales
1977–79, 22
1978–80, 28
supply 1977–80, 29
$35 ounce/gold, 253
Unstable components:
bullion demand, 11
communist sector sales, 9
official agency activities, 11

V

Volatility
in gold supply and demand, 5–6

W

West Germany:
private stocks of gold coin and bullion, 84–85
Williamsburg summit, 267
Wolfe, Tom, 71
World inflation series, 104–5
World liquidity:
in gold pricing model, 102–4
in revised gold pricing model, 110–17

Y

Year-end 1984 estimates
above-ground stocks, 89–96
coin and bullion, 94–95
communist sector, 94–96

Year-end 1984 estimates (*cont.*)
    karat jewelry, 94, 95
    noncommunist sector, 89

Year-end 1984 estimates (*cont.*)
    official reserves, 89, 95
    residual, 95